Critical Acclaim for
Humanistic HCI

The Bardzells' new book is an excellent contribution to the growing field of Humanist HCI. It's a comprehensive, thoughtful, provocative guide to work in this complex and sometimes unfamiliar field of ideas and methods. The carefully designed chapters provide just enough information and a critical take to make you want to go off and explore more deeply, without getting you bogged down in detail. The Bardzells' personal style draws you in as a reader, and the book is perfectly pitched for both young researchers entering the field and experienced researchers and teachers.

Peter Wright, Professor of Social Computing,
Open Lab, Newcastle University, UK

Given the importance of digital technologies in the world, the research field of Human-Computer Interaction is and needs to be interdisciplinary. But the marriage between different disciplines is not always easy. This book provides an important bridge between the humanities and Human-Computer Interaction, showing how, when, and where humanities can play a crucial and important role. A must-read for not only established HCI-academics, but also new Ph.D. students coming into the field.

Kristina Höök, Professor of Interaction Design,
Royal Institute of Technology (KTH), Stockholm, Sweden.

Synthesis Lectures on Human-Centered Informatics

Editor

John M. Carroll, *Penn State University*

Human-Centered Informatics (HCI) is the intersection of the cultural, the social, the cognitive, and the aesthetic with computing and information technology. It encompasses a huge range of issues, theories, technologies, designs, tools, environments, and human experiences in knowledge work, recreation and leisure activity, teaching and learning, and the potpourri of everyday life. The series publishes state-of-the-art syntheses, case studies, and tutorials in key areas. It shares the focus of leading international conferences in HCI.

Humanistic HCI
Jeffrey Bardzell and Shaowen Bardzell
September 2015

The Paradigm Shift to Multimodality in Contemporary Computer Interfaces
Sharon Oviatt and Philip R. Cohen
April 2015

Multitasking in the Digital Age
Gloria Mark
April 2015

The Design of Implicit Interactions
Wendy Ju
March 2015

Core-Task Design: A Practice-Theory Approach to Human Factors
Leena Norros, Paula Savioja, and Hanna Koskinen
March 2015

An Anthropology of Services: Toward a Practice Approach to Designing Services
Jeanette Blomberg and Chuck Darrah
February 2015

Humanistic HCI

Jeffrey Bardzell and Shaowen Bardzell

ISBN: 978-3-031-01086-6 print
ISBN: 978-3-031-02214-2   ebook

DOI 10.1007/978-3-031-02214-2

A Publication in the Springer series
SYNTHESIS LECTURES ON HUMAN-CENTERED INFORMATICS #31
Series Editor: John M. Carroll, Penn State University

Series ISSN 1946-7680 Print 1946-7699 Electronic

Humanistic HCI

Jeffrey Bardzell and Shaowen Bardzell
Indiana University

SYNTHESIS LECTURES ON HUMAN-CENTERED INFORMATICS #31

ABSTRACT

Although it has influenced the field of Human-Computer Interaction (HCI) since its origins, humanistic HCI has come into its own since the early 2000s. In that time, it has made substantial contributions to HCI theory and methodologies and also had major influence in user experience (UX) design, aesthetic interaction, and emancipatory/social change-oriented approaches to HCI. This book reintroduces the humanities to a general HCI readership; characterizes its major epistemological and methodological commitments as well as forms of rigor; compares the scientific report vs. the humanistic essay as research products, while offering some practical advice for peer review; and focuses on two major topics where humanistic HCI has had particular influence in the field—user experience and aesthetics and emancipatory approaches to computing. This book argues for a more inclusive and broad reach for humanistic thought within the interdisciplinary field of HCI, and its lively and engaging style will invite readers into that project.

KEYWORDS

HCI, human-computer interaction, humanities, philosophy, experience, UX, aesthetics, essay, social justice, activism, pragmatism, somaesthetics, Marxism, psychoanalysis, feminism, postcolonialism, critical theory, conceptual analysis, discourse analysis

For Tom Jennings, with love, gratitude, and admiration. —Jeffrey
To my sisters, Shaoying Lu and Sunako Liu, with love and fortitude. —Shaowen

Contents

Preface

Fifty years ago, computers lacked sufficient power to both do their tasks and also render a user interface; human specialists instead functioned as the interface between a human with a computational need and the system capable of performing it. Today, user interfaces capture our imaginations, drive economies, and are the very stuff of everyday life—be it delighting or frustrating. In those intervening 50 years, we witnessed the development of the graphical user interface, which meant that direct access to computing was directly available to most professionals, rather than only to specialist technicians. Driven by Moore's Law, falling prices led to PCs moving from the white-collar office to most workplaces, and then to our homes in the forms of workstations tailored for the home and video game consoles. The Internet took off, giving us the World Wide Web and email, persistent virtual worlds, social media, and online video. Soon, computers were in our pockets, dishwashers, cars, cameras, TVs, and today most of us don't know how many computers we own (or, thanks to complex laws and licensing agreements, whether we own them at all). Enabled by our smart devices and social media habits, algorithms now watch us online, in airports, via financial transactions to figure out whether we might be terrorists as well as which kinds of cheese we're be more likely to buy.

Jonathan Grudin describes this movement of the computer from a narrow technical specialist domain to something ubiquitously around us as "the computer reaching out" (1989). For those of us who have lived through this history, it's easy to see that the computer reaching out has enormous sociocultural consequences: practical, legal, ethical, financial, political, and aesthetic. Those who design information technologies are in the midst of adding a new dimension—virtuality—to the artificial world that all humans now must live in, it being nearly impossible to opt out (Vertesi, 2014).

No wonder, then, that the young field of HCI has seen enormous changes in its objects of inquiry, theory, and methods. In a little over three decades, HCI has already gone through three Kuhnian paradigms (Kuhn, 1996), that is, coherent concatenations of theoretical, methodological, and content-specific research structures (Bødker, 2006; Rogers, 2012; Harrison et al., 2007). In the 1980s, during its first paradigm or wave, HCI successfully developed and championed a concept of usability, which could be measured according to task completion time, error rates, learnability, memorability, and subjective satisfaction (Shneiderman and Plaisant, 2010). This remains a major intellectual achievement, but while usability offers an excellent way to evaluate professional systems, the field of HCI has long recognized that usability is weak at other evaluation criteria that are increasingly relevant as the computer reaches out. For example, usability is weak at capturing the social dimensions of collaboration, and also at the contextually specific dimensions of interaction; research in the second paradigm or wave of HCI sought to correct these shortcomings, and to do so turned to disciplines and theoretical traditions outside of HCI—social psychology, sociology, and anthropology in particular.

In the early 2000s, it became clear that whereas then-dominant theories and methods were optimized for workplace-based interaction, many of the most exciting developments in the field—such as mobile, domestic, and entertainment computing—were not amenable to such theories and methods. There were questions of experience, emancipation, domestic life, intimacy, sustainability, and the good life—issues that have come to dominate the third paradigm or third wave of HCI. Meanwhile, scholars in adjacent fields, including digital media studies, digital arts, video games, and science and technology studies (STS) were building a compelling track record of success with these issues by turning to humanistic theories and approaches. And so HCI made the turn as well to humanistic thinking—a sensible move, as we hope to demonstrate in what follows.

One final caveat to this brief narrative: it should not be read as teleological, as if the third paradigm of HCI is better than or somehow replaces the earlier two paradigms. Rather, all three paradigms now operate together, often in a complementary way. It would be absurd to argue, for example, that usability doesn't matter in an video game or a mobile phone app. Likewise, it would be foolish to dismiss the contributions of activity theory, distributed cognition, or ethnomethodology in researching collaborative behavior in a massively multiplayer online game, such as World of Warcraft.

WHAT IS HUMANISTIC HCI?

Chapter 2 offers a careful and substantive response to this question, but we'll aim to be pithy here in the Preface. We begin with a definition of the humanities.

> The term 'humanities' includes, but is not limited to, the study and interpretation of the following: language, both modern and classical; linguistics; literature; history; jurisprudence; philosophy; archaeology; comparative religion; ethics; the history, criticism and theory of the arts; those aspects of social sciences which have humanistic content and employ humanistic methods; and the study and application of the humanities to the human environment with particular attention to reflecting our diverse heritage, traditions, and history and to the relevance of the humanities to the current conditions of national life (http://www.neh.gov/about, accessed August 16, 2014).

We'll comment on this definition in Chapter 2, but we include it here simply to remind readers how wide-ranging the humanities are (extending far beyond obvious instances such as literary theory and philosophy to include archaeology, law, linguistics, and history) and also to show that even the U.S. National Endowment for the Humanities (the source of the above definition) sees the humanities as contiguous with and inseparable from certain aspects of the social sciences.

We agree. And in that spirit we offer our take on *humanistic HCI*.

> We understand *Humanistic HCI* to refer to any HCI research or practice that deploys humanistic epistemologies (e.g., conceptual systems) and methodologies (e.g., conceptual analysis; critical analysis of designs, processes, and implementations; emancipatory criticism) in service of HCI processes, theories, methods, agenda-setting, and practices.

A few clarifications (developed later in more detail) are in order. We do not understand humanistic HCI to be the same sort of thing as the Digital Humanities. The latter we understand to be contemporary humanities scholarship mediated by technological tools (e.g., text search capabilities, algorithms for pattern recognition and prediction). In contrast, *we understand humanistic HCI to be HCI scholarship*, supported or mediated by humanistic theories and methods. In turn, this means that *HCI researchers and practitioners do humanistic HCI*; it is certainly not limited to researchers and practitioners with advanced degrees in the humanities. Indeed, some of the most influential contributions to Humanistic HCI came from social scientists, including Paul Dourish, John McCarthy, and Peter Wright, and designers, such as Ann Light and Kristina Höök.

WHO SHOULD READ THIS BOOK?

Given our view that humanistic HCI is basically a style or mode of HCI scholarship, and that it is done by HCI researchers and practitioners, then one implication is that the whole HCI community is likely to benefit from resources that support its members in the uptake of humanistic HCI—to whatever degree they want to think about humanistic issues in their work, and starting from wherever they are in terms of humanities training. This book is intended as one such resource.

Specifically, we hope the book offers the following benefits to readers in the HCI community, regardless of background. The book should:

- demystify humanistic knowledge production processes (e.g., theoretical commitments, methodological predispositions, and standards of rigor) and humanistic knowledge outcomes (e.g., what constitutes a humanistic "contribution");

- offer an accessible and synthetic narrative of major contributions to humanistic HCI and a generous collection of bibliographic leads, to improve their accessibility to wider HCI readerships;

- provide immediate practical resources to help HCI researchers and practitioners to incorporate humanistic ways of knowing into their practice;

- highlight areas where humanistic approaches are particularly strong and/or influential in HCI practice, in particular, user experience and emancipatory HCI; and

- contribute toward the consolidation of humanistic HCI as one of the many coherent, if heterogeneous, subdomains of HCI, with the view that it can be further developed and improved internally and also that it has sufficient hooks to be able to function side-by-side with other HCI subdomains.

We have broader and longer-term hopes as well. Let us begin with the present state of the humanities. There is no question that the humanities have been in decline both in prestige and across a number of measures in recent decades. Academic disciplines come and go. The idea of a literature department or the academic study of literature is less than two hundred years old and emerged in a specific sociocultural moment. We are skeptical that what it would become in its heyday—the literature department of the 1940s–1970s, which taught "soft skills" such as critical thinking and deep and wide reading of "great books," to a professional white collar class, will come back again (or even that such an outcome would be desirable). But the intellectual virtues of the humanities, such as those in the box below should *not* be relegated to the past.

Key Intellectual Virtues of Humanistic Thought

➢ Critical thinking

➢ Mastery of one's own language (and others)

➢ Argumentative skill, including the accurate representation and analysis of ideas—one's own or those of others

➢ Sensitivity to historical patterns and genealogies, in particular their significance in the present and implications for the future

➢ Perceptiveness concerning false pleasures and ideological machinations

➢ Commitment to rational and democratic jurisprudence

➢ Imaginative connection to sociocultural others (e.g., people from the distant past, from other parts of the world, in different life stages, pursuing different forms of life)

➢ Reflectiveness about the conditions of one's own knowledge-producing capability

Our optimistic hope is that the humanities will in the coming years realign themselves with new major new disciplinary fields—informatics being one of them—to the mutual benefit of all of these fields and, far more importantly, to the benefit of the world we live in. In this regard, we as authors hope that we have readers beyond HCI, for instance, readers in the humanities interested in seeing the rise of humanistic HCI as a success story, one in which they can recognize themselves.

THE COMPUTER PUSHED OUT

We opened this Preface with a narrative of "the computer reaching out"—a powerful metaphor. But we in HCI are not just passively "being reached" by the computer. It is our profession that, along with others', *pushes* the computer out. This happens as researchers and practitioners identify new needs, explore new technological capabilities, design and release new things, construct new IT infrastructures, and imagine computation as a kind of approach to the very real problems we face. Nearly 15 years ago Paul Dourish (2001) wrote that the development and application of computational technologies is "most certainly also a philosophical enterprise," continuing,

> It is philosophical in the way it represents the world, in the way it creates and manipulates models of reality, of people, and of action. Every piece of software reflects an uncountable number of philosophical commitments and perspectives without which it could never be created. (vii-viii)

Dourish left tacit what we'll now ask directly: *Are we pursuing this philosophical enterprise competently?* Are we as a field merely waiting for the computer to reach out to us, running behind to study it after the fact, or are we owning up to our own agency as (at least one) party *pushing* the computer out? Can we even tell the difference in practice?

Our position is that humanistic theories and approaches, emerging out of and reflecting the values we just listed—of critical thinking, communicative competence, imaginative empathy, reflective self-awareness, etc.—not only *can* help HCI researchers and practitioners live up to their own utilitarian, ethical, and aesthetic ideals, but, as the following chapters show time and again, they *already have.* That's the story that we have to tell, and in doing so, we also hope our project brings into view some sense for *what comes next.*

But such topics aren't destined for humble prefaces.

Acknowledgments

The writing of this book was an enlightening and also a humbling process; it revealed to us just how much we didn't know about the stuff we're supposed to know the most about. Fortunately, we had a lot of help from some good friends. Above all, we want to thank our reviewers, all of whom advocated for you, dear reader, rather forcefully: Lone Koefoed Hansen, Kristina Höök, Ann Light, and Peter Wright. This book is much stronger for their constructive feedback. We are grateful to our Morgan & Claypool editor, Diane Cerra, for her guidance throughout this process. We also want to acknowledge Gopinaath Kannabiran, Tyler Pace, and Austin Toombs for helping us with the humanistic HCI literature review. It turns out to have been rather a lot of literature to review! Lastly, we wish to acknowledge the support of the Intel Science and Technology Center for Social Computing, which provided financial support for this work.

CHAPTER 1

Introduction

Many of the questions that occupy HCI researchers and designers now are such that there probably is no straightforward concept that can yield a set of practical measures, the way that usability did for workplace systems in the past. It is one thing to measure a particular system's contributions to employee productivity understood in terms of task completion time and error rates; it is another to measure a particular system's contributions to the emancipation of a dominated group, toward a balance between economic goals and sustainability, toward intimacy between family members, or to the good life. Each of these issues is endlessly complex. What counts as evidence or data? How are different types of evidence to be measured or weighed against each other? Who gets to make these judgments? HCI researchers and practitioners do, of course, whether we are up to it or not.

Another way to express this idea is that many of the questions that HCI researchers and practitioners find themselves needing to answer are *normative* in nature, rather than descriptive. That is, to answer them one must make value commitments about how things *should* be, rather than attempting to objectively describe facts as they are, which is a paradigmatic goal of traditional science. We must, after all, answer: What *should* we design? Let us take a common example. Western researchers and technologists have systems and technologies that could improve lives in the Global South. Yet communities in the Global South have their own ways of living: moral outlooks, laws, policies, practices, rituals, etc. In some cases, these local values/ways of life are contrary to Western values/ways of life; for example, in some communities only men are allowed to exercise political power, or because in some communities literacy is not widespread. What should be done? Do we attempt to impose our values, or do we act in opposition to our own beliefs? How should these conflicts be discovered and navigated? How will we know if we were successful (and by what criteria)? How should these projects be resourced? Who counts as a stakeholder, and what rights and responsibilities do they have? Who decides any of this?

Answering questions like these involves normative commitments. Continuing our thought experiment, we can say that an HCI project for a community in a developing region is likely involve a host of normative commitments.

- User needs come first.

- Whoever funds the project has a right to say something about it.

- The design should be based on rigorous science.

- People should know their place and respect authority.

- It is wrong to deny women the same rights as men.

- Literacy is a more basic need than computing.

- We need more data.

- We need to act.

- We (as designers, researchers, etc.) have professional expertise and need to assert it.

- We need to respect the wishes and expertise of our users.

- Governance (including design) should be participative.

These normative claims are not all compatible with each other and some even contradict each other. The complex layering of competing values is hardly limited to human-computer interaction for development (HCI4D): the same sorts of complexities among epistemological, moral, aesthetic, and other practical norms are common in social computing, mobile computing, ubiquitous computing, domestic computing, and so forth—wherever, in fact, the computer is "reaching out" (see Preface).

To work in HCI today is to design not just for usability, but for (and from within) a range of sociocultural norms. HCI researchers and practitioners hope to be competently skilled at perceiving, judiciously understanding, and wisely deciding among competing normative values. One of the paradigm features of the humanities is that they seriously engage these issues in a systematic, rigorous, dogged, and broad-minded way. This is not at all to say that the humanities have the answers to the sorts of dilemmas we've raised or that the humanities lack blind spots. It is rather to say that the humanities have tools and competencies that can serve as resources for researchers and practitioners to cope with these sorts of dilemmas and to discover and develop alternatives in light of blind spots. Indeed, humanistic HCI has been successful in bringing issues to the field's attention and helping shift the conversation, from the pioneering work of Terry Winograd and Fernando Flores (1986) and Lucy Suchman (1987) through to the present.

1.1   HCI AND THE HUMANITIES

As a result of the computer "reaching out" into everyday life (Grudin, 1989), from the late 1990s through the present, HCI has increasingly turned to humanistic theories and practices, and humanistic HCI has enjoyed significant impacts. Our initial background search (conducted in 2013–14) for humanities HCI papers, articles, books, position papers, etc., yielded about 500 total works, using inclusive criteria. Over 90% of them date from 2004 and after, which suggests that humanities HCI is strongly correlated with the third wave of HCI and that the HCI research community has indeed embraced humanistic approaches, but primarily in the past decade.

What is humanistic HCI?

Humanistic HCI refers to any HCI research or practice that deploys humanistic epistemologies (e.g., theories and conceptual systems) and methodologies (e.g., critical analysis of designs, processes, and implementations; historical genealogies; conceptual analysis; emancipatory criticism) in service of HCI processes, theories, methods, agenda-setting, and practices.

We would argue, however, that the humanistic HCI has been around for much longer, albeit without the critical mass that it now enjoys. For example, many of the seminal works in the field either make significant use of humanistic theories and methods or themselves could be characterized as making humanistic contributions. One of the earliest examples is Winograd and Flores' *Understanding Computers and Cognition*, first published in 1986. Flores is a philosopher who earned his Ph.D. under Hubert Dreyfus and John Searle, the former the author of arguably the most famous philosophical critique of artificial intelligence ever written and the latter the leading proponent of speech act theory after the untimely death of J.L. Austin. Among other contributions, Winograd and Flores' book offers a critique of "the rationalistic tradition" in HCI at the time, showing that the field tacitly embraced fundamental theories about rationality, decision-making, and cognition as the basis for its entire research program, arguing (in the footsteps of Dreyfus, Herbert Simon, and others) that this foundation was at odds with many of the key goals of HCI and design. As alternatives, Winograd and Flores introduce Heideggerian phenomenology, biological accounts of cognition and language, and speech act theory to the field. This book had enormous consequences for HCI, as thousands of researchers have subsequently embraced, for example, Heideggerian thought in relation to HCI. Offering an epistemological critique of the field as a whole and introducing an alternative epistemological stance is a philosophical activity *par excellence*, and it is easy to see that Winograd and Flores' seminal work was in fact humanistic HCI, even if no one was at that time using the term.

Many others followed in the tradition of Winograd and Flores by offering philosophical critiques of prevailing HCI theories, methods, and practices, and it is difficult to overstate their influence. They include Lucy Suchman's *Plans and Situated Actions* (1987), which reframes interaction in Heideggerian and semantics-influenced terms, having come out of the same intellectual circles as Winograd and Flores' work; Bannon and Bødker's 1991 "Beyond the Interface: Encountering Artifacts in Use," which offers a devastating analysis of the then-dominant cognitivism of the day and reframes HCI from within around issues of praxis and activity; Cooper and Bowers' (1995) "Representing the User" appropriates the methods of philosopher Michel Foucault to offer an analysis of "the user" as a discursive construct that HCI uses to legitimate itself (almost independent of actual users or needs); Harrison and Dourish's (1996) "Re-Place-ing Space" attacks the conceptual underpinnings of collaborative system design, arguing that it confuses "space" vs. "place," building on humanist geography to re-evaluate spatial systems. The cumulative effects of these works has been to argue that the field should move away from abstract models and logical representations toward a more situated and empirically grounded science. In other words, many of these articles were advocating for changes in HCI's scientific agenda, and for that reason it is easy to overlook their humanistic qualities. But inasmuch as each involved a critical analysis of one or more conceptual systems that underlie the science of HCI at the time, in every case using philosophy or other humanistic theories as resources to think beyond existing theories, they were also humanistic. Thus, even though humanistic HCI had little by way of critical mass before 2004, the fact is that the humanities have been contributing foundationally to HCI almost since the very beginning.

But it was in the early 2000s that humanistic HCI came into its own. The primary underlying cause, we believe, is that technologies had changed sufficiently—the Internet, mobile computing, etc.—that the field was more or less compelled to look beyond its existing theories and methods for new resources that could support it. In 2002, researchers at Aarhus University were fusing pragmatist aesthetics, digital media criticism, and HCI (Bertelsen and Pold, 2002). In the U. K., researchers offered a series of agenda-setting workshops that would eventually lead to a network grant entitled LeonardNet, including a CHI workshop on Funology (Monk et al., 2002) and a BCS HCI workshop entitled "Understanding User Experience: Literary Analysis Meets HCI" (Wright and Finlay, 2002). In 2003, HCI's (over-)emphasis on workplace computing was directly called to task in Blythe et al.'s (2003) *Funology: From Usability to Enjoyment* (see Chapter 5).

A year later, in 2004, the lid blew off, as dozens of significant humanist HCI papers and events happened all at once. These include a highly influential CHI 2004 workshop on "Reflective HCI," offered by Dourish et al. (2004) connected to LeonardoNet; John McCarthy and Peter Wright's seminal book *Technology as Experience*; important design papers by Bill Gaver, including a piece on cultural probes (Gaver et al., 2005) and the introduction of his Drift Table (Gaver et al., 2004); research papers foregrounding the role of interpretation in user experience (e.g., Höök, 2004; Sengers et al., 2004); and a number of other papers from what we now recognize as humanistic HCI researchers: Genevieve Bell, Olav Bertelsen, Alan Blackwell, Mark Blythe, Kirsten Boehner, Gilbert Cockton, Caroline Hummels, Jofish Kaye, Ann Light, Marianne Graves Petersen, Jennifer Rode, Thecla Schiphorst, Alex Taylor, and Ron Wakkary to name a few. 2004 was a watershed year for humanistic HCI.

Since then humanistic HCI has been well represented in the HCI community, finding homes in the Design subcommittee of the CHI conference, ACM Designing Interactive Systems (DIS), INTERACT, and in numerous journal special issues on humanities-friendly topics including experience, domestic life, aesthetics, feminism, participatory design, sexuality, and so on. Conceptual analyses of HCI research continued stronger than ever, analyzing and reframing HCI's treatment of topics such as emotion, context, sustainability, sexuality, and ubiquitous computing. Much of this book will be devoted to elaborating what these bodies of research have contributed. More recently, in perhaps the best evidence of all that humanistic HCI has reached critical mass, there have been a series of workshops and panels about humanistic HCI: it has achieved self-awareness and reflexivity (e.g., Blythe et al., 2006, 2008, 2010; Cockton et al., 2010; Bardzell et al., 2011, 2012).

Meanwhile, at the same time that humanistic approaches were moving into HCI, HCI researchers with other disciplinary backgrounds were moving into areas traditionally viewed as humanistic. For example, in the late 1990s and early 2000s, Noam Tractinsky wrote a series of highly influential papers that challenged and eventually overthrew the notion, promoted at the time by Don Norman and Jakob Nielsen, that aesthetics hindered usability and therefore that interfaces should be minimalist and transparent (see, e.g., Tractinsky et al., 2000). Using psychological methods, Tractinsky et al. showed how aesthetic judgments link to product perceptions and user experiences, and they (and many fellow travelers, including Marc Hassenzahl and Alistair G. Sutcliffe) have constructed models of aesthetic valuations that link together design choices, perceptual and experiential qualities, sociocultural context, and outcomes.

As Tractinsky and colleagues brought HCI research into aesthetics, so have Batya Friedman and colleagues brought HCI research into ethics. Their notion of "value-sensitive design seeks to provide theory and method to account for human values in a principled and systematic manner throughout the design process" (http://www.vsdesign.org/, accessed August 14, 2014). From that perspective they have undertaken a number of systems design projects as well as developed toolkits to support the values-informed design of interactive systems. As an example of this work, Friedman and Nathan (2010) have focused on the design of multi-lifespan systems, that is, systems that are operative longer than human lifetimes, intended to contribute to national memory and healing after the genocide in Rwanda. It is not hard to see such a project as having significant implications for cultural studies researchers, historians, and postcolonial cultural theorists.

The movement of HCI scholars like Tractinsky and Friedman (and there are many others) into areas of interest that are traditionally situated in the humanities is significant. Above all, it underscores our central argument that HCI needs and wants to engage humanistic topics, theories, and methodologies. Such work creates openings for humanists to participate in HCI, and, equally important, for HCI to influence the humanities by revealing new domains and issues that ought to be of interest to humanists, as we saw in the Rwanda example. At the same time, there are risks for non-humanist HCI researchers and practitioners entering into these domains: the risk of reinventing an already well-developed concept, of naively misappropriating technical vocabulary, and of failing to learn from hard-won achievements and debates—all of which have occurred to certain degrees in HCI already (see Chapter 3). Another challenge is that some HCI researchers, who are trained in the sciences but sympathetic to HCI contributions building on the humanities, don't know where to begin or how to use what's there.

What we want to argue for is rapprochement; that is, we believe that the field needs improved bridges to bring humanists (e.g., individuals with backgrounds in literature, philosophy, or history), humanistic HCI researchers (such as ourselves and those who contributed to the 2004 watershed), non-humanist HCI researchers who engage in traditionally humanities topics (such as Tractinsky and Friedman), and everyday systems and interaction designers more broadly. We hope this book can serve as one such bridge.

1.2   AIMS AND STRUCTURE OF THIS BOOK

In writing this book for a broad HCI and design readership, we aim to answer a number of basic questions as directly as possible.

- **What is humanistic HCI?** What is it not? Is it a domain of inquiry, a method, a discipline?

- **What makes humanistic HCI *humanistic*?** That is, how does it relate to traditional humanities? How does it relate to emerging humanities fields, including digital humanities, science and technology studies, and media studies? How do humanistic forms of rigor translate into HCI?

- **What makes humanistic HCI *HCI*?** How does humanistic HCI fit with HCI's scientific and design agendas? How do HCI researchers and practitioners use humanistic perspectives, theories, and research? What are their impacts on research and practice? How can HCI researchers evaluate humanities-based HCI research?

Each of these questions can be pursued descriptively and also normatively. That is, we can ask: How does the body of research in HCI that identifies itself with the humanities articulate its relations to the humanities, to HCI? But we can also ask: Given what we understand of the humanities and HCI, *how should* HCI best engage the humanities? Of course, the two senses overlap, since investigating the former requires judgments about what to count as humanistic HCI (on behalf of the original authors as well as the analyst), and since the normative question can only be seriously answered with reference to facts already on the record. We'll engage both the descriptive and the normative tasks, and we'll try to indicate when we're doing which.

This book is divided into two main parts, aside from the Introduction and the Conclusion. In the first part, we offer an account of what humanistic HCI is as a knowledge practice. In the second part, we work through two major impact areas of humanistic HCI: user experience/aesthetic interaction and emancipatory HCI.

In Chapter 2, we answer basic questions about the humanities, including some definitions, some accounts of what humanists do, and some accounts of the services the humanities provide for society at-large. In doing so, we reference a number of key historical and contemporary sources on the humanities from inside. Topics include historical awareness and the preservation (and criticism) of tradition; the theory and practice of interpretation; the reimagination of the social world and its translation into social action; the reflexive analysis of humanistic theories and methods; and pedagogical contributions toward the inculcation of critical thinking and creative expression and production. We discuss the understanding of humanistic HCI used in this book, consider it in relation to other HCI knowledge practices, and explore what is at stake with such definitions and distinctions.

Chapter 3 offers a general account of humanistic HCI methodologies, surveying the approaches by which it produces knowledge in HCI. We identify some of the distinctive potentials of humanistic HCI, including the humanities' strengths at evaluating competing normative claims and understanding the relationships between objects (e.g., artworks, designs, environments), individual subjective experiences of them, and the social situations of which such interactions are partly constitutive. It also surveys key epistemological and methodological commitments that are common in humanistic thinking and explores how such commitments play out in HCI research.

In Chapter 4 we focus on common research outcomes, both to help guide HCI researchers and practitioners integrating humanistic approaches in their projects and also to support peer review of such work, especially important for HCI given how interdisciplinary we are as a field. This chapter places a special emphasis on the role of the essay in humanistic knowledge-production. We argue that the essay is crucial, rather than incidental, to the articulation of humanistic rigor, because it is by means of the essay form that the deep connections between humanistic methods and knowledge outcomes become manifest. We distinguish the humanistic essay structurally and substantively from the scientific report to help explicate the essay's special fit for humanistic thinking. We end the chapter with specific peer reviewing guidelines for HCI research using humanistic approaches and/or offering humanistic contributions. Our hope is that our analysis of the essay explains and justifies these recommendations.

Part II, the portion of the book focused on major humanistic HCI impact areas, begins with Chapter 5, which traces the emergence of a humanistic conceptualization of user experience as a reaction to the usability movement. It focuses on two major approaches to user experience and aesthetic interaction: *a pragmatist vision*, heavily influenced by American pragmatist philosophers John Dewey and Richard Shusterman, and a *poetics-based vision* influenced (directly and more often indirectly) by Aristotle. The pragmatist vision theorizes experience—what it is, how it is structured, what distinguishes good from bad experiences, etc.—with plenty of implications for user research study design, data analysis, and design ideation. The poetics vision explicates the relationships between individual design elements, and the styles/themes that shape all of those elements into coherent wholes, and the anticipated experiential qualities that these lead to when people use them. We close the chapter with a reflective and critical stance on each of these approaches, the humanistic HCI project more generally as it pertains to experience and aesthetics, and the unfortunate rift that presently divides key contributions in humanistic vs. psychology-based approaches to user experience.

Chapter 6, "Social Change and Emancipation," summarizes four major threads of emancipatory thinking in the humanities: Marxism, psychoanalysis, feminism, and postcolonialism. It then surveys a range of HCI work that reflects these strategies. It confronts the fact that much of this work does not explicitly acknowledge its theoretical underpinnings—particularly those works that rely on Marxist and psychoanalytic theories and methods. It also introduces a major formulation of criticality in HCI—reflective HCI—which underlies virtually all emancipatory HCI. We close this chapter reflectively as well, considering the strengths and limitations of these diverse approaches, and what they imply about the road ahead.

We conclude the book by turning around and facing forward. What is next for humanistic HCI? How can HCI continue to build on humanistic HCI's strengths and deal with its weaknesses? What emerging HCI topics seem especially interesting from a humanistic perspective? How can we support the ongoing integration of humanistic HCI into the interdisciplinary field of HCI, so that it does not become a sealed-off niche area? How might humanistic HCI serve as a bridge between HCI and neighboring disciplines, such as video game design and studies, digital media, science and technology studies, and perhaps beyond to philosophy, comparative literature, and history?

1.3   COUNTERACTING THE GOD-TRICK: INTRODUCING YOUR NARRATORS

What follows is a scholarly historical genealogy and analysis of the humanities, which we then use to construct a certain view of humanistic HCI, and then provide a critical tour of the field situated in and guided by that view. Conventions of Western academic writing have us present all of this in the third person, rhetorically suppressing us—Jeffrey and Shaowen—and creating the illusion of what feminist philosopher Donna Haraway refers to as a "gaze from nowhere" and the "god trick." That is, the third-person academic voice suppresses writers' contingent identities and gives the writing what we'll call an *objectivity effect*, which in turn disempowers readers from assessing the roles we play as narrators constructing this story. One way to counter these effects is to disclose ourselves and our positioning as speakers, so that readers can understand our claims in relation to our contingent positions, rather than as the voice of a hidden all-knowing god.

Here are the relevant facts of our narratorial positionalities as relevant to this book (as we understand them). Both Shaowen and Jeffrey earned Ph.D.s in Comparative Literature in the early 2000s. Shaowen's dissertation focused on gender and rituals (e.g., of gift exchange) in medieval vernacular poetry. Jeffrey's dissertation focused on literary theory and ancient linguistics in ancient and medieval Latin poetry. By the late 1990s, we were both transitioning toward interaction design, putting ourselves through school as graphic and web designers and programmers and authoring books for Macromedia Press and similar publishers. In the mid 2000s, we both became academic

HCI researchers, and our research has focused on user experience and aesthetics (Jeffrey) and emancipatory approaches to HCI (Shaowen).

We anticipate several implications of our positionalities for the following narrative and the book as a whole. One is that our biographical trajectories are atypical in HCI—we are not aware of any other HCI researchers or practitioners with Ph.D.s in Medieval Studies, for example—and so we did not experience or contribute to the field's turn to the humanities in quite the way that others did.

Another is that our account of the humanities has a bias, in that it privileges literary sources and the study of literature as typical of the humanities. Had we been, say, historians or law students, our account of the humanities would likely be very different, and we would use different examples and framings. This bias is reflected, among other ways, through our extensive use of quoting in this book. The many block quotes throughout this book reflect our humanistic commitment to allowing our sources to speak for themselves while also allowing our readers to hear for themselves the voices we cite. The block quotes are a form of evidence, if you will.

Another bias is that we know "traditional" humanistic sources (i.e., humanistic theory and practice from the ancient world through the end of the 20th century) better than we know contemporary ones. Readers will find references to traditional literary figures such as Shakespeare and Joyce, and to classic theorists of the arts, including Aristotle and Matthew Arnold, but less to contemporary thinkers in the digital humanities and STS. The digital humanities were in their infancy when we were completing our Ph.D.s (mostly at the time focusing on creating electronic archives of important works), and (near-) contemporary digital arts activities, from Cybernetic Serendipity to SIGGRAPH and Transmediale, were simply not on our radars. This bias has a key advantage and a key disadvantage. The advantage is that we are able to situate humanistic HCI in a 2,400-year old conversation, highlighting the contiguities so that we do not reinvent wheels while teasing forward what is apparently new. The disadvantage is that we do not fully leverage parallel conversations in the digital humanities, STS, and the contemporary art scene today.

Knowing all of this, we sought to counter potentially negative effects during the research and writing of this book. We remind readers that it is we two writing, and not an all-knowing humanistic HCI god voice, by using the first-person quite frequently (much to the annoyance of our junior high school English teachers) and by trying to maintain a coherent voice and relation to you, our reader (much to the presumed approval of our undergraduate composition professors). We read up on areas where we knew we were weak, and we acknowledge and reference works outside of our immediate comfort zones so at least readers would have some pointers to that literature. But we also remain committed to the humanistic view that part of our contribution is precisely our ability to speak from our experience as a source of strength—and we lean on our experiences in Comparative Literature when and where they matter the most.

Thus, your narrators are introduced, *who prologue-like your humble patience pray / Gently to hear, kindly to judge, our play.*[1]

PART I

Theorizing Humanistic HCI

CHAPTER 2

What is Humanistic HCI?

To answer the question of what is humanistic HCI, we first take a step backward to consider the question, what are the humanities? Now, we assume that all of our readers have taken humanities courses at various points in their careers, that they are critical thinkers who are widely read, and that they already have a fairly sophisticated understanding of the humanities based on their own experiences. So it might seem needlessly pedantic to spend part of this short book introducing a topic that readers already know.

But we have several reasons for beginning with this question. Above all, we want to direct readers' understanding of the humanities into a relation to HCI. To do so, we want to offer an analytic (rather than intuitive and experiential) account of the humanities. A more analytic account has the benefits of allowing us to explicate relations between humanist and scientific approaches to knowledge and also to pull forward a set of themes that we will refer to throughout the book, which animate humanistic HCI. Creating this analytic account necessarily requires us to make choices about major categories, theories, historical contexts, and disciplinary boundaries, and to help us with this task, lest it be idiosyncratic, we will want the humanities to speak for themselves, so we will quote generously so readers can see how humanists account for their own practices.

Once we have our account of the humanities, we return to the question of what is humanistic HCI, offering a formulation of the term and exploring some of its consequences. In particular, we will consider what the term ends up including and excluding to assess whether the results fit with our expectations and understandings.

2.1 WHAT ARE THE HUMANITIES?

The humanities is an umbrella term that today is used to refer collectively to a range of academic fields or disciplines, including art history, classics, cultural studies, film studies, languages, law, literature, media studies, philosophy, religion, women's studies, and so on. The humanities are also associated with a range of key concepts, including humanism, the arts, critical theory, and culture. Beginning in the last century through the present, the humanities have come under heavy fire from outside and from within, for being tied to traditions that are either irrelevant, because we've moved beyond them, or politically regressive and therefore dangerous. We will survey all of these issues in the following pages, again with an eye toward HCI where appropriate, beginning with the social rationale for the humanities as we understand them today.

2.1.1   THE SOCIETAL CONTRIBUTION OF THE HUMANITIES

Humanistic practices have been around since the pre-Socratics in the west, and philosophy, literature, law, and the fine arts have been practiced continuously ever since. However, what we recognize today as a more or less stable set of academic fields, canons of works, and intellectual practices is much more recent. Our concept of "the fine arts"—a concept that unifies painting, sculpture, architecture, music, and poetry under a single concept (Art) and intellectual field (aesthetics)—dates only back to the 18th century (Kristeller, 2008). Liberal humanism itself—the notion that the arts can serve as the basis to educate and cultivate the free citizens of Western democracies—emerged in the 19th century. The first English departments in the United Kingdom started in the late 1820s, though it would take nearly another century before Oxford and Cambridge would have one (Barry, 2002). F.D. Maurice, Professor at King's College (which later would become part of London University), argued in 1840 that the study of English would "emancipate us … from the notions and habits which are peculiar to our own age" and would instead connect us to "what is fixed and enduring" (quoted in Barry, 2002, p. 13). The goal here, clearly an Enlightenment goal, is to move beyond our immediate context to connect to the universal.

In 1865, Matthew Arnold, the cultural critic and "founding father of modern criticism in the English-speaking world" (Trilling, cited in Leitch, 2001, p. 802), wrote a seminal essay called "The Function of Criticism at the Present Time" (Arnold, 2010, [1865]). In it, he would characterize "the critical power" as serving the following social purposes:

> to establish an order of ideas, if not absolutely true, yet true by comparison with that which it displaces; to make the best ideas prevail.… [T]o keep man from a self-satisfaction which is retarding and vulgarising, to lead him toward perfection, by making his mind dwell upon what is excellent in itself, and the absolute beauty and fitness of things.… [And to answer the question,] what will nourish us in growth toward perfection? (pp. 809, 816, 825).

As Peter Barry (2002) comments,

> You can see from [Arnold] that the study of English literature is being seen as a kind of substitute for religion. It was well known that attendance at church below middle-class level was very patchy. The worry was that the lower class would feel that they had no stake in the country and, having no religion to teach them morality and restraint, they would rebel and something like the French Revolution would take place. (p. 13)

It is interesting to note the contrast in tone and social agenda in Arnold's words and in Barry analyzing Arnold. For Arnold, criticism and liberal humanism are emancipatory, helping man [sic] elevate himself out of barbarity and pursue excellence in himself and greatness in his surroundings. For Barry, this agenda was in fact used as a mechanism to get the lower classes to buy into the status quo, thereby decreasing the chance of revolution. This tension—do the arts and humanities emancipate or are they subtle tools of oppression—remains debated today. Our view is that these options are not exclusive, that is, that the arts and humanities, as institutionalized and practiced today, can have both emancipatory and oppressive effects.

At any rate, the modern humanities are founded on a theory of the individual, one in which individuals can be cultivated "toward perfection" through access to the best ideas. A professional class is needed to identify which ideas were the best and to make those ideas accessible to the masses, which is the job of the critic or humanist to perform.

What we see in these nineteenth-century formulations is a concept of *enlightenment*—that humanities-informed engagement with the arts and sciences enlightens individuals, that is, brings us to transcend ourselves and moves us closer to perfection; and a parallel concept of *society*—that by giving all individuals a stake in their nation (i.e., their Englishness) the social order can thereby be protected from revolutions. There is no question, at least at the level of Maurice's or Arnold's explicit intentions, of cynically hoodwinking the masses into docility to maintain economic domination over them; rather, there is the optimistic hope that through universal education, defined as a carefully curated and explanatory access to the finest English (and later universal) ideas, the whole nation can be raised up.

This 19th century vision in some ways seems quaint today. And yet, the core commitment to individual enlightenment as a wellspring of a good society remains entrenched even now. Consider this 2014 description of the humanities from the United States' most significant federal funding source for the humanities, the National Endowment for the Humanities (NEH):

> Because democracy demands wisdom, NEH serves and strengthens our republic by promoting excellence in the humanities and conveying the lessons of history to all Americans…. The term 'humanities' includes, but is not limited to, the study and interpretation of the following: language, both modern and classical; linguistics; literature; history; jurisprudence; philosophy; archaeology; comparative religion; ethics; the history, criticism and theory of the arts; those aspects of social sciences which have humanistic content and employ humanistic methods; and the study and application of the humanities to the human environment with particular attention to reflecting our diverse heritage, traditions, and history and to the relevance of the humanities to the current conditions of national life (http://www.neh.gov/about, accessed August 16, 2014).

The notion of a *republic* depends on the wisdom of citizens, and the humanities are a national mechanism for ensuring that collective wisdom, with studies of what it means to be human conducted with a special focus on (in this case) American traditions, history, and national life. Here the NEH is embracing a view very close to that of Matthew Arnold, as discussed above. One could, of course, also argue that a U.S. government-funded humanistic agency also has the ulterior motive of building lower and middle class buy-in to its own regime.

While the humanities have, as we have mentioned, come under considerable fire in the past half century, it is not hard to find old school humanists still around expressing those values. One of the most notable is Harold Bloom, perhaps the most highly regarded literary critic of our times, a Yale professor whose dozens of books have deeply influenced academic and non-academic audiences alike. In a series of books, *The Western Canon* (1994), *How to Read and Why* (2000), and *Where Shall Wisdom Be Found?* (2004), he passionately defends the traditional humanities against its critics. He affirms the Arnoldian notion that literature is enlightening but expands Arnold's "good citizens make a good country" argument into an argument that reading brings us more fully in line with our humanity. Here is a selection of quotes from the Introduction of Bloom's *How to Read and Why* (2000):

> It matters, if individuals are to retain any capacity to form their own judgments and opinions, that they continue to read for themselves.… Ultimately we read … in order to strengthen the self, and to learn its authentic interests.… To read human sentiments in human language you must be able to read humanly, with all of you. (pp. 21–22, 28)

> We read deeply for varied reasons, most of them familiar: that we cannot know enough people profoundly enough; that we need to know ourselves better; that we require knowledge, not just of self and others, but of the way things are. Yet the strongest, most authentic motive for deep reading of the now much-abused traditional canon is the search for difficult pleasure. I am not exactly an erotics-of-reading purveyor, and a pleasurable difficulty seems to me a plausible definition of the Sublime, but a higher pleasure remains the reader's quest. There is a reader's Sublime, and it seems the only secular transcendence we can ever attain, except for the even more precarious transcendence we call "falling in love." I urge you to find what truly comes near you, that can be used for weighing and considering. Read deeply, not to believe, not to accept, not to contradict, but to learn to share in that one nature that writes and reads. (pp. 28–29)

For Bloom, reading is not about the transmission of great ideas (for that would foreground believing, accepting, or contradicting), but rather is about an almost Platonic participation in the form of (literate) human nature, a participation that is marked by acts of weighing and considering, that is, critical judgment.

From the standpoint of its social value, the humanities effectively rests on a double argument. The first part of the argument says that all individuals can become better or worse, can be ennobled or degraded, can become enlightened or remain in ignorance; that contact with the finest human ideas, expressed in artistic and scientific works, will do this work of education and enlightenment; and that this is valuable work to do because the growth and stability of democratic society depends on it. The second part of the argument says that it is the job of the humanities to serve this purpose, which it does by identifying what the best ideas are, and then by removing barriers to their public appreciation in the works in which they are found (e.g., a work of Shakespeare).

There are several criticisms of this formulation of the social value of the humanities, which we will get to shortly, but we note that after decades of attacks, the humanities, in a formulation like this, are making a comeback. Part of the reason for that comeback, we argue, is that not just nations, but science itself (including HCI!) depends on the best ideas enjoying wide currency, both within scientific practices and in the public at-large, which, after all, is expected both to fund scientific research and education and to supply universities with intellectually curious freshmen.

Speaking generally, we are inclined to argue that humanistic HCI can be seen to serve the sorts of social purposes outlined here. For example, humanistic pushback has occurred in HCI at times when the field appears to degrade users, e.g., by rendering them as mere "disembodied ratio-cinators" in Bannon and Bødker's (1991) memorable phrase, or as "a fragile beast under threat from technology" as Cooper and Bowers (1995) put it—both seminal essays calling for and contributing toward a kind of intellectual reform in HCI. The humanist stance also sees a link between the cultivation or enlightenment of the individual and the betterment of society or human nature, which is often expressed as a political and emancipatory stance. That is, if a good society is founded on the enlightenment of its citizens, then it follows that a society that has oppressed or degraded citizens is problematic. In this regard, HCI contributions informed by critical theory, feminism, and postcolonialism have shown how the design of technologies participates in oppression and degradation, e.g., of women, of racial minorities, of citizens of the global south, etc., both harming individuals *qua* users and society at-large in the process. Moving toward a more meta stance, when HCI seems to be committing itself to theoretical and methodological perspectives that are problematic, humanistic HCI has used conceptual analysis to expose weaknesses and create opportunities to introduce alternative conceptual frameworks for the field (e.g., Winograd and Flores, 1986; Boehner et al., 2005; Harrison and Dourish, 1996; Erickson and McDonald, 2008; Moggridge, 2007). Of course, science has its own mechanisms for theoretical and methodological redirection, but the use in the above cases of both philosophical methods (e.g., conceptual analysis) and philosophical concept systems (e.g., Heideggerian phenomenology) has a distinctly humanistic character, even if it unfolded within and for a scientific research context. In short, not only has humanistic HCI shaped HCI, but it has done so in recognizably humanistic terms.

2.1.2 CHARACTERISTIC FEATURES OF HUMANISTIC PRACTICE

There are several features that are common, if not universal, to humanistic knowledge contributions. In this section we discuss how the humanities contribute to our ability to learn from history and tradition, the central role of critical interpretation in humanistic thought, the intentional intermingling of social activism and knowledge production, and the humanities' contributions toward the development, clarification, and justification of concepts. As we will show in the main body of this book, each of these is carried forward into humanistic HCI.

History and Tradition

It is thanks to art history, for example, that we have a historical narrative of art; that we can distinguish among impressionism, neo-impressionism, post-impressionism, and expressionism based on qualities intrinsic and extrinsic to individual works; that we can defend judgments about art works, artists, and artistic innovations; and that we can explain the social benefits and even market values of individual works. Languages are also important: a scholar of French literature who couldn't read French, or a classicist who didn't know Greek or Latin is a contradiction in terms. Even when a humanist is attacking tradition, as often happens, it is inconceivable that the humanist wouldn't know it intimately. Thus, it is easy to find literary scholars denouncing the patriarchy of the Western canon, but impossible to find any literary scholars that haven't read extensively from that canon; indeed, a scholar of English literature who hadn't read Shakespeare is also a contradiction in terms. It is by means of the humanities that "the lessons of history" that the NEH builds itself around are available at all.

In short, one of the services of the humanities is to offer historical accounts, including articulations of important past events and also narratives of artistic traditions and canons—not to fetishize or preserve the past but to enliven our sensitivities to the present and to the nature of social change (e.g., how quickly it unfolds, how it is rationalized, what its long-term effects are viewed in hindsight). These contribute to a systematic reconstruction of the available knowledge and background of the original act of creation and/or audience for a given work: language, styles, genres, sociocultural and historical details, knowledge of what they would have available as background knowledge or readings, etc. This makes possible the interpretation of individual works in relation to traditions and canons. It also not surprisingly gives rise to criticisms, revisions, and defenses of historical accounts, traditions, and canons.

HCI is an interesting field with regard to history and tradition. Having emerged only in the last 40 years, it doesn't have the millennia-long histories of literature, painting, or even certain design disciplines, such as fashion. Many HCI systems are presented with little to no reference to their own historical genealogies, and the field itself has no significant histories, beyond a generally shared sense that HCI has had three paradigms or waves (Bødker, 2006; Harrison et al., 2007; Rogers, 2012). Yet other design fields—including architecture, product design, graphic design, and fashion design—do have significant histories, and practicing designers know and use them. Our expectation is that interaction design and/or HCI (whatever their relation is or will become, exactly) will develop much more of a historical sensibility in the coming decade.

Interpretation, Hermeneutic Analysis

The objects of inquiry of the humanities are complexly layered and defy simple understanding. We look at Andy Warhol's *Brillo Box* and wonder why it is art at all. A high school curriculum planner needs to justify why *Hamlet* is better for 9th graders than *Richard II*. A believer wonders how an erotic poem that makes no reference to God found its way into the Hebrew scriptures and how she is supposed to make sense of it spiritually. A college student watches a classic movie and wonders what all the fuss was about. The state takes a publisher to court over the purported obscenity of a novel: but is it obscene? Making headway with any of these situations requires skilled *interpretation*, and the development and dissemination of that skill is a paradigm contribution of the humanities.

Interpretation

Interpretation is a word with a wide range of applications, and accordingly it can be difficult to define. Below, we offer two major formulations of "interpretation" to provide some cognitive handles on this slippery term. The first addresses why we interpret and what interpretation achieves. The second addresses the mechanisms of interpretation—what we do when we interpret.

One is that of political philosopher Charles Taylor, who writes:

> Interpretation … is an attempt to make clear, to make sense of an object of study. This object must, therefore, be … in some sense confused, incomplete, cloudy, contradictory—in one way or another unclear. The interpretation attempts to bring to light an underlying coherence or sense. This means that any science that can be called [interpretative] … must be dealing with one or another of the confusingly interrelated forms of meaning. (Taylor, 1971, p. 6)

The other is from aesthetic philosopher Noël Carroll, who characterizes interpretation in relation to works of art:

> Interpretation … goes beyond the given in order to establish the significance of what has been given. Interpretation is concerned with significance—for instance the thematic significance or the narrative significance of an artwork or the significance of the behavior of a character in a fiction or the interrogation of the import of a metaphor […] Typically, interpretation involves the process of abduction—hypothesizing from the various parts of an artwork to the theme or message or idea or concept that best explains why the assemblage of parts before us coheres together as a whole […] Interpretation aims at excavating the sense of the work. (Carroll, 2009, p. 110)

The humanities have contributed to this goal in three basic ways: *interpretations of particular works*, which remove barriers to their appreciation or comprehension; the *development of frameworks and theories of reading* (e.g., close reading, reader-response theory, the New Criticism, psychoanalysis, and deconstruction); and the *development of justificatory accounts of interpretative theories*, that is, metacriticism.

The most conspicuous application of interpretation in HCI has been in experience design, particularly the cultural strand of experience design (Blythe et al., 2003; McCarthy and Wright, 2004; Sengers and Gaver, 2006), Höök, 2010; Pace et al., 2010, among others). This strand of research has argued that usability measures are insufficient to characterize experience in sufficient rich or broad terms, especially given the move of computing to all parts of everyday life. Experience itself is the kind of "confused, incomplete, cloudy, contradictory" phenomenon that demands interpretation, which includes the users interpreting their own experiences with technology as well as researchers interpreting technological experiences.

Additionally, interpretation has come up in other areas of HCI. Ubiquitous computing research is vision-driven, that is, underlying the possibility of ubicomp research is an interpretative vision of what the future will or should or could be like (Weiser, 1991; Bell and Dourish, 2007; Rogers, 2006; Bardzell and Bardzell, 2014; Blythe, 2014). Aesthetic interaction is another area where skilled acts of interpretation have been foregrounded (e.g., Bertelsen and Pold, 2004; Löwgren, 2006; Bardzell, 2011). Humanities-supported interpretations have also had significant impacts on HCI4D (Irani et al., 2010), games and play (Nardi, 2010; Fernaeus, 2012), self-expression and identity (Akah and Bardzell, 2010; Tanenbaum et al., 2012).

Social Action

With the exceptions of movements such as art-for-art's-sake decadence and postmodern skepticism, the belief that the arts and humanities serve a higher social purpose has been a main thread of humanistic thinking. The concept of *emancipation* is at the center of much of this work. Emancipation refers to delivery from bondage, and humanists typically take a broad and inclusive view of bondage, ranging from the emancipation of slaves to far more subtle forms of domination, exploitation, and abuse. The latter would include the abuse of one's own body to fit patriarchal norms of feminine beauty (in the case of anorexia), or making fun of lower class accents as a way to reinforce social class distinctions.

As we discuss in Chapter 6, Marxism, psychoanalysis, feminism, and postcolonialism are all emancipatory perspectives and approaches. Each focuses on a different formulation of a hegemonic status quo, analyzing its tactics of self-perpetuation, and analyzing and/or proposing tactics of resistance.

- **Marxism** analyzes the ways that capitalism establishes an exploitative system of labor, economic production, and wealth distribution and then embeds it in a self-reinforcing way of life that seems both natural and inevitable.

- **Psychoanalysis** posits profound conflicts between our embodied selves with instinctive drives on the one hand and our social selves subjected to a common language and heavily codified way of life.

- **Feminism** considers how biological sex is interpreted and performed as socially constructed gender norms, which are themselves exploitative and seemingly natural and inevitable.

- **Postcolonialism** focuses on the ways that Western culture unilaterally establishes the Middle East as a homogenous cultural "other," failing to recognize how the diverse peoples of the region understand themselves or even letting them speak for themselves on the matter. This cultural other is then used to justify the West's ongoing political, economic, cultural, intellectual, and military engagements in the region.

These kinds of emancipatory critiques are well represented across many areas of HCI research and practice. The computer's "reaching out" has touched much of the planet: it's in our bedrooms, in our pockets, in diverse societies across the globe, and so forth. For those of us who research and design systems, it's easy enough to see that we have social power. Whether we want it or not, we have the power to inscribe social norms, gender roles, everyday practical assumptions into technologies—and we do. The idea that "user needs come first," when the power to understand and interpret "user needs" is unilaterally (self-)granted to Western scientists, is colonial. That "the user" lacks gender, that is, that HCI is "gender blind," flies directly in the face of the core value proposition that feminists bring to the table. That the planned obsolescence baked into Apple's environmentally disastrous business model seems perfectly natural and reasonable is a function of capitalist hegemony. HCI researchers are leveraging the concept systems and critical interpretative methods of the humanities both to expose HCI's complicity in practices of domination and oppression while seeking to develop alternative HCI theories and methods to combat them.

Conceptual Analysis

Around the turn of the twentieth century, it was clear that science had risen as the privileged form of knowledge production, eclipsing other knowledge disciplines, including the humanities. This development put considerable pressure on the prior center of all intellectual knowledge, philosophy: What was philosophy's role in a scientific era? Did science eliminate the need for philosophy? Or was philosophy to serve in a secondary role, serving as a handmaiden to science? Perhaps philosophy needed to become more scientific. It was a lively period for philosophy and the first part of the twentieth century burgeoned with new ideas about the relations between philosophy and science, and a two-part answer was developed, which in many ways is still with us today.

The two-part answer is to identify what philosophy is and to situate it in relation to science. One thing was clear and that is what philosophy is not: a discipline that can give us doctrines about how the world is (science had preempted that role). Instead, philosophy became an activity directed at the clarification of thoughts, as the early Wittgenstein wrote in this passage from his *Tractatus Logico-Philosophicus*:

> The object of philosophy is the logical clarification of thoughts.
>
> Philosophy is not a theory but an activity.
>
> A philosophical work consists essentially of elucidations.
>
> The result of philosophy is not a number of "philosophical propositions", but to make propositions clear.
>
> Philosophy should make clear and delimit sharply the thoughts which otherwise are, as it were, opaque and blurred. (1999 [1922], Section 4.112)

Or as Bertrand Russell put it,

> The business of philosophy, as I conceive it, is essentially that of logical analysis, followed by logical synthesis … The most important part [of philosophy] consists in criticizing and clarifying notions which are apt to be regarded as fundamental and accept uncritically. (cited in Glock, 2008, p. 6)

This philosophical activity had two components for Rudolf Carnap, one positive and the other negative: "Negatively, it reveals metaphysical nonsense. Positively, it turns into the 'logic of science', namely the linguistic analysis or explication of scientific propositions, concepts and methods" (Glock, 2008, p. 141).

Philosophy was thus moving away from producing original systems, as Aristotle had done, and which seemed now to be quaint dogmas, grand pronouncements, and metaphysical nonsense, and toward the disciplined analysis of the concepts we use to think with, and "we" in this case refers to everyday citizens, philosophers, and scientists alike. Thus, if scientists use a concept uncritically, it is the job of the philosopher to step in and offer a conceptual (or logical or linguistic) analysis and set the scientist on stronger conceptual footing. "Philosophy, in fact, is the activity whereby the *meaning* of statements is established or discovered," Glock writes. "Philosophy elucidates propositions, science verifies them. … Even this separation is not feasible, and that the definition of concepts is part and parcel of the work of unified science" (2008, pp. 135–6). Another role for the philosopher is to investigate those aspects of reality that are not understandable using the methods of empirical science (see Glock, 2008, p. 135). In these ways, philosophy retains a distinctive role in knowledge production, one that cooperates with rather than competes against science.

We have already written in the Introduction of how works considered seminal in HCI, such as Winograd and Flores (1986), Cooper and Bowers (1995), Harrison and Dourish (1996), and others can be described as doing conceptual analysis. That is, they offer an analysis of how HCI researchers use a concept, critiquing its shortcomings, and proposing better alternatives, many of which themselves are drawn from elsewhere in philosophy. Some of the key HCI concepts that have been analyzed in this way include aesthetics, affect, cognitive models, context, criticality, design implications, probes, reflection, sexuality, space and place, sustainability, and the user. In Chapter 3, we will return to conceptual analysis in HCI, but suffice it to say for now that many of these works have had tremendous influence on the field.

2.1.3   AGAINST THE HUMANITIES

Even as the humanities flourished in the 20th century, they also came under considerable attack, both from without and from within. But we will argue that none of the attacks is decisive, as each has its own limitations and confounds. These attacks, and the sorts of responses they prompt, in many ways shape the humanities today, and humanistic HCI carries forward hallmarks of these debates.

Scientism: An Attack from Without

The primary attack from without is that relic of logical positivism known as *scientism*. It is a doctrine like scientism that makes philosophical writings and literary speculations seem like "metaphysical nonsense" in the first place, because they involve neither the discovery of new facts nor the derivation of propositions based on facts. The prestige of science, and with it the dominance of a theory of knowledge based on "facts" has dominated Western intellectual circles since the late nineteenth century, and HCI has in many ways inherited that preference. See, for example, how Noam Tractinsky categorically dismisses over two millennia of thinking about aesthetics in favor of scientific data collection to construct a new theory of visual aesthetics in HCI (Tractinsky, 2012). Similarly, we've heard anecdotally from humanistic HCI researchers in industry that a common response to their contributions is, "that's interesting, but where's the data?"—a common way that scientism manifests itself in everyday professional discourse.

Scientism

Scientism is "the doctrine that *only* the methods of the natural sciences give rise to knowledge," that is, "only the factual propositions of science are empirically verifiable and hence that only the propositions of science are cognitively meaningful" (Stroll, 2000, pp. 1, 68).

There are two fundamental problems with scientism, for all of its entrenchment in Western knowledge discourse and industry. First, because there is no empirical fact or set of empirical facts that does or even could justify scientism, it is on its own terms "metaphysical nonsense" and "dogma." Indeed this led philosophers of science sympathetic to scientism, such as W.V.O. Quine (1951), ultimately to dismantle logical positivism and reconstruct science in terms of a "post-positivism" that seeks to preserve the strengths of empirical science without its dogmas, and in doing so re-opens the door to a positive, albeit limited, role for philosophy and the humanities. Second, as Frankfurt School critical theorists were quick to point out, if knowledge is strictly limited to facts, and since facts can only be present or past, then it stands to reason that knowledge must be forever backward-looking and thus regressive (How, 2003), an argument repeated in McCarthy and Wright's *Technology as Experience* (2004). But if the goal is to transform society, to emancipate citizens, then knowledge should be a forward-looking enterprise, and scientism narrowly construed simply cannot get us there. Because design is also intrinsically a forward-looking enterprise, it follows that scientism, narrowly construed, offers a problematically limited epistemic basis for design.

Politics and Postmodern Skepticism: Attacks from Within

The humanities have also been attacked from within. Two attacks in particular have had extraordinary influence in the humanities: the neo-Marxist political attack on the regressive underpinnings and effects of liberal humanism in spite of itself, and the postmodern attack on the ability of language to tell us anything about the world at all (i.e., an extreme form of skepticism).

We begin with the political critique. One common type of argument is that "the canon" of great works and books on which the humanities depends was constructed during a time of aristocratic control of the social world, and that even after the decline of the aristocratic world, the canon "has retained its self-image as the aristocracy of texts" (Guillory, cited in Freedman, 2000, p. 358). This has led to a political split on the canon: the view from the right is that works in the canon represent the most timeless and most noble accomplishments humankind has ever created (Harold Bloom, although often fiercely critical of the right, does defend the canon on these terms). The view from the left is that works in the canon represent the values and norms of dominant social classes, are used to marginalize alternative ways of life, and therefore should be opened up to be more inclusive of works by marginalized groups, such as women, indigenous peoples, racial minorities, and so forth.

Canons

The notion of "the canon" in a given field is the corpus of works that meet some combination of the following criteria: they are the best works in the tradition; they best represent styles, movements, or themes in a given cultural moment; everyone in the field is expected to master them; they reflect what is most commonly taught.

➢ The Western literary canon typically includes Homer, the Bible, Virgil, Dante, Cervantes, Montaigne, Shakespeare, Goethe, Whitman, Proust, Joyce, etc.

➢ The Western fine arts canon typically includes Leonardo da Vinci, Michelangelo, Velázquez, Rembrandt, Monet, Kandinski, Pollack, etc.

➢ The Western philosophy canon typically includes Plato, Aristotle, Descartes, Hegel, Marx, Nietzsche, Wittgenstein, Heidegger, etc.

Canons are always contentious, always subject to change, as different constituencies seek to influence what is taught and/or regarded as the best or most important. However, in the 1970s and 1980s the *very idea* of canons came under heavy attack.

But John Guillory (1995), an English literature scholar who focuses on the history and sociology of the discipline, sets aside both views and asks instead what the canon *does*. His answer is that the canon historically has been used to teach literacy, that is, when teaching children grammar, "great books" are used as models. But the written word that literate children learn in school evolves far more slowly than the oral word that they speak in everyday life. Out of this tension, a third dialect emerges, one that mediates between contemporary oral usage and "high" written usage; this third dialect is seen as "proper" usage. The point, though, is that only those with formal schooling are able to speak this "proper" dialect; as Guillory writes, "Since the eighteenth century the social stratification of speech has corresponded roughly with the level of class" (p. 242). Thus, the entire institutional apparatus of the humanities—its schools, its canons of works, its theoretical and methodological apparatus, and its pedagogical goals—can be seen as serving and maintaining class stratification and social domination. This could hardly be further from the aspirations expressed by Matthew Arnold in the 19th century and Harold Bloom at the beginning of the 21st, which embrace a universal emancipation through difficult but rewarding encounters with great works.

This political critique is impossible to dismiss, but it's also not without problems of its own. One problem with the political view is that it tacitly posits that there is a body of canon-legislators who decide by fiat what counts as canonical (Lamarque, 2008). Yet we know no such body exists, and, moreover, we have some idea of who does make these decisions in an ongoing and hardly coordinated way: schoolteachers, about which works they teach; curators, theater managers, and editors, about which works they present to the public; and authors, artists, and other creative individuals, who make decisions about which prior works they want to take on and rework. One can retort that all of these groups fit within a system of institutions (universities, schools, policymakers, public museums) and are themselves members of a higher social class, which is true. Yet the "West's greatest writers are subversive of all values, both ours and their own…. If we read the Western Canon in order to form our social, political, or personal moral values, I firmly believe we will become monsters of selfishness and exploitation" (Bloom, 1994, p. 28). And as Arthur Danto once noted, the history of art and the history of censorship cannot be understood without the other. If aristocrats were using literature as a tool of domination, they seem to have made some very eccentric choices.

Another objection is that the political view makes it impossible to establish any notion of aesthetic value, since the category itself becomes suspect. Yet few dispute that some works offer more aesthetic value than others. If that is the case, then it follows that some professional practice is needed to make and defend such judgments, and these judgments will need criteria, which, whatever its limitations, old-fashioned liberal humanism provides: there are cognitive, spiritual, and/or moral benefits to the serious study of the arts, which enlightens and emancipates individuals, and which at sufficient scale leads to a better society.

The other internal attack on humanism comes from postmodernism, and the details of its argument are quite technical, based on a combination of post-Kantian epistemology further developed by Nietzsche and post-Saussurian linguistic theory. The gist of the attack—and Jacques Derrida's "deconstruction" and Michel Foucault's "archaeology of knowledge" are central theory-methods here—is to question the very possibility of any connection between language (e.g., of science, social policy, philosophy, literary arts) and the world. Once these core assumptions are taken away, what remains is a relational notion of meaning, in which words come to be meaningful as a result of the relationships (e.g., institutional, oppositional, complimentary, hierarchical relationships) that they enter into with other words. Yet these relationships are neither bounded nor stable, and an analyst can "deconstruct" the ways that words enter into these relationships. This in turn opens up the possibility of imagining or inventing new kinds of relations, which in turn can reveal new ways of being and thinking, which then, according to this theory, supports emancipation. On this view, liberal humanism is another construct that, once pressed, cannot hold itself together and loses any coherence. Thus, whereas the neo-Marxist views the liberal humanist as well intentioned but ultimately regressive, the postmodernist reviews the liberal humanist as incoherent and senseless.

Postmodernism has gone on quite a ride, but there is an emerging consensus, which began to gain momentum in the 1990s, that its heyday is past. From the start, it faced accusations that it leads to relativism, which its proponents fiercely denied but which nonetheless dogged this line of thinking. For feminists, for example, who were drawn to his account of power, Foucault's postmodernism was frustrating because even as it could function as a powerful critique of institutions, knowledge, and social domination, at the same time and for the same reasons it seemed also to pull the rug out from under the possibility of activism (McLaren, 2002). That is, if power is so pervasive and systemic, then if feminism can exist at all, it's because the system of power can accommodate it, meaning that feminism must be always already toothless. Indeed, the toothlessness of emancipatory academic agendas has become a topic of concern within the humanities. Bruno Latour laments that postmodern critique has become a tool of the right wing, enabling it to relativize scientific debates about, for example, climate change by dismantling the binary between science and pseudoscience (Latour, 2004). Marxist literary critic Terry Eagleton observes that decades after the heyday of emancipatory theory the whole movement seems to have achieved very little (Eagleton, 2004). Another concern is that postmodern thought is too textual: it treats everything—art works, institutions, power, human bodies, etc.—as "texts," with the result that it is comparatively weak on issues of embodiment that are central to any form of activism as well as for design.

Many of the debates just summarized are also active in HCI. Are HCI's *emancipatory agendas toothless*? As we summarize in Chapter 6, Paul Dourish (2010) suggests that much of HCI's work on sustainability effectively puts the onus of responsibility on individuals and obfuscates corporate and government responsibility—effectively preempting many of the most important questions and contributing to toothlessness. How about *canons*? As the HCI community continues to stabilize as a field, a certain set of examples tend to bubble up time and again, e.g., VisiCalc, Spotfire, Tangible Bits, Drift Table, etc. It is likely that these are constituents of an emerging canon, bringing with it all of the benefits (e.g., community-wide shared exemplars) and disadvantages (e.g., aristocratic tendencies) of canons. Finally, the risk of *scientism* is more subtle; we see it as hindering, for example, the theoretical and methodological development of research through design, critical design, and so on, as many in the community appear to feel a need to legitimize their processes and outcomes according to the rhetorics and virtues of science. We also see scientism as hindering constructive discussion between psychology-based and humanistic conceptualizations of user experience, as we discuss in Chapter 5.

2.1.4   FINAL THOUGHTS ON THE HUMANITIES

We have devoted considerable space in this chapter to an account of the humanities. In a predominantly scientific discipline such as HCI, it is understandable that an appreciation for humanistic research contributions, social value, and intellectual integrity or rigor can be elusive. As Yvonne Rogers writes in her contribution to the *Synthesis Lectures on Human-Centered Informatics* (Rogers, 2012, p. 72):

> What this means in practice, is to understand HCI from a number of different angles, such as "linguistic, ideological, gender-based, institutional, environmental" and to develop multi-faceted knowledge constructs that are, "diverse, complex, intentional, subconscious, implicit, genealogically layered, ideological, linguistic and ritually structured—all at once"

(Bardzell, 2009). This seems like an art form and skill set that takes much to practice to develop and hone…. For those unfamiliar with this form of multi-layering and interpretative position, it can appear daunting and unwieldy.

Here, Rogers uses one of our earlier papers to express the multi-layered complexity of the humanities. It is true that in this book, as in elsewhere, we want to recognize that humanistic approaches confront their objects of inquiry in their complexity, rather than atomistically as is common in science (i.e., by breaking down a complex concept into ever-smaller and more tractable sub-concepts, for example, by dividing "experience" into "need fulfillment," "positive affect," and "hedonic quality," with further subcomponents and operational measures for each of those). But the last thing we want is to mystify the humanities or make their practices seem impossibly complicated. In fact, there are shared social objectives, theoretical stances, hermeneutic methods, and objects of inquiry that make the humanities coherent as a practice; they are teachable, which brings people into that practice; and they are evaluable in terms of rigor.

By way of summarizing this section, here are some of those shared commitments. What follows is an optimistic picture, but it should be understood as constituting the core normative goals of most humanists, rather than a description of actual achievements; science could likewise be accounted for by relating its intended contributions to society vs. actual consequences.

The humanities, through their underlying humanism are primarily committed to *the improvement of thinking*, including the cultivation of our abilities of perception, imagination, discernment, conceptual clarity, intellectual coherence, and judgment. This knowledge goal is distinct from the knowledge goal that drives the sciences, namely the expansion of existing knowledge through the discovery of new facts. Of course, the humanities also discover new facts, and science is likewise deeply concerned with the improvement of thinking; the difference is one of emphasis.

The improvement of thinking, enacted collectively by a citizenship or population, is believed to be *emancipatory*, because it exposes forms of injustice and reveals more just alternatives that people are able to work toward individually and collectively, and it reveals alternative forms of life as viable and even desirable. The humanistic improvement of thinking is also *enlightening*, because individuals have access to a great and diverse repertoire of ideas, ways of life, and the tools to weigh and to judge their inevitable conflicts and contradictions, which helps them perceive their own situations empathically and imaginatively. An enlightened and emancipated public leads to a better society, which is more stable because it is more just.

The improvement of thinking is achieved through diverse activities, some of which we have summarized. These include critical and historical accounts of tradition, with objectives of collecting humanity's best ideas and achievements and also keeping in our consciousness our worst ideas and crimes, to serve as a resource for the present. It includes the practice and theorization of interpretation, because real life practices, including science, policymaking, parenting, and citizenship all depend on it. It holds itself directly accountable for its contributions toward (or against) emancipation and social justice; that is, in contrast to the scientific normative goal of objectivity in service of truth, humanists generally commit to a normative goal of justice and right action, which necessarily unfolds within subjective agency, which the humanist seeks to maximize. This is where reflexivity enters the picture, and our account of attacks on humanism shows that the attacks from within are more compelling and harder to defend against than the attacks from without. Finally, we talked about the role of conceptual analysis, which exists not only in analytic philosophy, but which also unfolds in aesthetic critique (e.g., using Milton's Satan in *Paradise Lost* to analyze concepts of rebellion or using Botticelli's *Primavera* to contribute historical genealogies of the concept of feminine perfection).

Humanistic HCI is research or practice within HCI that inherits a critical mass of these commitments and practices. Let us now turn to what that has meant and what it could mean.

2.2   WHAT IS HUMANISTIC HCI?

This term, "humanistic HCI," is not used in the field in any sort of formalized or coordinated way, and the majority of writings we summarize in this book as comprising humanistic HCI do not use the term at all. Now, as the authors of a book called *Humanistic HCI*, we feel considerable pressure both to define the term (which seems like the least we can do for readers) and also to be able to provide excellent criteria by which to decide which works to include in the book, which ones to emphasize, and how to articulate their significance as humanistic HCI.

As humanists ourselves, we are also well aware of the dangers of proposing any such definition. We've read enough philosophy to be certain that we would fail to provide an adequate definition—no one has yet offered satisfactory necessary and sufficient conditions for important concepts, such as art. We've read enough emancipatory theory to have absolute confidence that whatever we come up with will be political, overvaluing some contributions and undervaluing others, in a way that makes it even harder to rectify afterwards. As evidence of these problems were the disputes (occasionally heated) that the two of us had about which works to include, how to handle borderline cases, and so forth. What do we do with significant HCI research that seriously engages traditionally humanistic concepts but in a distinctively non-humanistic way, such as Tractinsky's work on aesthetic interaction? Or a design research project using a healthy injection of humanistic thinking to support it, as is often the case of Dunne and Raby's work?

We came up with the following, which we have already cited in our Introduction.

Humanistic HCI refers to any HCI research or practice that deploys humanistic epistemologies (e.g., theories and conceptual systems) and methodologies (e.g., critical analysis of designs, processes, and implementations; historical genealogies; conceptual analysis;

emancipatory criticism) in service of HCI processes, theories, methods, agenda-setting, and practices.

We view this as a candidate or working definition. That is, we doubt that this is a final or adequate definition, but we do believe it is sufficient for our immediate need to determine what to include vs. exclude, what to emphasize and what to treat as borderline, in this book. But there are bigger issues as well: we hope that this book helps consolidate and build momentum for humanistic HCI. To do that, we will have to communicate something to readers that they can get behind, identify with, and take forward. We also hope that this book helps community members make good decisions, say, about when, whether, and how to take up humanistic approaches in their HCI research and practice; and also to support good decision-making in the all important peer review process. For these reasons, we have decided to share the criteria we came up with to help us decide what counts as, what exemplifies, humanistic HCI.

Guiding our criteria for inclusion as *humanistic* are the following criteria, the presence of each of which motivates toward inclusion but by itself does not guarantee it. We stress that each of these is offered descriptively, but not normatively; that is, the presence or absence of any of these criteria in a research or design product makes it more or less easy to identify as "humanistic," but it does not in itself make it more or less easy to identify as "good."

- The research is in a traditionally humanistic *domain* of inquiry, such as aesthetic experience, ethics, hermeneutics, law, history or tradition, and philosophy.

- It considers its objects of inquiry *holistically*, rather than atomistically. For example, it views user experience as a holistic phenomenon to be critically interpreted (e.g., McCarthy and Wright, 2004), rather than a complex structure that can be analytically decomposed into measurable parts (e.g., Hassenzahl, 2010).

- It relies on traditionally *humanistic methodologies*, including critical analysis, interpretation, history/genealogy, conceptual exploration and analysis, and mastery of relevant canons and commentaries.

- It relies on and/or develops one or more mainstream *humanistic theories* (e.g., Deweyan experience, reader-response theory, Heideggerian phenomenology, psychoanalysis, Foucauldian identity theory) in a central or substantial way.

- It embraces the humanist stance of *expert subjectivity* over that of scientific objectivity. Philosopher Stanley Cavell (2002) characterizes the serious interpreter or critic of art as seeking to master, rather than bracket aside, her subjectivity, a position fundamental to hermeneutics (Gadamer, 1975) and also put forward in HCI by Greenberg and Buxton (2008).

- The paper, book, or article and/or one or more of the authors *self-identifies* as a humanist work or researcher. For example, Christine Satchell's (2008) CHI paper, "Cultural Theory and Real World Design" explicitly calls itself cultural theory.

Each of the above motivates for what we count as humanistic.

There is also the question of whether or not the work is HCI. Guiding our criteria for inclusion as *HCI* are the following criteria, again which motivate toward but does not guarantee inclusion.

- It addresses its primary claims/contribution to the HCI community, heavily references HCI research/practice as its research base, and/or explicitly claims to speak from within HCI.

- It addresses itself to specific problems that are focal points of the HCI community, including research on use and users and the design of interactive systems.

- The research is published in a venue institutionally recognized as doing HCI, such as ACM SIGCHI, *ToCHI, Interacting with Computers*, CSCW, DIS, TEI, Creativity and Cognition, NordiCHI, OzCHI, HCII, British HCI, etc.

To be humanistic HCI, then, is to meet a critical mass of *both* of the above sets of criteria. Again, deciding whether a work is humanistic HCI is an interpretative judgment, and indeed we as authors had numerous disagreements about what to count (one of us tended to be more inclusive and the other to be more exclusive). Neither do we expect our readers to agree with us completely about where we ended up. What is important is not asserting some abstract ontological fixed point; what is important is to be able to grasp the phenomenon well enough to get on with what one is doing. In our case, we had to decide what to include and what to emphasize in this book, and so we developed these criteria for doing so. The community also faces similar pragmatic situations all the time, e.g., when choosing peer reviewers for a submission, when deciding which evaluative criteria are appropriate for peer review, when seeking to ensure representation of different perspectives at a grant evaluation panel. These are not arid philosophical hypotheticals, but rather practical issues that professionals in this community deal with on an everyday basis.

In addition to dealing with the practical problem we had in deciding what to include in this book, this activity also helped with another practical problem, which is to distinguish humanistic HCI from digital humanities, science and technology studies (STS), game studies, and third wave HCI, all of which seem to overlap humanistic HCI in certain ways. Simply, our sense is that digital humanities, STS, and game studies are not humanistic HCI, because they are institutionally and discursively distinguished from HCI (on all sides), and (at least for the purposes of this book) our scope of inquiry is humanistic research or practice *within* HCI. For example, digital humanities refers to humanistic research that is mediated by digital technologies, including archiving humanistic work, developing toolkits to support humanistic analysis of art, literature, documents, and law, etc. (Berry, 2012). Although there are clearly HCI-relevant issues in such work, most of our colleagues who self-identify with digital humanities do not publish in HCI venues, use common HCI research methods or theories, or even read HCI research. Now, there are many important exceptions where STS and DH styles of knowledge production and research outcomes have made contributions to HCI, and our intention is *not at all* to legislate let alone police any boundary; rather, we are reflecting what we believe is a relevant distinction among the research communities themselves.

To summarize, the notion we are putting forward of humanistic HCI in this book is intended to be descriptive and not normative; it is meant to reflect meaningful distinctions available in relevant research discourses; it is intended to be provisional and we expect and hope it will be superseded; it is intended to support practical decisions. These practical decisions include the following: which works do we (or might the community) recognize as exemplary of humanistic HCI; whom an editor or paper chair should invite as appropriate peer reviewers; which peer reviewing criteria are appropriate for a submission; and above all how to generate buy-in and identification with a movement within HCI to take it forward into the future, without freezing the topic in a way that inhibits growth or discourages researchers and practitioners on the edges from joining the party.

CHAPTER 3

Humanistic HCI and Methods

Methods play a central role in all knowledge disciplines, including the humanities. But the nature and meaning of the concept of *methods* differs between the humanities and the sciences. We both completed Ph.D.s in Comparative Literature, and in our experiences theories and methods were not well distinguished from each other. Further, methods—often called "approaches" or "tactics"— were typically not well formalized, to leave room for creative adapting for the research and specific object(s) of inquiry in question. In contrast, in the sciences, methodologies are crucial to ensuring the rigor and legitimacy of inquiry, and many of them are formalized to a high degree (e.g., content analysis). The apparently different attitudes toward methods in the sciences and humanities is a case of important but relatively surface differences masking some equally important underlying similarities; both are disciplined approaches to inquiry and knowledge production, have forms and standards of rigor, theories and methods, research products, benefits to society, and so forth. We believe that for an interdisciplinary field like HCI, with researchers and practitioners of diverse disciplinary backgrounds and predilections, it's worth disentangling these issues to help scientists and humanists in HCI communicate to each other.

3.1 METHODS AND THE SUBJECTS AND OBJECTS OF INQUIRY

A geologist collects data about the behaviors of the earth—earthquakes and volcanoes, the movement of tectonic plates, the chemical compositions of different geological materials, and so forth. An education researcher collects data about first grade reading outcomes based on a diverse set of pre- and post-grade measures, data about which teaching methods were used, data about the demographic composition of the students, and data about the school's prior year performance. A medieval historian pores through archives to collect facts about the early origins of what would become the modern university system in twelfth-century Parisian church schools, while collecting socio-economic data, data concerning ecclesiastical labor at the time, evidence concerning literacy rates, as well as contemporary or subsequent accounts/perspectives on this event. The geologist, education researcher, and medieval historian all analyze and interpret what they have collected, set in relation to existing knowledge in the discipline, which could include any combination of theory (e.g., tectonic plate theory), policy (e.g., education policy), and domain knowledge (e.g., knowledge of 12th-century schooling in Paris). Typically, this knowledge contribution is expressed in writing, via articles, papers, books, conference presentations, and so forth. From this perspective, the humanities are not so different from either the natural or the social sciences.

Methods

We understand "methods" in a generic way to name the coherent bundles of activities scholars *do* (a) to seek out, acquire, or discover new information, facts, ideas, or items of interest; or (b) to analyze, interpret, make sense of information, facts, ideas, or significant texts; or (c) to present to their peers these facts/texts and/or analyses/interpretations as research contributions.

The natural sciences, social sciences, and humanities all use "methods."

Now—and still speaking at a very high level of generalization—the main difference between the sciences and the humanities regarding methods has to do with the *relations* among theory, methods, and data on the one hand, and the relation between the researcher and theory/methods/data on the other. A common scientific mindset holds that researchers, methods, and data are categorically separate, that what makes a method legitimate is that it has been validated using more than one comparable data set by different researchers. On this view, the data, sometimes characterized as "brute data," represent the objective facts that are "out there," whether or not anyone ever sees them, much like we now believe gravitational pull on Earth has always been a constant, independent of historical beliefs about it. Methods on this view are valid actions that one can do with that data which should produce replicable results: for example, given a data set, any two researchers can use a chi-square test of significance and should yield the same result.

In contrast, a common humanistic mindset holds that that the "text" is *sui generis*—no other work is just like it and it needs explaining, at least to some degree, on its own terms. A humanist includes virtually any human-made work as a "text," including novels, films, paintings, scientific reports, data visualizations, and designs. Any methodological approach to access a text on its own terms will need to be reworked specifically for that text; otherwise, that perspective will be seen as reductive. For example, a Marxist interpretation that merely points to a text and says it is ideological is not very interesting as criticism; in such an analysis, the methods (i.e., the deployment of Marxist concepts) and results (i.e., that the text is ideological or alienating) are circular; such a reading has thus failed to access or account for the text itself adequately. Some literary theorists (i.e., reader-response criticism) go even further, holding that each *act* of reading is a unique performance—no other individual act of reading, even by the same person of the same work, is the same—and so will need to be explained on its own terms. The scientific notion of replication is thus excluded from norms of literary criticism, since what is replicable in a literary analysis is at the most obvious and banal level of plot details, the use of specific diction, the names of the characters, etc., and fails to get at the deeper levels of what is specifically literary or of enduring value in this work.

Texts vs. Works

The term "texts" has come to replace the earlier term "works." Both "texts" and "works" denote the same things—individual paintings, movies, poems, performances, sonatas, etc. Counter-intuitively, "texts" in this sense is not limited to verbal works. The difference is the theoretical stance implied by these terms.

➢ "Works" belongs to a romantic paradigm that focuses on "high culture" (e.g., literary works, operas, etc.) and views artistic works as the work of genius. The goal of criticism or analysis is to make its worthiness accessible to audiences (e.g., students).

➢ "Texts" belongs to a postmodern paradigm that focuses on all cultural products, often denying or at least not concerning itself with distinctions such as high vs. low culture, for example, Roland Barthes studies of spaghetti ads, sumo wrestling, and plastic toys as "texts." Texts are not the result of individual artistic genius, but rather reflect certain positions within signifying systems, and it is the job of criticism to explicate the semiotic play that constitutes the text.

Humanists frequently use the terms "theory" and "approach" to get at two different stages of their "methodology."

• The *theory* stage refers to a cogent initial stance, constituted by a set of concepts, common general procedures, expected outcomes, and norms of use. Psychoanalysis, reader response theory, deconstruction, Marxist criticism, semiotic readings all operate at this organizing level.

• The *approach* stage refers to the ways that the researcher creatively reworks and uniquely applies that stance to bring out whatever it is in the text that needs interpreting.

A Marxist critic, for example, might start with concepts of ideology, false consciousness, class struggle, base, superstructure, alienation, with the intention of exploring the ways that the text contributes to the naturalization of ideology and/or resistance to or emancipation from that ideology (this is the *theory* level). Yet the particularities of the text also demand some creativity; specificities of the text (including the text's unique linguistic structures and diction, thematic development, use of genres and conventions, and positioning in its sociohistorical contexts) are explored in their relation to Marxist concepts, which if successful should both help express something important about that text and also change Marxist theory, however slightly (this is the *approach* level). For these reasons, Marxist literary critics do not view Marxism as a methodology, but as a "theory," which might be viewed as a conglomeration of theory, standard methods, and standard expected outcomes.

In the same way that humanist theory/text does not stand in the same relation as the scientific method/data, so the role of the researcher is also different. Rather than donning the metaphorical white lab coat and seeking to maintain objective distance from the facts with the goal of obtaining truth, the humanist researcher is explicitly and unapologetically subjective. As F.R. Leavis, one of the great literary critics of the 20th century, writes on the matter,

> My critical judgment is mine, in the sense that I can't take over anyone else's (and if I did, it would cease to be a judgment). But it is not merely and possessively 'mine'; my implicit assumption being that it is right, 'I know that it is not mine'—and that my responsibility is to mean it as universally valid. Of course, it has training behind it; one that has entailed a complexity of necessarily collaborative frequentation—a matter of exercising sensibility and responsive thought on the work of creative writers (Leavis, 1975, pp. 46–47).

Leavis is here expressing the humanist notion of the *expert subject*. It is subjective insofar as it is situated in "exercising sensibility," in offering "judgment," and in being "mine" in a way that cannot be transferred to another. And yet this subjective judgment is also "right" and strives to be "universally valid" (today most of us would scope "universally valid" to within a community of practice), by which Leavis means that his expert judgments will be in-line with the expert judgments of others in his community of practice. Most literary critics would agree that *King Lear* is superior to *Titus Andronicus*, and they would be able to defend that judgment to other members of the community by offering diverse arguments that reflect literary standards and reasoning within that community. In contrast, the community of ice cream eaters would not find a reasoned consensus on vanilla's superiority to mint chocolate chip, and no one could produce arguments of the sort that a mint chocolate chip-preferrer would be intellectually persuaded to change her mind and now prefer vanilla. Making the subject an "expert" subject, then, requires a community of experts with intersubjective theories, methods, exemplars (e.g., a canon), and values; mechanisms to inculcate new members into that community, e.g., via "training," and so forth. Such communities are not exclusive to the humanities. Traditional design fields (and education) fit this model, as do advanced wine drinkers.

The reason for the difference between the science's objective research and the humanities' expert subject has to do with the nature of the object of inquiry. Whereas science seeks to discover laws and patterns that are hidden from everyday observation, humanistic "theories concern *what human beings already know and do*" (Turvey et al., 2005, p. 25, italics in original). When a biologist looks through microscope or a geologists measures tectonic plate movement over a period of time, she is accessing information not available without those tools, measures, and so on. But when we watch a jazz performance, for example, we have no trouble distinguishing it from heavy metal, folk, or a violin sonata; we know how to behave as audience members; we know how to attend to its melodies and rhythms (although jazz aficionados, as expert subjects, will presumably be better at this than novices).

Yet in a chapter of *Technology as Experience*, John McCarthy describes his experience attending a jazz concert that nonetheless left him with questions. Noting that this concert was a transformational experience for him as a listener, McCarthy writes of the performer, "whatever he did that day got me in the gut" (McCarthy and Wright, 2004, p. 5). For a transformational experience, described by an internationally recognized expert on experience in his seminal work on the subject, "whatever he did that day" may seem like a surprisingly inarticulate summary. Although McCarthy continues in that passage to attempt to put into words various characteristics of the music, the visuals of the event, the social context of how he ended up there, and the energy of the crowd, in the end, McCarthy is not, in this short passage, able to convey "whatever" it was that "got me in the gut." Instead, he concludes, the "concert had layers and layers of sound, feeling, and meaning." We have all experienced something like this. We know that the answer to McCarthy's question is not merely something hidden in the music that he failed to attend to, as if some kind of jazz hearing aid fell out. It is rather something in himself, in his own lifeworld, the way that he sense-makes that work, in all of its "layers and layers of sound, feeling, and meaning." His point is that what happened to him at the jazz concert is typical of all human experience, that to capture an experience in its specificity, one has to *interpret* it and accept it, and not merely decode it as if there were a single correct answer to be received. Recall how Charles Taylor defines interpretation, cited in Chapter 2: "Interpretation … is an attempt to make clear, to make sense of an object of study. This object must, therefore, be … in some sense confused, incomplete, cloudy, contradictory—in one way or another unclear" (1971, p. 6)

Because the answer to such questions cannot be found objectively out there (i.e., "in the text"), but rather in the way that the text enters into one's lifeworld, how the text is experienced by one as an experiencing subject, humanistic questions tend to have strongly subjective dimensions. But we know that some subjects are better than others at understanding and expressing such issues: we expect the jazz aficionado, the wine connoisseur, the opera buff, and the literary critic all to be better at encounters with texts in their areas of expertise than novices. This is why Stanley Cavell writes, "The problem of the critic, as of the artist, is not to discount his subjectivity, but to include it; not to overcome it in agreement, but to master it in exemplary ways" (Cavell, 2002 [1969], p. 94). This mastery is an ideal that humanists aspire toward but never expect to meet, and our encounters with texts change us; the point is that our ability to understand texts is a lifelong act of cultivation, one where the significances of texts, our own interpretative strategies, and ourselves all change together. Becoming a jazz aficionado, wine connoisseur, or opera buff is not merely a question of hearing lots of jazz, drinking lots of wine, or going to many operas (though that is prerequisite); these experiences transform how we think and who we are: "we must be careful not to lose sight of our main purpose," philosopher Monroe Beardsley writes in the spirit of late Wittgenstein, "which is not primarily to increase our knowledge of the arts, but to improve our thinking about them" (1981, p. 5). Long-term engagement with an art (or, we would argue, design or any other domain of experience) not only adds to our knowledge, then, but it changes how we think.

Today, HCI is devoting considerable scholarly resources to developing methods and metrics for the evaluation of user experiences, motivated in part by the rise of mobile, entertainment, and social computing. HCI researchers are interrogating the concept of digital materiality, motivated in part because of the rise of ubiquitous computing. Researchers are asking how their designs are contributing toward or inhibiting emancipation among diverse groups. HCI is using research through design, that is, using the process of design as an inquiry methodology to research possible futures, possible desiderata, possible alternative ways of being. Common to all of these questions—and there are others in the field like them—is the fact that there is no answer "out there" awaiting our discovery of it. All of these are questions, rather, of how technologies have, do, could, or should enter our collective lifeworld, how we do, could, or should experience them as experiencing subjects. That is, just as any attempt to respond to McCarthy's question of "whatever [the jazz performer] did that day got me in the gut" would tell us as much about McCarthy's subjective experience as it would about the notes hit that day, so these HCI questions of experience, materiality, social justice, and the future are as much about our collective subjectivity as they are about actual technologies and design choices.

Perhaps the best way to understand humanistic HCI methodologies is to survey them and map out how they have been used.

3.2   HUMANISTIC HCI METHODOLOGIES: A SURVEY

We now survey some of the types of methodology—i.e., theorized clusters of individual methods—that have been used in HCI, and then offer some comments about what sorts of epistemic stances they have in common. Specifically, we will step back and offer some thoughts on the nature and roles of "criticality" in the contexts of HCI and design, as well as the epistemic goal to contribute to knowledge not with new facts and information, but with different and improved ways of thinking about and knowing what we do know.

3.2.1   IMPORTING A HUMANISTIC CONCEPT INTO HCI

Arguably the most basic strategy (it is probably overstatement to call this a "methodology") that HCI researchers and practitioners have used is to import a concept or theory from the humanities and then apply it in a domain of inquiry in HCI. For example, McCarthy and Wright (2004) import American Pragmatist philosopher John Dewey's theories of experience into HCI, countering then-prevailing notions of experience as an iteration on the "subjective satisfaction" criterion of traditional usability evaluation. The Deweyan notion of experience (discussed in detail in Chapter

5), as McCarthy and Wright deployed it, had far-reaching consequences, both influencing how we theorize what "an experience" is, what research methods are appropriate to build an understanding of it, and what sorts of agency designers have to design (for) it. We have seen other examples of this as well, including Thecla Schiphorst's (2009), Lee et al. (2014), Kristina Höök's et al. (2015), and Jeffrey Bardzell's (2012) use of Richard Shusterman's philosophical system of somaesthetics (2000, 2008); Ann Light's (2011) use of queer theory; and perhaps the most classic example, Winograd and Flores' (1986) introduction of Heideggerian phenomenology to HCI.

In the best cases, research and design practices that import concepts are able to open whole new areas of HCI inquiry and practice, by revealing new territories and offering conceptual tools to render these new territories tractable. In the worst cases, they risk piecemealism, that is, ripping a concept out of its richly situated original context and thereby stripping it of its original explanatory power, or surfing from one cool concept to the next without developing it, that is, without exploratively discovering its capabilities, while also critiquing its limitations.

We see two research strategies to resist piecemealism. First is to demonstrate that the original richly situated context in which the concept was first developed is brought into a substantive relation with its new context in HCI. For example, Dewey's notion of "experience" was developed partly in response to what he saw as the deadening of experience—in classrooms, factories, and even museums—as the result of certain technocratic management practices shaping how we live day-to-day. McCarthy and Wright introduce Dewey's notion of experience at a time when HCI's increasing interest in experience was framed in the technocratic terms of usability, with its measures, optimizations, and emphases on functionality and performance. Thus, McCarthy and Wright's motivation to propose an alternative way of thinking about experience was in many substantive ways similar to Dewey's own motivations, generations earlier.

Another way to resist piecemealism is to present the imported concept in a way that is not oversimplified, but which reflects in an appropriate amount of detail and sophistication the content and use of the theory in the humanities. That was one of our primary goals when we were working on "What is 'Critical' about Critical Design?" (Bardzell and Bardzell, 2013), in which we sought to offer an understanding of *criticality* that reflected the most recent 150 years of its actual practice in the humanities. In that work, we sought to demonstrate that notions of criticality prevalent in HCI discourse tended to belong to a limited subset of a much broader practice in the humanities; by reintroducing that broader practice into HCI, we reasoned, we might open up space to pursue critical design with a more diverse, yet fully resourced set of norms, strategies, theories, and methodologies.

Of course, both of these strategies to resist piecemealism entail judgment, since some abstraction is needed: critical design is not the same as 20th century literary criticism during the era of high modernism, for example, and neither are Dewey's factories and schools exactly the same as McCarthy and Wright's critique of usability-based formulations of experience. And it can always turn out after the fact that a different balance of abstraction and fidelity would have been better.

3.2.2   CRITICAL ANALYSIS OF DESIGNS AS THEORY-BUILDING

Another humanistic form of HCI entails the critical analysis of individual or small collections of designs. A common activity in design processes is to collect exemplars relevant to the current design project and to critically analyze these designs for insights, inspirations, formal and material considerations, and other forms of problem framing (Blevis, 2012). The research analogue of this is *interface criticism* (Bertelsen and Pold, 2004; Andersen and Pold, 2011) or *interaction criticism* (Bardzell, 2009, 2011). Both advocate for close "readings" of designs, not unlike scholars in the traditional humanities offer close readings of literary, painted, musical, or dance works.

What, exactly, is criticism as practiced in the humanities? Philosopher of art Noël Carroll (2009) defines art criticism as follows:

> criticism, properly so called, is not merely a matter of evaluating an artwork–of giving it a thumbs-up or a thumbs-down. Critics are expected to supply reasons–indeed, good reasons–in support of their evaluations. […] For me, the primary function of the critic is not to eviscerate artworks. Rather, I hypothesize that the audience typically looks to critics for assistance in discovering the value to be had from the works under review…. [T]he critic also occupies a social role. In that social role, the primary function of criticism is to enable readers to find the value that the critic believes that the work possesses. It is the task of criticism to remove any obstacles that might stand in the way of the reader's apprehension of that value. I do not intend […] to imply that criticism is not also concerned to identify disvalue in artworks. However, I do think that this is a lesser charge than that of isolating what is valuable. Value is what we look for most of all in criticism. (pp. 13–14; 45–46)

Many students and colleagues who talk to us about criticism and criticality seem to believe that it is fundamentally negative. But we did not pursue literature degrees as 20-year-olds because we hated literature and hoped to spend the next 50 years writing about how bad it is! Carroll's formulation emphasizes that criticism is above all a positive practice, *a reasoned yet personal search for value*, and readerly sensitivities capable of accessing it, that seeks to reach out and engage others on the basis of that value. And, compatible with the discussion earlier in this chapter, Carroll also makes clear that although criticism is subjective, it is also reasoned. He spent much of his book explicating the critical activities that form the basis of criticism's rationality, activities that include aesthetic *description* (e.g., of the work's features or qualities, such as plot details of the novel, the subject of a painting, or the meter of a poem), *classification* (e.g., of the work's genres and themes), *contextualization* (e.g., of its historical, geographical, and social situatedness), *elucidation* (e.g., of its difficult to understand features or passages), *interpretation* (i.e., producing accounts of the work's meaning and significance), and *analysis* (i.e., producing accounts of how all of the foregoing cohere or add up to offer the best theory of that work).

Criticism

Criticism refers to an expert of a given domain's informed exercise of judgment. This expertise is based a lengthy engagement with relevant works/examples, theories, and other expert perspectives within the domain. The ongoing engagement is both sensual/perceptual and intellectual. The critic's particular judgments (e.g., of a given work or example) are typically based on a holistic, non-reductive reasoning. Common purposes of criticism include the following: explaining how aspects of a work function together to achieve certain subjective effects (e.g., *katharsis*); evaluating works or aspects of works; accounting for works' significance and/or meanings; revealing hidden but important aspects/effects of works (e.g., how they perpetuate racist values), analyzing key themes or forms that span many works (e.g., a historical style or movement).

One of the earliest sustained and explicit uses of criticism in HCI appears in Bertelsen and Pold's 2004 paper, "Criticism as an Approach to Interface Aesthetics" and Andersen and Pold's edited book, *Interface Criticism: Aesthetics Beyond Buttons* (2011). In this work, the authors observe that as HCI increasingly takes aesthetics seriously that criticism should not be far behind. To support the uptakes of criticism, they offer an 8-part framework developed to support the aesthetic critique of interfaces:

- stylistic references;

- standards and conformance to tradition;

- materiality and remediation;

- genre;

- functional versus cultural dimensions of an interface;

- representational techniques;

- challenges to user expectations; and

- capacity for unanticipated use.

As this list suggests, aesthetic criticism of interfaces is a practice that attends to diverse features, functionalities, social and semantic contexts, experiential qualities, rhetorics, materials, and forms, and that it does so *holistically*. It is also clear that considerable skill—an expert subject, specifically—is required to use a list like this well.

Bardzell and Bardzell (2008) and Bardzell (2011) propose a framework for interaction criticism that was derived from, and intended to be faithful to, criticism as practiced in the humanities.

They proposed that criticism commonly avails itself of one or more of the following four entry points to analysis.

- **Creator**, including author, composer, sculptor, designer, etc. What was the creator trying to express or intending to do? How do the creator's other works help us understand this work? Does this creator have a certain "style," and how does that style contribute to our understanding of her or his work?

- **Artifact**, including text, painting, performance, interface, etc. What type of work is this? What is its subject matter? With what techniques, styles, implicit attitudes, conventions, or materials is this subject matter presented? How is the work structured? How does it exhibit and/or resist existing genres, conventions, styles?

- **Audience**, including reader, viewer, listener, user, etc. How is this work experienced? How does the work achieve its cognitive, emotional, or experiential effects on the reader? How does the work project an ideal audience, that is, what is the audience expected to know, think, or feel to get the most out of this work? Who are actual audiences of this work? How do actual audiences respond to this work?

- **Social context**, including historical setting, class, ideology, gender, etc. How does this work reflect and/or resist contemporary (race, class, gender, nationalist, etc.) ideologies? Why is this work believed to represent something important about, for example, the African-American experience, or the working class experience during the Industrial Revolution?

They visually represent these entry points to critical analysis and their relations to each other (and most of humanistic critical practice) in Figure 3.1.

Given this sense of what criticism, in general, and interaction criticism, in particular, is as a practice, we now turn to how it has been used in HCI. In other words, we seek to answer the question, paraphrasing Carroll, what is the value that HCI researchers have identified in designs, and by what means have they sought to remove barriers to enable the HCI research and practice communities to perceive it?

In the late 1990s, system designers were told to aspire toward transparent interfaces, e.g., in works like Norman's *Design of Everyday Things* (1988) and Nielsen's then widely circulated "10 Usability Heuristics for User Interface Design" (Nielsen, 1995). In Norman's famous formulation of interface transparency, designers should help users bridge the "gulfs" of evaluation and execution. The "gulf of evaluation" is the distance between the user's understanding and what state a system is in, and a transparent interface therefore makes system state clear to the user. The "gulf of execution" is the distance between what users want to do and how to do it in a system, so a transparent interface makes it clear what users can do and how they are supposed to do it. For Norman, this involves bringing into a structural alignment designer intentions, the user interface, and user mental models. Or, as Nielsen (1995) wrote much more directly, systems should aspire to a minimalist aesthetic, "Every extra unit of information in a dialogue competes with the relevant units of information and diminishes their relative visibility."

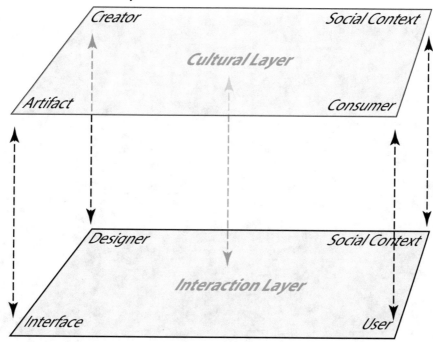

Figure 3.1: Interaction criticism understood as analyzing the mutual influences of the interactional and cultural aspects of a design.

Yet by the 2000s, this value was coming under fire. In an essay entitled "Transparency and Reflectivity: Digital Art and the Aesthetics of Interface Design," Bolter and Gromala (2006) show how interfaces might be non-transparent, not in the sense of lousy design, but in a sense that contributes to, that improves upon, a design. As part of their analysis, they spend a few pages critiquing Daniel Rosen's Wooden Mirror (Figure 3.2). Wooden Mirror is an exhibit at SIGGRAPH 2000 that uses thousands of 1-in (2.5 cm) square wooden tiles, which can be tilted more or less to reflect available light. A camera mounted in its center captures an image, which the computer then reproduces by tilting each of the wooden tiles so that, like pixels, they reproduce the image. Like a mirror, the device changes its "reflection" in real-time depending on what is in front of it. But (obviously) very much unlike a mirror, the wooden tiles are not reflective in the way that silvered glass is. Despite its very conspicuous lack of transparency, Bolter and Gromala (2006) note that it "has the simplest possible interface, one that is grasped immediately by the viewer/user without any instructions" and further note that passersby were generally unable to resist it and indeed very quickly developed into "a playful relationship between the viewer/user and the interface." Here we see descriptions of the object as an interface as well as descriptions of its use, broken into two moments—the seductive moment that pulls user to it, and the playful moment that emerges af-

terwards.

Figure 3.2: "Wooden Mirror" by Daniel Rosen, used with permission.

After these descriptions, Bolter and Gromala (2006) move to the next level of analysis, arguing that the device raises a number of interesting research questions, including "How much information is needed to convey an intelligible image?" And it "asks us to consider the interface as a mirror that reacts to and reflects its viewer. The viewer is not a clear and perfect illusion. [...] If the conventional mirror seems to be transparent, a window onto another world, Wooden Mirror suggests the irony of an opaque image" (p. 375). This leads the authors toward the outcome of their critique,

> Wooden Mirror, then, shows how a user interface can be reflective in at least two senses of the word. It reflects the user on its "screen." [...] In addition, it causes the user to reflect on the process by which the digital and the analog come together and on his or her relationship to the interface (p. 375).

This then prompts a discussion of the treatment of transparency in HCI literature, Norman's views, in particular, and allows them to build a theory of reflectivity in interfaces that they go on to develop through and apply to other interfaces.

Using a similar logic but exploring a different formulation, Sengers and Gaver (2006) explore a design norm around the idea of being open to interpretation. Here, Norman's gulfs of evaluation and execution are not problems resulting from bad design, but instead might also be understood as a means to design with the plurastic, emergent, and unpredictable nature of computer use in mind. Thus, rather than controlling user experiences from beginning to end, designers can design intentionally to be "open to interpretation." But rather than working out an *a priori* argument, the authors turn to several recent designs intended to probe the notion of ambiguity. Analyzing these designs individually, the authors infer six different ways that designs can be (and already are) open to interpretation: "Designs can clearly specify usability, while leaving interpretation of use open; Designs can support a space of interpretation around a given topic. Designs can stimulate new interpretations by purposefully blocking expected ones. Designs can gradually unfold new opportunities for interpretation over the course of interaction. Designs can make space for user re-interpretation by downplaying the system's authority. Designs can thwart any consistent interpretation." (p. 102).

Several methodological features of Bolter and Gromala's and Sengers and Gaver's design criticism are worth stressing here. First, they do not focus on the stated intentions of the original designers (e.g., Rosen, in Bolter and Gromala's case). They read the designs to help them think through a research question relevant to themselves and their research community. Second, their design criticism is deployed as a theory-building methodology. It is not the case that they already had the theory and simply found a design that conveniently illustrates it. Rather, they were troubled by normative guidelines in the field about transparency, and they sought example designs that seemed successful in some sense while also not transparent in some sense, and by engaging with these designs, they arrive at potential distinctions, new technical vocabulary, and new practices that had not been visible to them before, and which are responsive to the initial research question.

This use of a small group of carefully selected designs to think through a difficult research problem is both typical of the humanities and general and typical of design critical practices in HCI and design in particular. In *Hertzian Tales*, Dunne (2008) challenges the normative assumptions underlying human factors. Building on concepts of emancipation developed in critical theory, he proposes that usability breeds passivity. But he does not conduct an empirical study (i.e., social science); neither does he systematically analyze formulations of emancipation and formulations of usability (which might be philosophy); instead, he curates a collection of contemporary designs that challenge norms of usability and then analyzes them to synthesize successful design tactics that are not usable, but which instead constitute "a form of gentle provocation": defamiliarization, design as text, bypassing the self, and functional estrangement, explaining and exemplifying each of these tactics with designs.

The Bolter and Gromala and Dunne uses of design criticism all function in a way that resists or even attacks prevailing theoretic and/or design norms. But design criticism is not always adversarial or confrontational in its tone. In a series of papers, synthesized in Löwgren (2009), Löwgren seeks "to add some clarity to our task of unpacking the beauty of interaction" by identifying four aesthetic qualities common to interaction. The four that he identifies are pliability, rhythm, dramaturgical structure, and fluency. For each, he offers a definition and then explores and demonstrates the quality in specific designs. For example, he defines "pliability" as follows: "When an interaction feels tightly coupled and highly responsive, almost to the point of shaping a malleable material with your hands, then the interaction experience is one of high pliability" (p. 5).

He then explores this in some detail by referencing two designs, Liquid Browsing, a 2004 design by Waldeck and Balfanz, and BumpTop, a 2004 design by Agarawala and Balakrishnan. Liquid Browsing is an interactive information visualization of thousands of films, and BumpTop is a stylus-based alternative desktop UI. Each uses a combination of pressure-sensitive user inputs and physics-inspired behaviors of output visual elements to create the sense of interactive pliability, as Löwgren summarizes his analysis of BumpTop: "the key element in the design with respect to pliability is the almost exaggerated quasi-physicality of the objects that are manipulated with the stylus. They can be pushed, dragged, flicked around and they collide, bounce and pile up just like so many slow-motion domino bricks" (Löwgren, 2009, p. 7). Soon after this work was being done, Apple released the iPhone and the iPad, thus bringing this interaction quality to a mass market in an attractive product. The point is that during the years preceding the release of a commercial technology that exploited it well, there was a combination of computer science contributions and analytical work exploring how these diverse interactional elements might come together and cohere as both an interaction paradigm and as a certain type of aesthetic experience. In this way, Löwgren's work is anything but adversarial, and instead it functions alongside and as a part of mainstream computer science and technological progress.

Design Criticism

Design criticism refers to rigorous interpretive interrogations of the complex relationships between (a) the design, including its material and perceptual qualities as well as its broader situatedness in visual languages and culture and (b) the user experience, including the meanings, behaviors, perceptions, affects, insights, and social sensibilities that arise in the context of interaction and its outcomes.

That Löwgren's work is not adversarial is a point worth stressing, because our experience in HCI is that many seem to believe the role of critique is to be confrontational, dystopian, and adversarial, and while that indeed is one common application of critique, as we have shown from the critical humanities (e.g., in the Carroll quote above), in HCI theory of criticism (e.g., in Bertelsen and Pold's and our own work) and through to actual works of interaction criticism in HCI (e.g., in Löwgren's work), criticism can be, and commonly is positive, rather than adversarial. Design criticism is better understood as a search for value in design, as an interpersonal cultivation of the sensitivities required to access it. As we discuss in Chapter 5, design criticism can also contribute to the identification and theoretical development of "strong concepts" (Höök and Löwgren, 2012). Denaturalizing hegemonic powers through expository critique is certainly one way to do critique. But so is attentively analyzing how a subject matter is skillfully presented via designerly techniques and conventions, and how that presentation achieves experiential effects in the reader/viewer/user, and how all of that is significant to a society in a time and place and/or the tradition of which that design is a constitutive member. And if one looks at the great body of actual criticism of art, literature, and film (as opposed to handbooks summarizing grand theories of criticism), one will find that positive critiques are much more common than adversarial ones. Löwgren's analysis gives its readers conceptual handles to understand, appreciate, and design for the aesthetic values he advocates, interactional pliability and fluency being the two he has most thoroughly developed.

3.2.3 CRITICAL ANALYSIS OF HCI DISCOURSE

Critical analysis is not limited to art or design objects; it can be applied to any cultural "text" or group of texts (i.e., discourses). In critical discourse analysis, the analyst critiques discourses, such as the collection of published ACM papers about HCI and sustainability or about HCI's appropriation of cultural probes.

Research unfolds within social praxis, in communities of individuals who often share intellectual backgrounds, theoretical and methodological sensibilities, notions of what are appropriate topics of inquiry, and so forth. It often happens that communities of researchers, engaged in a diverse yet also broadly coherent inquiry practice, have shared blind spots, faulty assumptions, or other weaknesses, the discovery of which can lead to significant changes in the research agenda. The problem, of course, is being able to see into the blind spots, to perceive the assumptions as faulty, etc., in the first place. One technique, humanistic in its repertoire, is the critical analysis of HCI as it is manifested with a scientific discourse, which is known as critical discourse analysis (Fairclough, 1995). Although superficially similar to a literature review, a content analysis of a discourse, and synthetic accounts of scientific theory, critical discourse analysis is distinct from each in its critical purpose, as follows.

Distinguished from a literature review. A common feature of scientific reports is a literature review. The lit review summarizes research relevant to a given study; it is also frequently used to establish the need for the present research report. A literature review is similar to a critical discourse analysis in that each leverages prior research to support and contextualize its knowledge contribution. The key difference between a lit review and a critical discourse analysis is that normally a lit review itself is not offered as a novel contribution, but rather as the background of a different and new contribution. Additionally, the sources in a literature review are usually not interpreted in a critical sense; rather, their relevant findings are straightforwardly reported. In a critical discourse analysis, the goal is to identify underlying organizational patterns or coherences, raise them up for critical interrogation, and propose new ways forward.

Distinguished from content analysis. As outlined in Krippendorf (2013), content analysis (CA) is a research technique that methodologically analyzes the contents of a corpus, that is, a systematically collected body of literature. As with critical-reflective analysis, and unlike a literature review, the results of CA are generally offered as a novel scientific contribution. However, the intellectual goal of CA is to discover and/or reveal features of interest in a corpus, to enable us see "what gets said" in a way that makes it amenable to empirical data analysis, making possible the discovery of patterns in the corpus (e.g., correlations) that would be hard to spot simply by reading it. In contrast, critical discourse analysis seeks to discover discursive features in order to critique and transform them. As Vlastos writes, critical discourse analysis "is anything but a lexicographical inquiry into contemporary … usage. It involves an analysis of the concepts named by those words—an analysis which may lead … to a radical revision of the meaning which attaches to those words in unreflective current usage" (cited in Hanfling, 2000).

Distinguished from synthetic accounts of scientific theory. Scientific theories are "systems [that are] explicitly stated bodies of propositions, universal in scope, that can be axiomatized and deductively organized" (Kincaid, 1996). They explain (not just describe) a phenomenon of interest, and they are supported by data. The theory of creativity in psychology research is an example of this: part of a continuous tradition going back many decades, psychology researchers have relied on thousands of empirical studies to assemble and validate the field's ongoing understanding of different aspects of creativity, including individual artistic creativity, developmental childhood creativity, and organizational creativity, to name a few. Sometimes the status quo of a major theory is expressed in synthesis form, for example Sternberg's *Handbook of Creativity* (1999), which surveys creativity theory in all of its major aspects, as developed by and through innumerable empirical studies. A critical discourse analysis, in contrast, is generally a single study of the way a community uses a concept. Thus, to continue the psychology of creativity example, whereas psychologists working on traditional theory would seek to understand *what creativity is in such-and-such a* situation (e.g., in a fourth grade classroom, in a design firm, in a painter's studio), a critical discourse analysis would investigate *what a given community of psychologists means when it talks about "creativity"* and how those meanings are, e.g., ideologically and/or epistemologically circumscribed. A critical discourse analysis has a reflexive relationship to a disciplinary tradition; it would make no sense without it.

Broadly speaking, there's two different ways to critique a discourse: systematic and non-systematic critiques. We do not intend to imply that systematic are superior to non-systematic; rather, the difference describes a difference in emphases. In systematic critiques, authors collect a large set of papers, usually intended to comprehensively cover a subdomain of the field; this set of papers is then known as the corpus, and it becomes analytically fixed, that is, frozen at the time analysis is begun. The analysis itself uses an explicit and fixed set of procedures to analyze that corpus. Its primary emphasis is disclosing tendencies of the corpus as a whole, with the intention of demonstrating their epistemic or ideological limitations. In non-systematic critiques, authors generally take on an assumption in the field that in many ways is understood as given, and instead they focus their efforts on critiquing the assumption. Thus, the systematic critiques emphasize demonstrating that the problem exists more than they do proposing solutions or ways forward, while the non-systematic critiques deconstruct a given problem, and through that deconstruction emphasize ways forward.

Non-systematic critiques of HCI discourse

Two examples of influential non-systematic critiques of HCI discourse are Greenberg and Buxton's (2008) challenging of the exalted position of "usability" in HCI, and Dourish's (2006) challenging of the assumption that ethnographic work in HCI must have explicitly stateable "implications for design." In neither case do the authors conduct a systematic analysis to demonstrate to the reader that HCI exalts usability or that ethnographers are normatively expected to provide explicit implications for design (though they do offer some evidence). Instead, they focus on their critical analysis of the troublesome state of affairs in question. For Greenberg and Buxton, for example, this entails demonstrating that usability is "weak science"; demonstrating that an uncritical belief in usability crowds the subjective expertise of designers that is well known and taught in design disciplines; and demonstrating that usability works better for later, rather than earlier, phases in the design process (i.e., that it better supports refining and validating than it does ideating).

Closer to the systematic approach is a survey approach used to reflect on a broad range of texts without explicitly using a corpus. For example, Rogers (2004) and later in her *HCI Theory*

(2012) in this Morgan & Claypool series, synthetically organizes HCI theory by linking it back to its development in other fields, such as ecological psychology, activity theory, cognitive science, ethnomethodology, etc. Her goal is to survey what has been presented as "theory" in the field, to assess its contributions to research, and to investigate why its uptakes among practitioners has been limited. In Abowd and Mynatt's (2000) "Charting Past, Present, and Future Research in Ubiquitous Computing," the authors survey dozens of research papers in an attempt to present the state of the art and to clarify major research threads moving forward. Again, neither uses the notion of a "corpus" or identifies an explicit set of analytic procedures. In fact Rogers, Abowd, and Mynatt might be surprised to discover their papers cited in a chapter on humanistic methods. However, we argue that both are performing an important critical purpose, by curating and synthesizing the vast and sprawling archive of papers into a sensible and useful form. "It is the business of the critical power" Matthew Arnold wrote in 1865, "to establish an order of ideas, if not absolutely true, yet true by comparison with that which it displaces; to make the best ideas prevail" (Arnold, 2010, [1865] p. 809). There is little question that Rogers, Abowd, and Mynatt were performing such a service, and neither is it a coincidence that this service was performed by three of the most senior members of the community, reflecting a trust (their own as well as that of the research community) in their subjective expertise.

Systematic critiques of HCI discourse

One influential form of systematic critique in HCI today is the "epistemological survey" used by Phoebe Sengers and colleagues in several papers to critique important concepts in HCI, including the use of cultural probes (Boehner et al., 2007), affective computing (Boehner et al., 2007), and sustainable interaction design (DiSalvo et al., 2010). An epistemological survey collects a corpus of the works in HCI on a given topic; it then *critiques* that corpus. In one example of an epistemological survey, DiSalvo et al. (2010) describe their method as asking the same set of questions to the roughly 70 HCI papers on sustainable HCI in their corpus:

> (1) how does the paper define and justify attention to sustainable HCI? (2) what disciplinary orientation is used? (3) how is the problem of sustainability and its solution framed? [...] (4) How is the role of the researcher framed? (5) Who takes action, or is supposed to take action? (6) Who is considered the 'expert,' and whose point of view is questionable? (7) How do the authors deal with political disagreements about the environment? (8) Does the paper aim to establish a definitive truth, or does it leave open the possibility of serious differences of opinion about its subject matter? (9) What constitutes success?

As these questions suggest, this mode of analysis is meant to explicate what action is and means, and how this constitutes the discourse. What counts as action? When is a project successful? Who has the power to do sustainable interaction design? Who is affected by it? Who is part of the problem and who part of its solution? "Our goal," the authors write, "is to provide a reflective lens for practitioners of sustainable HCI which will allow for principled, reflective discussion of how we have, until now, defined sustainable HCI, and how we might best choose to do so in going forward."

The "epistemological survey" has affinities to *critical discourse analysis*, a methodology widely used in the humanities and social sciences (e.g., Fairclough, 1995; Wodak and Meyer, 2001; Rogers, 2004) itself resting on the "archaeological" and "genealogical" methodologies developed by Michel Foucault (1972, 1977 [reprinted in 1998]; see also Mills, 1997). Critical discourse analysis is a methodology intended to reveal how power and domination operate within and through "discourse," and how they become productive or generative of knowledge practices within the discourse (the revealing of these conditions of knowledge production is presumably why Sengers uses the term "epistemological").

Arguably, its most theoretically robust form builds on the work of French philosopher, sociologist, and historian Michel Foucault, who developed his methodology in a series of studies on the institutionalization of the social sciences (hospitals, prisons, schools, etc.) before naming and theorizing the methodology itself, first as an "archaeology of knowledge" (Foucault, 1970) and later as the "genealogy of knowledge" (Foucault, 1998). Foucault has a specific and technical theory of discourse, which underlies his methodology. Discourse is "the general domain of all statements, sometimes as an individualizable group of statements, and sometimes as a regulated practice that accounts for a number of statements" (Foucault, 1972). On this view, discourse is a set of regulated practices "that systematically form the objects of which they speak" (Foucault, 1972). We summarized his theory in Kannabiran et al. (2011) as follows.

- *Discourse* is understood as a corpus of statements that is both regulated and systematic.

- The production of such statements is governed by a set of rules that is internal to the discourse itself. This set of rules includes within itself the rules of combination with other discourses (for example, how does sexuality interact with tangible computing) and rules that help to establish the differences from other categories of discourse (for example, scientific versus literary).

- These rules delimit what can count as a legitimate statement inside a specific discourse.

- These rules create discursive spaces within which new statements can be made. Thus, like a grammar, they simultaneously delimit what can be said but also make possible new statements, in this case by providing the conceptual frameworks, models, analogies and theories, these rules with which research operates.

A discourse analysis, then, aims not at providing a summary of what is said per se, but rather an attempt to expose the discursive rules, demonstrate their operations and consequences, and subject them to the possibility of intentional change. Stated more concretely, the rules help us understand what can/cannot be said about a given topic in HCI, and we hope that by making them visible, we, as a community, can change the rules and make room for new kinds of research contributions, hitherto lacking a grammar allowing their formulation.

In our critical discourse analysis of sexuality in HCI (Kannabiran et al., 2011), we found that sexuality in HCI manifested itself in two circumscribed framings: (1) where sexuality becomes a lens to understand a domain of inquiry (e.g., domestic computing) that is discarded once it has served its initial purpose; and (2) where sexuality is a problem for technology to solve, typically positioned as a research domain cordoned off from other technology domains. Thus, we argued, both (1) and (2) yielded insights of relevance to domestic and affective computing, and yet domestic and affective computing are not seen as "sexual" any more than they were before, thus perpetuating a separation between sexual HCI and all other HCI, suggesting that sexuality is not relevant to computer practices, thereby alienating users from an aspect of everyday lived life.

Common to all of the work described in this section is that the research does not seek to add new domain-specific facts, so much as improve thinking about that domain. That is, critical discourse analyses on sustainable HCI did not design new sustainable technologies, conduct empirical studies to reveal unsustainable behaviors or technologies that can be improved upon, or propose new algorithms or interfaces to persuade individuals to behave more sustainably. Instead, these papers ask critically how the research community is going about its business in a given domain—the "rules" by which research is established to be "legitimate"—and seeks to expose blind spots or other problems in such a way as to propose new or refined research and practice agendas moving forward.

3.2.4   BLENDED CRITICAL AND SOCIAL SCIENTIFIC METHODOLOGIES

Another humanistic methodology that has been used in HCI involves the critical interpretation of empirical data. That is, it reads data sets collected via social science—most frequently qualitative social science—as if the data comprises "texts" that can be subject to critical interpretation. This approach blends social sciences and humanistic approaches, and in some ways it might seem to blur the distinction between qualitative social science and hermeneutic approaches to data analysis. However, as with many blends, it's helpful analytically at least to maintain the distinctions between the elements being blended.

Conveniently, Blythe and Cairns (2009) offer side-by-side qualitative social scientific and critical-hermeneutic analyses of the same data set, in this case YouTube user comments about the release of the then-new iPhone. The authors explain their methodology in traditional social scientific terms, explaining the data population as a whole, how they arrived at their sample, and how they used grounded theory to analyze their sample, to arrive at an account of what YouTube users were saying about the iPhone, which they broke into several categories: amateur reviews, demos and hacks, unboxing, advertisements, reporting on launch day queues, and satires of iPhone mania. They then take the additional step of doing a focused analysis of the user responses to the single most popular iPhone-related video on YouTube at the time of their analysis, "Will It Blend?" which puts the iPhone in a blender and destroys it, and again using grounded theory, they chart three types of reaction to it: confusion, dismay, and celebration.

At this point, the article pivots. In a section called "Limitations of Social Science-based Approaches," the authors observe that their analysis has given them a good sense for the main threads of response to the iPhone, the combination of excitement and anticipation on the one hand and critical reviews and even haters communicating the public's ambivalent reaction to the device. But the authors note that there is another category of response that is "puzzling," one that their qualitative analysis has given them less insight into. These are videos that have such "a surplus of meaning," that interpreting them isn't straightforward, such as the blender video or the video of the man telling everyone in line to buy an iPhone that they are all going to Hell. Using the theories of critical theorist Slavoj Zizek as a springboard, the authors offer a critical analysis of the "Will It Blend?" video, demonstrating how it achieves its comic effects. The authors offer a critical genealogy of the persona in the video who blends the iPhone, linking him to educational science films, sitcom and game show soundtracks from the 1950s and 1960s, television advertisements, and incongruous juxtapositions. Underlying all of this, Blythe and Cairns (2009) claim, is the cultural logic of consumerism, with the iPhone serving as its present-day avatar, and society's ambivalence to consumerism—its awareness of how and why marketing works, its awareness of the costs to the climate and planet, and, of course, its actual love of the iPhone all swirling around in a pleasingly destructive conflagration. By critically interrogating a symbol (the iPhone in a blender) of a symbol (the iPhone as fetish object) of a symbol (consumerism and its social costs), the authors offer an analysis that complements, but does not replace and could not be replaced by, qualitative social science.

That Blythe and Cairns' piece pivots on a "puzzling" example is not a coincidence. Philosopher Charles Taylor, in his 1971 "Interpretation and the Sciences of Man," argues that the puzzling is the starting point of all interpretation:

> Interpretation … is an attempt to make clear, to make sense of an object of study. This object must, therefore, be … in some sense confused, incomplete, cloudy, contradictory—in one way or another unclear. The interpretation attempts to bring to light an underlying coherence or sense.

This helps clarify a key difference between the types of question that grounded theory-based qualitative social science asks and the types that a critical interpretation asks. Social science helps us understand what is typical or representative of a population, with qualitative social science shedding light on the nuances and important variations or interconnections within those responses. But sometimes we are also interested in understanding the *finest* rather than the most representative responses. Of the thousands of videos about the iPhone, "Will It Blend?" somehow struck a nerve, resonating with millions of viewers in ways that other representative videos did not. Likewise, among the thousands of user comments, presumably a small number of responses were also more thoughtful, on-point, witty, etc. How, then, do we come to understand the best videos or the best responses in the best possible way? This sounds like a humanities question. Which literary works are the best in the English language tradition? Which works at the Venice Biennale best represent our techno-cultural moment? By setting these two approaches toward qualitative data side-by-side, Blythe and Cairns help clarify the different methods and also research outcomes associated with each.

In our research on online sexuality and intimacy, we asked users of online virtual worlds World of Warcraft (Pace et al., 2010) and Second Life (Bardzell et al., 2014) to tell us, in as much detail as possible, about an online experience that they considered to be "intimate"—and we offered no definition of intimacy in our prompt. We received about 150 responses, averaging about 100 words in length. As social scientists, we were interested in patterns among the responses of how people defined intimacy, and in particular how people handled the relationship between their offline and online selves. But, as we did this work, we couldn't help but notice that a handful of the answers really stood out—perhaps in their subject matter, level of detail, emotional honesty, narrative sophistication, etc.—and these challenged, that is, puzzled, us.

Explication de texte (aka Close Reading)

Explication de texte is a method of close reading of a literary passage. Often formalistic in nature, it attends to diction, figures of speech (e.g., metaphor, metonymy, synecdoche), acoustic qualities (e.g., rhyme and rhythm), symbols and images, style, tense, voice, syntax, and themes.

For example, one subject wrote, "My avatar is a female raccoon and I wear a tux. It was a dj and ball gown affair. There was a white fox at the club—male. He clearly did not realize I was a female until I pointed this out to him. We got very friendly after that." What were we to make of a statement like that? How do we adequately understand the significance of her in-world appearance as a raccoon in a tux, including the fact that her partner couldn't even discern her gender during her sexual encounter? For passages like this, we switched into a critical and hermeneutic mode, reading the responses almost like they were lyric poems.

- Why this word and not that word?

- Why did the voice change from active to passive tense right there?

- What is the significance of this metaphor here?

- How are conventions of online play mediating the intimate experience here?

- Why are these apparently heterogeneous items presented in a series, as constituents of a coherent group?

- Of all the ways the research subject could have presented that narrative to us, why that way?

- How do we gain access to the full complexity of the experience being communicated here?

Beyond this mode of close reading, we also deployed some critical theory to help direct our attention analytically, in this case philosopher Michel Foucault's concept of the "care of the self," a theory strong at explicating the relationships between external laws and norms that subject us to control (e.g., sexual laws, norms, and mores) and the private subjective experiences we have as we navigate and act as sexual beings within those laws and norms. We won't delve into the results of the analysis here, but the point for our purposes here is that this poetic shift in our analysis strategy, supported by a relevant critical theory, helped us gain certain types of insights not so much about what is typical in or representative of online intimate experiences, but rather some of the experiential heights that certain individuals had achieved, expanding our sense for what is possible (and thereby what could or should be designed).

So far we have addressed analyzing data as if it is a text to be read or interpreted. We have seen instances were data collection itself is deeply informed by humanistic approaches. One such example is Light et al.'s (2010) work on interview methods for experience design. Broadly embracing McCarthy and Wright's (2004) advocacy of more critical, rather than atomistic, approaches to studying user experience, Light et al. (2010) point out a significant methodological problem, which is that in relating their experiences to others, people interpret and repackage those experiences, and in doing so introduce a reflective layer of significance that was not present during the experience itself. Thus, user experience research runs the risk of being based on post-hoc reflection as much as or more than the qualities of the experience itself.

Building on phenomenological theory, and prior work in other fields, Light et al. (2010) propose an approach to user experience interviews called the "explicitation technique." The goal of this technique is to facilitate the research subject's giving an account of an experience in such a way that "there is no room for interview-time reflection" (p. 4). To achieve this, subjects are asked to recall specific details of the experience without being asked to supply judgments; questions that might put the subject in an analytical position are avoided; the interviewer "is on the side, helping the subject to be in contact with the past activity, remembering the situation and lived experience as vividly as possible" (p. 5). Light et al. do not naively believe that this method actually arrives at a "pure" account of the "actual" experience; rather, they more plausibly claim that a critically theorized understanding of experience exposes a methodological opportunity to adjust interviewing practices to facilitate user's production of experience accounts that foreground details of the experience over post-hoc reflection thereby improving researchers' access to technology experiences in an important way.

A broader approach to introducing a humanistic perspective into social science can be found in Bell et al.'s (2005) "Making by Making Strange: Defamiliarization and the Design of Domestic Technologies." In it, the authors point out a methodological problem with doing ethnographies of the home in support of domestic computing, that is, that we're all already experts in the home, and that this expertise is likely to inhibit ethnographers' perceptive and analytic abilities in the home. As a counter to this, they propose the concept of defamiliarization, a concept from early 20th century literary theory. A literary author can present a subject in such a way that we don't recognize it right away, or at least not as we usually do. Art "removes objects from the automatism of perception," the authors cite literary theorist Victor Shklovsky as saying, before summarizing what they have in mind for HCI research:

> Defamiliarization then is a literary technique and can be used as a method which calls into question our usual interpretations of everyday objects. In HCI, one example of defamiliarization is the use of extreme characters [Djajadiningrat et al. 2000] or designing applications for the viewpoint of a particular, idiosyncratic, and unusual user. Djajadiningrat et al. argue that such design strategies uncover and alter underlying assumptions about users built into applications, suggesting new options for design that may be useful or interesting even for normal users. (p. 154)

The authors also stress the humanistic, rather than scientific nature, of the method they are proposing, "Defamiliarization is explicitly *not* a scientific method" (p. 154, emphasis in original), before continuing.

> It is important to note that this role differs from the one usually assigned to ethnography in HCI. Normally, [ethnography] is used to better understand our target users and their practices so that our designs can better address their needs. In this article, we are instead suggesting that it can provide alternative view- points on assumptions in the design process itself. (p. 154)

Again we see the distinction, raised throughout this chapter, between scientific approaches that seek to tell us something about reality itself, to give us new facts, and humanistic approaches that seek to improve how we think about or understand the facts that we have. Defamiliarization, then, does not supply us with new facts; rather, it works by introducing a critical distance in between ourselves and our facts, so that we can perceive them afresh, rather than with our habitual automation of perception. This, in turn, is generative, because it helps us imagine new possibilities—both for inquiry and for design itself.

Throughout this section, we introduced examples of critical interpretation and critical theory "playing nice" with social science. Taking neither a skeptical stance that denies epistemic value in science, nor an adversarial stance that accuses science of collusion with hegemonic forces, instead these approaches show how critical interpretation and the sciences achieve complementary ends, how each can supplement the other in interdisciplinary forms of inquiry into aspects of experience, sexuality, domestic life, and so on, that are so hard to pin down adequately with any single method or mentality.

3.2.5   HUMANISTIC THINKING AND DESIGN FUTURING

Because design takes time, there is inevitably a degree of futurity to it. In many (maybe even most) cases this is trivial, as when a car company puts out a new model year making only minor and cosmetic changes: the new model is designed for next year (i.e., the future), but the future it projects is basically the same as the present, and nothing about the car is intended or expected to change that. Such design typically entails relatively little humanistic influence. At the other extreme are designs that envision ambitiously, even radically, a different future, for example, in traditional utopian thinking. Given their literary and philosophical nature, traditional utopias are more closely aligned with humanistic thinking than they are to design.

But designers often focus on what is in between these two extremes—a future not far off, one that is plausible and even likely, but which is different from our present-day mundane reality, and a key reason for this is technological change. A classic example of this in HCI is ubiquitous computing, which seems to be perpetually stuck in a proximate future, as Bell and Dourish (2007) write:

> [ubiquitous computing research] motivations and frames are often written not merely in the future tense, describing events and settings to come, but describe a proximate future, one "just around the corner." The proximate future is invoked in observations that "Internet penetration will shortly reach..." or "We are entering a period when..." or "New technological opportunities are emerging that..." or "Mobile phones are becoming the dominant form of..." (p. 2)

Ubiquitous computing is hardly unique in the world of design, because many designers think along similar horizons. For example, Intel has to engage in futuring, because it takes a certain number of years to design a processor, which has to be optimized for computing needs in the future when it is released, rather than in the present when it is being designed. In design research, similar preoccupations with the future can be found. For example, Dunne and Raby (2013) position their interest in the "preferable" future, one which is situated within plausible and probable futures. For Dunne and Raby (2013), the future is less a state of affairs to be predicted and instead serves in an epistemic role:

we are absolutely not interested in [predicting "The Future"]... What we are interested in, though, is the idea of possible futures and using them as tools to better understand the present and to discus the kind of future people want, and, of course, ones people do not want. They usually take the form of scenarios, often starting with a what-if question, and are intended to open up spaces debate and discussion; therefore, they are by necessity provocative, intentionally simplified, and fictional.... For us futures are not a destination or something to be strived for but a medium to aid imaginative thought—to speculate with. Not just about the future but about today as well, and this is where they become critique, especially when they highlight limitations that can be removed and loosen, even just a bit, reality's grip on our imagination. (pp. 2–3)

In HCI research, several stakes have been identified concerning "the future" as a register for design thinking. Most fundamentally is the notion of technological imaginaries, that is, our capacity to look beyond individual technologies, which come and go, and improve our capacity to imagine futures, and specifically futures that can be made possible through technologies and technological imagination. How can we enact and improve this capacity? This question is posed in the Introduction of a special issue on "Science Fiction and Ubiquitous Computing" in a 2014 issue of the journal *Personal and Ubiquitous Computing* (Kaye and Dourish, 2014). Several of the essays included in the special issue offer answers to that question.

Dourish and Bell (2014) offer readings of five "indexical" science fiction television shows, which reflect a range of assumptions about technology and society: *Doctor Who*, *Star Trek*, *Blake's 7*, *Planet of the Apes*, and *The Hitchhiker's Guide to the Galaxy*. They use these shows as a lever to investigate the technological imagination within pervasive computing research.

Bardzell and Bardzell (2014) turn to the literary theory of science fiction—the work of Darko Suvin, Carl Freedman, and Ursula LeGuin in particular—to explicate what makes science fiction "cognitive," that is, a legitimate mode of inquiry. They develop Darko Suvin's concept of "cognitive speculation" in the context of ubiquitous computing, to argue that key texts in ubiquitous computing, including and especially Weiser's founding texts, are impactful more because of their literary qualities than because of their of their scientific qualities.

Blythe (2014) uses literary theory as a way to reread Weiser's Sal narrative: deconstruction, psychoanalysis, and feminism. Each of these three readings brings forward important issues that are mostly latent in Weiser's narrative but which are crucially important to ubiquitous computing. In doing so, Blythe is clear that he is not trying to decode or reveal the "correct" reading of Weiser, but is rather demonstrating how different takes on Weiser have diverse implications for the framing and pursuit of ubiquitous computing research.

Besides the special issue on science fiction in *PUC*, other HCI research has considered the future. Blythe and Wright (2006) take on the challenge of user experience design: How can we understand and design for the "felt lives" of users of technologies that don't yet exist? They propose a method called "pastiche scenarios," which imagines user scenarios with fictional personas. However, unlike Cooper's notion of a persona—commonly constructed as an aggregate of market and/or user research data—Blythe and Wright suggest the use of literary characters, e.g., Ebenezer Scrooge or Bridget Jones. The reason is that these characters have come to life in such a rich way that it becomes possible to imagine how they would act within a given use situation.

Offering a more political take, Ann Light (2011) argues that technology design embeds social values, and that without reflection and intervention it is likely that the values HCI researchers and practitioners inscribe in research and designs will simply replicate the hegemonic status quo, whether it is capitalism's need for low-cost production and high consumer demand or the tendency of the powerful to dominate the marginal. Light turns to Queer Theory, and its notion of "troubling" as a kind of intellectual mischief-making that plays at the seams of the status quo (a classic example being Judith Butler's analysis of gender by studying drag queens). She proposes a number of design tactics to support these acts of troubling. (See Chapter 6 for more on this paper.)

Design Fiction

Design fiction is a hybrid of science, design, and science fiction. In the words of Julian Bleecker (2009), "Design fiction is a conflation of design, science fact, and science fiction. It is a ... way of exploring different approaches to making things, probing the material conclusions of your imagination, removing the usual constraints when designing for massive market commercialization.... This is a different genre of design.... As much as science fact tells you what is and is not possible, design fiction understands constraints differently. Design fiction is about creative provocation, raising questions, innovation, and exploration.... In this way design fiction is a hybrid, hands-on practice that operates in a murky middle ground between ideas and their materialization, and between science fact and science fiction. It is a way of probing, sketching and exploring ideas." (pp. 6–8)

The linkages between science fiction, science, and design have been made more explicit in design fiction, a hybrid approach that combines the latest in scientific research, the material fabrication practices of design, and the speculative imagination of science fiction. Common to all of these readings is a view that technological innovation happens within and is reflective of sociocultural moments, and that to disengage from the sociocultural is a form of denial (see Dourish and Bell, 2014). Science fiction author Bruce Sterling (2014) expresses this idea provocatively:

> in the long run, it's not about speculative technologies. It's all about *law, culture, governance, and money!* You'll get perfectly adequate results in thinking about computation of any kind,

if you blow off the deep geeks and the laboratory work, and concentrate fully on the puissant interests of lawyers, activists, bureaucrats, and bankers. (p. 767)

We can find less provocative versions of the same idea in Weiser's work; his Sal narrative could almost be described as science fiction itself, except that it tends to play down the significance of social conflict in its projected world (Blythe, 2014).

At any rate, there are two deep strategies we see at work in design futuring with a humanistic bent:

- to fabricate fictional prototypes from the near future, which embody near-present materials, infrastructures, and capabilities using present-day design methods in ways that push present understandings and conventions; and

- to help researchers/designers and also users/public think critically and holistically about sociotechnical possibilities of the near future to inform debate and to gather momentum for (or against) agendas.

The above two strategies are typically intertwined and supported by a range of critical and/or design tactics, including the following:

- the construction of what-if scenarios—using any combination of designs and fictions—as prompts for reflection and dialogue (Dunne and Raby, 2013);

- the use of a fully realized fictional character as perspective through which to view technosocial change (Bardzell and Bardzell, 2014; Blythe and Wright, 2006; Blythe, 2014; Weiser, 1991);

- the invention of new words, neologisms, portmanteaus, and so forth as a way of disrupting everyday language's role in limiting our imagination (Blythe, 2014);

- treating undesirable or unorthodox uses and behaviors as paradigmatic of an alternative way of being worthy of exploration (Djajadiningrat et al., 2000; Light, 2011); and

- critical re-readings of scientific texts and especially design scenarios supported by literary theory (Bardzell and Bardzell, 2014; Blythe, 2014).

Common to all of this is a critical relationship between a prompt and some viewer (the designer, the researcher, the public), such that the prompt helps the viewer move beyond the mundane familiar and into a more critical and imaginative space. The prompt varies, and can include literature, design, user behavior, and even new hybrid forms—such as design fictions—that are custom created to achieve these effects. That this relationship is critical is what secures its humanistic quality, even if it is (e.g., in the case of Dunne and Raby) above all a design methodology. For the ways that Dunne and Raby (2013) and Bleecker (2009) characterize the epistemic role of their designs—to provoke, probe, sketch, defamiliarize, spark discussion or debate—is in deep alignment with a classic humanistic conception of the role of the arts. In a chapter entitled "Literature and Truth," in which he considers the cognitive value of literature, philosopher Peter Lamarque (2008) quotes several major statements on the topic, including the following:

> One thing that happens to us [when we read fiction] is that our conceptual and perceptual repertoire becomes enlarged ... This enlargement of our stock of predicates and of metaphors is *cognitive*; we now possess descriptive resources we did not have before. (Hilary Putnam, cited in Lamarque, 2008, pp. 248–9)

> "Truth" is something we recognize in good art when we are led to a juster, clearer, more detailed, more refined understanding... Critical terminology imputes falsehood to an artist by using terms such as fantastic, sentimental, self-indulgent, banal, grotesque, tendentious, unclarified, willfully obscure, and so on. The positive aspect of the avoidance of these faults is a kind of transcendence: the ability to see other non-self things clearly and to criticise and to celebrate them freely and justly (Iris Murdoch, cited in Lamarque, 2008, p. 226)

> ...works of fiction, rather than providing new ways of thinking, sometimes lead us to places of obscurity or untested areas in entrenched ways of thinking. In getting us there, the work provides a context in which we can think fruitfully about the conceptual issues raised, where the line of inquiry we pursue is integrated into our efforts to judge the characters and events. (Eileen John, cited in Lamarque, 2008, p. 249)

Each of these quotes describes something about how the prompt (in this case, literary fiction) helps the viewer (in this case, reader) move beyond her mundane present. Although these quotes all link to literary art, it is clear that these could also apply to design, e.g., as criteria to evaluate the critical and speculative designs of Dunne and Raby or to evaluate the contributions of Bleecker's design fictions.

- Does the design enlarge our perceptual repertoire, our stock of predicates and metaphors (about the future or the domain of the design)?

- Does it offer a more refined understanding of non-self things (including future ways of life), allowing us to criticize and appreciate them justly?

- Does it help us think fruitfully in a place of obscurity (e.g., the future)?

In short, the relationship between the design fiction or speculative/critical design on the one hand and the interpreting audience on the other is a *critical* one, which should shape both the design practices and the interpretative practices once the designs are made and viewed.

3.3   SUMMARY: THREE KEY THEMES OF HUMANISTIC APPROACHES

We close this chapter with a few reflections on what the diverse humanistic methods and methodologies surveyed here have in common, and specifically what makes them humanistic. We point now to three key themes: the foregrounded role of critique, the intention to improve knowledge not with new facts but rather improved thinking, and the use of speculative reasoning to disclose new forms of life.

3.3.1   CRITIQUE: ROOTING OUT THE STALE AND ILLUMINATING WORTH

We have talked about two major formulations of critique.

One is *to challenge what is perceived as dominant or normal*. This can be an adversarial transgression against a hegemonic power. It can also be an epistemological transgression against automated and habitual perceptions, as in the case of defamiliarization. It can be to reveal how an entire research agenda has a blind spot, which might be ideological and/or epistemological, as occurs in critical discourse analyses. It can be the introduction of the right new concept at the right time, as McCarthy and Wright's use of Dewey's theory of experience helped reorient experience design after the heyday of usability and workplace productivity. It can confront a disciplinary expectation, e.g., that social science in HCI is valuable insofar as it has "implications for design," or that usability is adequate as a guiding norm for the field.

The other is *to perceive and illuminate what is the best, richest, or most significant* about an object, practice, experience, or phenomenon of interest. This often entails taking on a puzzle, such as the conflict between transparency and reflectivity in cultural interfaces, the astonishing popularity of "Will It Blend?" upon the release of the iPhone, or the sexuality of a tuxedo-wearing raccoon online. It might also entail seeking to put one's finger on those features of something complex that matter most, be it teasing out the right dimensions of an experience in an interview, as Light et al. sought to do, or explicating what it is about an interaction design that works so intuitively, so tangibly, so aesthetically—as was the case for Löwgren's ruminations on Liquid Browsing and BumpTop.

3.3.2   EXTENDING KNOWLEDGE VS. IMPROVING THINKING

The second key theme is the aim not to extend our knowledge with new facts about the world, but rather to improve our knowledge by transforming how we understand and use the facts we have. "The problems are solved, not by coming up with new discoveries, but by assembling what we have long been familiar with" (Wittgenstein et al., 2009 [1953], Section 109), or, adapting the words of philosopher of art Monroe Beardsley (1981) to our purpose: "we must be careful not lose sight of our main purpose, which is not primarily to increase our knowledge of the arts, but to improve our thinking about them" (p. 5).

The synthetic papers of Rogers (2004) and Abowd and Mynatt (2000) clearly were in this vein, both assembling what we are familiar with and also improving our thinking about them. Sengers' and colleagues' epistemological surveys also do not aim give us new information about probes (Boehner et al., 2007), affect (Boehner, et al., 2005), or sustainability (DiSalvo et al., 2010), but rather to help the research community see, by assembling its own products in front of it, that it has fallen into a kind of rut in how it thinks about them. Also in this vein is closely attending to an actual design in use, its constitution, its qualities, its effects, i.e., using design criticism to help think through an existing theory or develop a new one, as we saw with Bolter and Gromala's and Löwgren's theory-building through interaction criticism. It can come from cognitive speculation, such as Weiser's vision for ubiquitous computing, by providing an image that a community agrees is worth collaboratively pursuing. It can come in the form of switching from viewing data as representing a population or a phenomenon to viewing a selection of data as poetic, as Bardzell et al. (2014) did with Second Life user accounts of intimacy, perceiving within that data an unsuspected experience of luminousness, representing not so much what everyone experiences, but rather what it is now possible for us as designers and researchers to hope for.

3.3.3   DISCLOSING NEW FORMS OF LIFE

The third key theme is the aim to reveal new ways of living, being, and doing. If we cannot imagine alternative forms of life, we cannot design to support them—or even use design, policy, law, education, and so forth, to facilitate their coming into being. Dunne and Raby begin *Speculative Everything* (2013) with a famous provocation of Marxist literary and cultural critic Frederic Jameson, who claimed that it is easier to imagine the end of the world than an alternative to capitalism. Dunne and Raby wonder if design can serve as a medium of speculation that might one day help us find that alternative. Philosopher Michel Foucault used drugs and consensual sadomasochism as a means for himself as a philosopher to explore alternative ways of being. Feminists have struggled against the constraints that link biological sex to socially constructed gender, and "queering" or "troubling" became a means of resistance. Canadian feminist political scientist Shannon Bell (2010) engages in a "philo-porno-political practice" literalizing the notion that resistance begins with one's body. Set in this context, design fictions and critical and speculative designs are not so much on some new cutting edge as they are situated within an ancient tradition of thinking-otherwise supported by practices of thing-making and aesthetic performance.

One of the reasons humans have turned to arts and crafts across history and cultures is because these practices and the objects they produce have the potential to reveal to us alternative ways of life. This is not only true of contemporary work, but also of the fact that we have access to global histories of art and craft. One only has to read Homer or see an ancient vase to experience at a gut level alternative ways of being. Of course, for such revelations to work, we have to be competent viewers: if all I can see in an Impressionist painting or Islamic sculpture is an affirmation of my own beliefs, I am wasting my time. Indeed, this is why so much of art, literary, and historical criticism is about revealing and explicating the significance of works' contemporary contexts: they help us to encounter them *in their otherness*, as "non-self things" (as Iris Murdoch put it, cited in Lamarque, 2008, p. 226) which expand our horizons and disclose new possibilities.

We believe that it is this relationship between design and humanistic ways of knowing that has formed a large part of the backbone of so-called "third wave HCI," with its emphases on aesthetics, experience, sociotechnical systems, futuring, and social change. Underneath it all is a desire—a need—to explore alternative ways of being, to imagine their potentials both good and bad, and to build research and design agendas that guide humans toward preferred ways of being. One way to meet that need is to make—to design, to craft, to make art, to prototype—and then to engage such works with critical rigor.

CHAPTER 4

Enacting the Struggle for Truth in Full View: Writing and Reviewing Humanistic Research

In any research discipline, the linkages between research methods and research products run deep. In the previous chapter, we surveyed a range of humanistic HCI research methods, and in doing so inevitably also surveyed their knowledge outcomes. We discussed how the timely importing of a humanistic concept gave new energy and direction to the field, asking new research questions and providing new leads. We saw how the critical interpretation of challenging designs can be used to produce new theories. We surveyed ways that the critical analysis of our own research discourses can reveal blind spots and generate new agendas. We showed that humanistic and social scientific methods could be blended to deal with methodological confounds. We also considered how forms of speculation common in the humanities are being leveraged in support of design speculation and futuring.

In this chapter we turn to the ways that these outcomes are typically manifested as research products—especially research articles, and we address the question of ways that humanistic HCI contributions should be evaluated, both internally (i.e., within the research team) and externally (especially in the peer review process). To take on these questions, we need to devote some attention to writing, specifically the typical form of humanistic research writing, and by that we mean the essay.

Our position is that the significance of the essay as a genre of writing is insufficiently understood and underdeveloped in HCI today. The form of our research writing shapes how we motivate, give shape to, account for the methods of, and provide the evidence supporting our research contributions—this claim applies equally to all knowledge disciplines. The issue before us now is that the *scientific report* has been the dominant written genre of HCI since the field's inception, and even as HCI has become more—much more—interdisciplinary, we have not collectively revisited the dominance of this genre of writing. It is time we did.

A typical social scientific paper in HCI is basically a report, and it has a straightforward and direct structure, as follows:

- *Introduction*, which sets the background, motivates the project, invites the reader's interest, etc.;

- *Literature review*, which maps the research terrain and identifies a specific gap, problem, or opportunity for this paper's intended contribution;

- *Statement of research hypothesis or research questions*, often explicitly;

- *Methodology*, which describes in replicable detail the methods used (sample, data collection, analysis, etc.) and justifies their appropriateness for the intended contribution;

- *Results/findings*, which reports the brute facts discovered and/or offers a lightly interpreted exposition of the facts discovered);

- *Discussion*, which puts the results/findings back into dialogue with the literature review, research questions, and motivations, to assess, assert, and/or interpret their significance to the research community; and

- *Conclusion*, which commonly minimally summarizes the key take-homes of the report.

Social scientists have settled on this rhetorical form for strong pragmatic reasons. To be considered a legitimate scientific contribution, a given project needs to demonstrate a number of scientific virtues, including commitments to transparency, replicability, and objectivity. *Transparency* refers to the ability of anyone to know exactly what the scientist did, what exactly they found, and so forth. These are articulated in the Methodology and Results sections. *Replicability* is a similar value that means that another scientist should be reasonably able to replicate the study and derive comparable results; this too is commonly articulated in the Methodology section. *Objectivity* is a commitment to "an unbiased, disinterested pursuit of the truth [such that] our beliefs indicate the way the world is rather than the way that we want it to be" (Kincaid, 1996, p. 33). These virtues are manifested throughout both scientific processes and products. Importantly, they are not manifested individually in isolation, but rather as a kind of across all aspects of the project, for example, in the way that the selected methods and population are expressed as a fit for the research question/hypothesis, or in the way that the claims advanced in the Discussion are tightly linked with the Results, and so forth.

The scientific report itself is a highly utilitarian genre, embracing the aesthetics of clarity, directness, and transparency. A scientific report accommodates different levels of attention, from a careful read to a quick skim. Its skimmability is manifested in several ways, including descriptive (rather than poetic) titles and heading; the presence of an abstract; the explicit structuring of its contents (with hierarchically organized and numbered headings); a conclusion; and a predictable structure. This skimmability encourages researchers to access a very high number of relevant papers, skim them, and from there select the ones that merit closer attention. This skimmability likewise lends itself to the writing of literature reviews, because it is easy months or years later to go back and capture the gist of a paper's contribution quickly and accurately. That said, if one wants to read a scientific report with a very high level of care, its commitments to transparency and disclosure support such a usage. The scientific report also has the benefit of being a relatively easy template to use as a writer, which is important in a global discipline where leading researchers often are not native speakers of English, and where findings are prioritized over expressiveness. All of these observations explain why the traditional social scientific template is a fit: it structurally provides the information required to express, find, evaluate, and learn from the writeup in accordance with the highest scientific standards.

4.1   THE HUMANISTIC ESSAY

The successful humanistic essay, although profoundly different from a scientific report in its structure, style, and contribution, nonetheless also demonstrates a strong pragmatic fit between its discursive form and the rigor and appropriateness of the research it articulates.

In contrast to the scientific report, a typical essay has a highly eccentric structure, one that can be impossible to see by skimming. Most essays are structurally *sui generis*, so readers cannot expect it to follow a shared template. Essays often have poetic/evocative titles, rather than descriptive ones. They typically lack an abstract. If they have headings at all, they are used sparsely, and when they are, they are as likely to be poetic as they are descriptive. So the question then is, how is the form of the essay epistemically suited to the intellectual virtues of humanistic research, comparable to the way that the scientific report is epistemically suitable for reporting science?

Essayist and essay theorist Philip Lopate (1995) claims that the essay form is itself experimental. That is, the act of writing itself it often serves as the medium of its writer's thinking; the essayist is not reporting knowledge gained through prior acts, but in some senses is constructing the knowledge in the act of writing itself. Film critic Stephanie Zacharek characterizes serious essay writing "in terms of rigorously thinking an argument through, of shaping a piece of writing into something that will be interesting, entertaining, and possibly lasting" (Zacharek, 2008). In her comments, Zacharek stresses that film essay has two key features: it reveals a *process of thinking*, and it is *shaped and crafted* as a work of writing. The two go hand-in-hand.

Lopate (1998) writes of the essay that it "tracks a person's thoughts as he or she tries to work out some mental knot, however various its strands. An essay is a search to find out what one thinks about something" (p. 281). And the essay-as-search is also a form of dialogue: "Readers must feel included in a true conversation, allowed to follow through mental processes of contradiction and digression, yet aware of a formal shapeliness developing simultaneously underneath" (Lopate, 1998, p. 282). Thus, rather than reporting a truth already discovered, as presented in the standard scientific report, the essay can instead be seen as "enacting the struggle for truth in full view" (p. 282). The essay thus discloses, rather than represses, the inquirer as a subject with a point of view performing the inquiry right before our eyes.

In summary, the author of the essay has a distinctive *voice*. This voice reflects that she is an expert subject, that is, someone who has mastered the domain, but who also speaks subjectively of her or his own experiences and processes of thinking. *Structurally*, essays are fluid and idiosyncratic; it would be all but impossible to present the common structure in a bullet list. What structure is there is *crafted* (Zacharek and Lopate frequently use the metaphor of "shaping" and "shapeliness"); there is a literary quality to the essay. In terms of its *tone*, the typical academic essay is conversational, inclusive, and provisional. It does not typically use the "god trick" or "voice from nowhere" the way that objective scientific writing does—the essay is more intimate, personal, individual.

4.2   THE ESSAY IN HCI

With some sense of how essays are understood by their own theorists and practitioners, let us return to HCI. As we have already claimed, the HCI community does not appear to appreciate or make full use of the essay as a scholarly discursive genre. This is visible in the templates we are given, the advice given on what constitutes a good research contribution, and the advice given to paper reviewers about how they should be evaluating submissions.

Perhaps the most conspicuous evidence of HCI's essay problem can be found in how its flagship conference—ACM CHI—defines an essay, though it refers to it as an "argument paper":

> Argument papers contribute provocative essays. They present the author's well-supported arguments about a topic of significant interest to a relatively broad segment of the CHI community. They have well supported claims, including consideration of other perspectives, and/or data from research or practice, if applicable. They are expected to have a stimulating effect on the CHI community—http://chi2015.acm.org/authors/contributions-to-hci/ (accessed March 22, 2015).

This brief description is not outlandishly incorrect or anything like that. However, its admonition to be "well supported"—offered twice in two sentences—possibly betrays an anxiety that essayists have to be told that their reasoning should be well supported. This presumably reflects an anxiety concerning the overtly subjective nature of essayistic writing. Similarly, the recommendation that "argument papers" include "data" is also arguably scientistic. "Data" to us at least implies the scientific conceptualization of objectivity, in which the data and its interpretation are in some key ways always kept separate from one another. Effective academic humanistic essays offer plenty of evidence, but it is typically not conceived of as "data." One can present a careful *explication de texte* of a Shakespeare sonnet, offering textual evidence throughout the analysis, without appealing whatsoever to the concept of data.

But deeper than its subtle scientism, the ACM CHI description appears to be oblivious to key virtues of the academic humanistic essay, and in particular the shapeliness of the essay structure, of the author as expert subject experimentally "enacting the struggle for truth in full view." Insofar as these have been recognized for centuries as important qualities of essayistic writing, and given our belief that the forms of academic writing are appropriate to their content, we think this is a problem. It implies that the HCI community is not yet able to fully enjoy the cognitive potentials of essay-based research, because it is tacitly expecting it to offer the same types of argument, evidence, and outcomes as scientific reporting.

What we wish to contribute to this issue here, then, is the point that the knowledge producing methods and contributions that we surveyed throughout Chapter 3—the role of critique in knowledge production and the related intent to change how we think about what we know as opposed to extending our knowledge—are a good fit for a style of writing that is unapologetically subjective (albeit also expert in a publicly recognizable sense), whose structure is crafted specifically and uniquely for this particular instance of inquiry, and whose contents reflect doubts, dialogism, dead ends, and other signs of "enacting the struggle for truth."

Underlying this rhetorical form is a reflexive awareness of the fallibility and frailty of human thought, that the essayist, in spite of his or her best efforts, might still miss something important, make a mistake, or write something that is self-delusional. Lopate writes of the founder of the modern essay, 16th century writer Michel de Montaigne, that he saw himself as an average human being, a typical member of a human condition that is "constantly in flux, vain, ashamed of itself, and contradictory. Rather than condemning people, however, he recommended a generous self-forgiveness" (Lopate, 1995, p. 44). By rendering his fallibility explicit, by opening his own processes of thinking to his reader, warts and all, Montaigne, according to Lopate, allows his readers to set their own guard down, and to set aside the skeptic's question of whether Montaigne has arrived at the truth, and instead to sit alongside him and ponder the truth with him. This generosity and collaboration is a different author-reader relationship than the constructive skepticism of the scientific reader. For questions of how best to think about what we know, and for questions that reflexively challenge our habits of mind, our favorite dogmas, and our own intellectual and moral integrity and authenticity, this stance—of collaborative, post-lapserian, humble, and yet still ambitious thinking—is well suited to the literary form of the essay.

The preceding paragraph might appear to suggest that a key quality of essayists is that they don't know what they're doing. There is some truth to that; however, we argue that rather than seeing this uncertainty as a vice (e.g., comparable to a half-baked scientific paper), that it should be seen as a virtue (i.e., because it entails an honest appraisal of the relationship between understanding and doubt that stands at the core of any disciplinary pursuit). For it is doubt and uncertainty that drives us.

Recall McCarthy's inability to articulate "whatever it was" that the jazz performer did that got him in the gut (as described in Chatper 3). This was not his apology for having done poor science; it was an acknowledgement that his theoretical grasp was not as robust as his experiential capacity—the awareness of which spurred him to pursue theory and motivate us to join him in that project. We presume (we have not interviewed them) that when Greenberg and Buxton (2008) began their project critiquing usability that they began with a hunch, a doubt, a disturbing intuition, which prompted them to start thinking seriously about it. When we wrote "What is 'Critical' about Critical Design?" (Bardzell and Bardzell, 2013), the titular question was anything but rhetorical; the whole project reflected our effort to answer that question for ourselves, sustained by a belief that others in the community would be interested in our answer.

Consider, by way of example, an essay published at the annual Ubiquitous Computing conference by Gregory Abowd, entitled, "What Next, Ubicomp? Celebrating an Intellectual Disappearing Act" (Abowd, 2012). In this paper, Abowd—one of the most influential researchers in ubiquitous computing—proposes that ubicomp should be abandoned. His reason is not that it has failed, but that it has become so wildly successful that it has effectively become "all computing," and the reason for treating it as a niche area deserving its own name, conference, and subcommunity, has dissolved in that success. There are several essayistic qualities of this essay. Abowd liberally refers to himself and even addresses his reader directly as "you" at several points. It is structurally *sui generis*. Abowd offers doubts and uncertainties and acknowledges the fallibility of his predictions. We would add that this essay could only have been written by Abowd or someone of his stature; had a first-year Ph.D. student written the same collection of words, it almost certainly would have been rejected; this type of argument demands a publicly recognizable expert subject as its speaker. But in spite of this paper's overt subjectivity, fallibility, and uncertainty, none of the reviewers (presumably) voted to reject it as half-baked or asked the author to come back in ten years once he had more data on whether ubicomp did in fact disappear.

Again, we stress that the relationship between the humanistic impulse toward *interpretation*—which we (again) we resort to when the object of inquiry is "in some sense confused, incomplete, cloudy, contradictory" (Taylor, 1971, p. 6)—and the *experimental form, tone, and voice* of the essay is an epistemic fit.

4.3   HUMANISTIC HCI AND PEER REVIEW

If readers accept our argument that humanistic epistemologies, methods, contributions, and verbal products are distinct from scientific ones, then it should also be obvious that the criteria for evaluating and peer reviewing such contributions will also differ in certain respects from scientific contributions. What's needed is an evaluative approach that takes into account the epistemological, methodological, substantive, and rhetorical fit of a good humanistic project.

A Common Approach to Scientific Peer Reviewing

When we review scientific submissions, most of us begin with the contribution. Scientific contributions tend to be expressed (or at least be expressable) as propositions: "we found that X." So we begin: *What is the intended contribution of the work?* From there, we commonly pursue a range of questions to help us assess the extents to which this contribution was successfully made.

➤ *Is the contribution well motivated?* Does it reflect a gap, opportunity, problem, or need in the research literature? Does it situate itself adequately within the current state of that research, for example, by citing relevant papers appropriately? Does the paper persuade the reader that the gap, opportunity, or problem ought to be addressed?

➤ *Is the methodology a fit for the intended contribution?* That is, were the data collection methods deployed, the sampling, the data analysis methods, and so forth appropriate to the object of inquiry? Were the methods rigorously used? Was the sample representative of the object of inquiry? Could another research team replicate these methods?

➤ *Are the results novel and appropriately derived from the methods?* Did they speak to the object of inquiry? Were they presented in a way that readers can see the data for themselves? Do the authors assess (or provide measures of) room for doubt (e.g., tests of significance)?

➤ *Are the results analyzed transparently and rigorously?* Are interpretive claims and asserted implications tightly coupled with the results? Do the authors acknowledge and assess the significance of the study's limitations?

➤ *Is the reporting clear and appropriate?* Did the authors actually deliver what they promised in the introduction? Is the writing lucid and easy to understand? Is it easy to find relevant information (e.g., the methodology, the research question/hypothesis, the actual results)?

We already have and do this in scientific reviewing (see box). It should be easy to see that the scientific report as a genre of writing fits very well with an approach to peer reviewing that looks like this. It should also be increasingly clear that the standard practices of scientific peer review are unlikely to be a fit for humanistic reviewing. The question we confront now is what is the equivalent reviewing approach for humanistic essays, one that assesses the rigor and novelty of humanistic contributions in essay form?

We begin with the question of *agreement*. Scientific contributions, broadly speaking, are designed to demand the reader's agreement (which is not to say that they always do, of course). They make this demand through the tight coupling of methods, results, and implications. Scientific claims have to meet very high standards, and there is little room for speculation (unless it is clearly and explicitly marked as such). A medical result amounting to "it's our gut feeling that it's probably not a good idea to X" is no medical result at all. A legitimate clinical trial is an enormous undertaking and usually results in carefully scoped claims made with a high level of confidence.

But if we look at the examples we've pointed to just in this chapter and in Chapter 3—Abowd's reflections on ubicomp, McCarthy's reflections on his experience at the jazz festival, Greenberg and Buxton's concerns about the centrality of "usability" in interaction design practice, and Bardzell and Bardzell's uncertainty about what would make a design "critical"—we see a very different sort of inquiry. Here, the knowledge is often provisional, in doubt, and provocative. It is unlikely that any of these writings seriously demand their reader's agreement. Agreement must not be what they are after. As philosopher Stanley Cavell ruefully notes, no one ever agrees with another philosopher, but that is not the undoing of philosophy. Going a step further, Michel Foucault wrote that he never even agrees with himself in his last book, which is why he keeps on writing!

We have repeatedly distinguished between contributing new facts to a knowledge domain on the one hand, and changing how we think about a domain on the other. Contributing to the former objective will require an argument with evidence that the proposed new knowledge merits being added to the domain, and the scientific report and scientific peer review process are geared toward such a process. Contributing to the latter objective—changing how we think about a domain—does not require proof so much as provocation that is hard to dismiss (even if one is inclined to disagree with it). Interestingly, the verb "to prove" in English has two distinct senses, as William Ziegler writes:

> The practice of experimenting, or trying something out, is expressed in the now uncommon sense of the verb to prove—the sense of "testing" rather than of "demonstrating validity." Montaigne "proved" his ideas in that he tried them out in his essays. He spun out their implications, sampled their suggestions. […] To "prove" an idea, for Montaigne, was to examine it in order to find out how true it was. (Zeiger, cited in Lopate, 1995, p. xlv, emphasis in the original)

This reminded us of a passage in the work of Cavell, where he writes, "The philosopher appealing to everyday language turns to the reader not to convince him without proof but to get him to prove something, test something, against himself" (Cavell, 2002 [1969], p. 95). By now, appropriate criteria for reviewing humanistic essays is coming into view. Let us remove several inappropriate criteria from contention.

- Do I agree with the essay (or argument paper)?

- Is this argument convincing?

- Is the author fully justified in making that argument?

- Did the author cite all the authors or theories that I would have, were I making this argument?

These criteria all assume an epistemic value of correct assertion, a notion of truth supported both by method and evidence. These are scientific values, and they are fully appropriate within a scientific peer reviewing process. But to apply them unreflectively to humanistic contributions is a form of scientism, and our sense is that this is often happening in HCI, not because peer reviewers are epistemological bigots consciously asserting scientific virtues over humanistic ones, but simply because this is the reviewing methodology they were trained to write for and trained to use themselves and their use is simply second nature.

The following is a first attempt at articulating an approach to reviewing humanistic research contributions in a way that holistically engages humanistic epistemologies, methodologies, substantive contributions, and expressive idioms. We doubt that we've got this quite right on the first try—surely we missed, exaggerated, or understated certain issues—but the intent is to put a view "on the table" so to speak, in hopes that the HCI community will reflect on it and continue to improve it.

A Proposed Approach to Humanistic Peer Reviewing in HCI

When we review humanistic submissions, we should begin with the contribution, which is commonly expressed as a *position*. Now, a *position* is not merely a proposition; it instead holistically comprises an expert-subjective voice; a theoretical-methodological stance; its own situatedness within a domain; and a pragmatic purpose. So, we begin: *What is the intended position of the work?* To understand the position, and to assess its contribution to the research dialogue, we commonly pursue the following range of questions.

➢ *What is the purpose of the position?* How does this position manifest itself as a research contribution? What does it seek to challenge, displace, provoke, iterate on, clarify, propose, or bring into being? Does it work out an idea or stance that should be in our collective repertoire? Does it offer new resources (conceptual, historical, exemplary)? Does it shed new light on familiar examples? Does it give us reason to revisit established or overlooked ideas or examples? Does it offer new ways of thinking about or approaching a relevant problem?

➢ *What are the effects or consequences of the position?* Does the essay entice the reader into the author's thinking space? Does the position provoke a response from the reader (negative or positive)? Does this position force the reader to clarify or iterate on her own position(s) (even if she disagreed with the essay's position)? Does it provoke the reader to want to try it out?

➢ *What or who is the voice offering this stance?* This is not necessarily a biographical question, but rather: Who is the expert-subject speaker inscribed in the essay? Is that voice coherent, honest, and internally consistent? Is that voice contingent, situated, and present to the reader? Do author and reader come across as equals, sharing a common goal, if not necessarily in agreement? Is the finitude of the speaker and the project visible?

➤ *What are the theoretical and methodological substrates of the position?* Are they appropriate to the object of inquiry? Are they leveraged coherently and robustly? Do they merely determine the position or do they serve as a launching pad for creative and original thinking?

➤ *What is the topic or domain of inquiry?* What is it about this domain that makes it appropriate for humanistic inquiry? Are the selected objects within that domain not representative, but rather resonant, salient, or otherwise rich in potential but in an as yet unclear or muddled way?

➤ *Does this meet humanistic standards of rigor?* Does the work demonstrate insight, imagination, perceptiveness, sensitivity? Is there evidence of mastery of the domain, theory, methodology, relevant history, relevant scholarship? Does the essay communicate reflexive qualities of the project, that is, does it reveal its own conditions of knowledge production?

We believe that all of the papers cited in this and the previous chapter—and almost all of the works cited throughout this book—in fact, do very well according to these criteria. Moreover, in judging them by criteria such as these, we are better able to bring what is good in them into focus.

For example, Abowd's paper on ubiquitous computing is not a scientific report: it simply doesn't speak well to scientific virtues or to scientific reporting or reviewing criteria. What it does do is speak well to humanistic expression and evaluation criteria. It is provocative, fallible, perspectival, and expert. It invites readers into that perspective and challenges them to form their own responses. Its contribution should not be read as a proposition that can be assessed in terms of its correspondence to external reality—"ubiquitous computing is obsolete"—but rather as a position, a position that invites us to reflect on how we have been treating ubiquitous computing (i.e., as a niche), to consider why that once was the case, whether it still is a constructive framing, and to imagine an alternative view and extend that into implications for research practice. Ubicomp becomes an object of interpretation, and Abowd's contribution consists of both hermeneutic and speculative moves. Along the way, the paper exudes an almost casual mastery of the domain. Throughout, Abowd's voice and perspective are made explicit to the reader and maintains a consistency and honesty throughout.

4.4   HUMANISTIC HCI AND INTERDISCIPLINARY PRACTICE

Of course, in an interdisciplinary field such as HCI, we have as many blended projects and papers as we do "pure" ones. That is, besides humanistic essays, we have papers with scientific reporting and essayistic discursive elements, for example the Blythe and Cairns (2009) paper we discussed in Chapter 3, in which the authors provided side-by-side grounded theory and psychoanalytic interpretations of a set of YouTube comments on the (then new) iPhone. The appropriate blending of scientific, designerly, and humanistic approaches requires professional judgment on the part of authors to determine how best to articulate the role, scope, justification, outcomes, and limitations of humanistic theories, methods, and other inputs into their research. Similarly, it requires professional judgment on the part of readers (including peer reviewers) to read humanistic aspects of the work in appropriate ways, including their relation to non-humanistic aspects of the work (e.g., the social scientific or design aspects).

Such judgment can be supported through the use of any combination of the following integrative tactics.

- Demarcating the humanistic from other epistemological approaches, for example, the way that Blythe and Cairns conduct and report on their grounded theory vs. psychoanalytic analyses separate from each other. Such demarcations help readers read each of the different elements of the project—social scientific, humanistic—on its own terms.

- Indicating how, why, and where any blending is occurring. For example, in Schiphorst (2009), discussed in Chapter 5, the work is presented as a practice-based example of somaesthetic design. The humanistic element—somaesthetic philosophy—is the concept behind and generative of her design thinking. The paper does not offer, nor attempt to offer, any critical analysis of somaesthetics—such is out of the scope of the work. Instead, Schiphorst traces her moves starting in the philosophical theory, toward a design framing, to the design itself; in this way, the scope and purpose of her use of somaesthetics is clear to the reader.

The main argument of this chapter is that humanistic approaches holistically incorporate common epistemological commitments, methodologies, objects of inquiry, and research questions—and that all of these are a pragmatic epistemological fit for the dominant form of humanistic writing: the essay. As HCI appropriates humanistic theories and methods, we believe it should also be taking seriously humanistic discursive conventions and genres—both as writers and as readers (including reviewers). This applies to research and practice that is predominantly humanistic as well as research and practice that is interdisciplinary. We hope this chapter has offered some practical guidance on how to do so.

PART II

Major Topics in Humanistic HCI

CHAPTER 5

User Experience and Aesthetics

By the end of the 1990s, the usability movement in HCI was in full swing. In a major outcome for HCI, the concept of "usability" had stabilized as an important concept in both research and practice. Part of the reason for usability's success was that it supported interface design in a way that was both powerful in making design issues tractable, and also practical in the sense that teams of virtually any size or budget could deploy. Industry projects with significant budgets could develop elaborate models to predict usability outcomes at scale using these measures, while much smaller teams (including student teams in undergraduate HCI courses) could do simple experiments on themselves or their friends. Either way, usability evaluation tended to deliver actionable results.

Usability

Usability comprises five evaluative measures of interface design: time to learn, speed of performance, rate of errors by users, retention over time, and subjective satisfaction (Shneiderman and Plaisant, 2010, p. 14).

5.1 FROM USABILITY TO USER EXPERIENCE

Perhaps usability might have worked a little bit *too* well, as we saw in Chapter 3 in Greenberg and Buxton's (2008) critique of usability and the design process. In tracing the history of the usability movement in HCI, Kari Kuutti (2009) observes that it began in the form of psychological laboratory experiments, but as it simplified over time,

> the scientific content of the experiments (like theory, modeling, factors, control, statistics) was totally discarded. What was left was just observation of actual users in simulated tasks to identify potential problematic moments encountered in the process. Very simple, but also very efficient in practice: the emergence of such working methods directed the whole course of HCI for at least the next decade: usability became the central concept in HCI and better methods to evaluate and design for it the major research topic. Unfortunately this also meant a certain intellectual impoverishment: calls to discuss about HCI theoretical foundations lost the audience, when the somewhat a-theoretical (and originally sometimes even anti-theoretical) usability movement took over. (pp. 6–7)

The part of usability that linked to the topic of this chapter—user experience—was, of course, the fifth of the five usability criteria, "subjective satisfaction." This concept remained theoretically and methodologically thin. Shneiderman and Plaisant (2010) write, "How much did users like using various aspects of the interface? The answer can be ascertained by interviews or by written surveys that include satisfaction scales and space for free-form comments" (p. 14). HCI researchers Whittaker et al. (2001) characterize it in this way: "users made comments about the experiential quality of the interaction, leading to the criterion of *subjective satisfaction*" (p. 179, emphasis in original). These characterizations suggest that "experience" was theoretically undeveloped, and that methodologically, subjective satisfaction could be accounted for using self-report tools, such as interviews, satisfaction scales, and so forth.

But even as usability was settling in, the computer was reaching out (Grudin, 1989). Weiser (1991) was already forecasting a new era of ubiquitous computing. A decade of CSCW research and practice had demonstrated beyond any doubt that spatial and social environments were fundamental design considerations. The massively multiplayer online role playing game *Everquest* was transforming the gaming industry and anticipating much of what we know understand as social media. With the Internet in people's homes, the emergence of mobile computing, and the rise of domestic computing—all of these were challenging a deep assumption of the usability movement: that interfaces could be evaluated in terms of task completion (i.e., productivity) and individual psychology (i.e., learning and satisfaction with those tasks). In studies of online behavior, for example in Sherry Turkle's landmark *Life on the Screen* (1995), issues of identity construction and performance, play, social competence, disability, pleasure, fantasy, and a whole range of socio-aesthetic qualities had come to the fore: issues that the usability movement had not even begun to acknowledge let alone engage.

A paradigm change was in the air. By 2000, industry practitioners and researchers alike were beginning to reframe "interface design" as "interaction design," and shortly thereafter "experience design" (McCarthy and Wright, 2004). Although questions of product experience are fascinating intellectually, we must remember that in an applied field, closely aligned to industry needs, what was happening was the increasing recognition that experience sells. Consumers were demanding not just functionality but good experiences, and this helped drive the agenda.

It's one thing to call for more emphasis on user experience and quite another to develop a mature practice of it. Experience is a notoriously difficult concept to grapple with; as our graduate students will ruefully acknowledge, experience can be embarrassingly difficult to define or explain. This difficulty is visible in practitioner and research texts in this era. In his *Observing the User Experience* (2003), Mike Kuniavsky admits, "It's hard to capture what creates the surprise and satisfaction that comes from using something that works well, but it's definitely part of the best product designs" (p. 20). Kuniavsky tries to articulate why the concept of experience resists definition:

> "defining 'the user experience' is difficult since it can extend to nearly everything in someone's interaction with a product, from the text on a search button, to the color scheme, to

the associations it evokes, to the tone of the language used to describe it, to the customer support" (p. 43).

Kuniavksy's characterization here conforms closely to qualities of the interactive artifact and users' immediate reactions. In contrast, design researchers Schifferstein and Hekkert (2008a) emphasize the subjective side of the equation in their characterization of product experience.

> Notwithstanding the fact that the way in which people interact with a product is clearly product-dependent, they always use their senses to perceive it, they use their motor system and their knowledge to operate or communicate with it, and during the interaction they process the information they perceive, they may experience one or more emotions, and they are likely to form an affective evaluation of the product. (p. 1)

Product experience on this account, then, is largely an issue of affective evaluation, arising out of the human perceptual apparatus. Casting the nets even wider, user experience practitioner Nathan Shedroff (2003) accounts for experience design in this way.

> Because Experience Design encompasses so much new territory for designers (such as social issues, business strategy, the senses, emotions, and the creation of value), designers need to learn new ways of understanding their audiences in order to better prepare for their needs. Some would argue that it's a designer's responsibility to understand user needs such as fulfillment of desire, pleasure and enhanced capability, as well as business needs such as viability, sustainability, and (usually) profitability. (p. 155)

These texts anticipate a number of the challenges that the subsequent decade of research and practice would take on: the nature of experience, the role of products in causing experiential reactions, the role of the user completing the experience for herself, the roles of society and culture on the reception and experience of products, and the business environments in which all of the foregoing take place. Accordingly, user experience was not an easy concept to operationalize or deploy in practical design work—most understandings of it are so holistic and expansive that it seems to include everything: the interface, the history of all interfaces and communications media, the user's skills (and affective state, predispositions, etc.), culture, society, fashion, the immediate physical/spatial context, the social context (ranging from immediate collaborators to sociopolitical forces), and so on.

The lack of clarity about experience raised a number of practical questions for researchers and practitioners throughout HCI and interaction design.

- What, then, should a user researcher look for when analyzing user experience?

- Are users able to articulate the qualities of good experiences, and if not, then what?

- Which aspects of experience are designable?

- Is it even *possible* to design experience?

- Do *designs cause* experiences, or do *users creatively fulfill* potential merely latent in the design?

The first decade of the 2000s witnessed considerable research in user experience, which included a combination of theoretical and methodological innovation. Fundamentally, though, we see two deep types of questions that underlie the whole project.

- *What is experience?* What distinguishes a good from a bad experience? What are the subjectively felt qualities of experience? How do sense perceptions, imagination, affective dimensions, and so on contribute to a good or bad experience?

- *How do objects—especially artworks and designs—cause/contribute to experience?* How do we design (for) experience? What design features or qualities can we shape or manipulate to contribute toward good experiences?

Note that the first question gets at the *subject* of the experience, that is, the person experiencing, including the psychological structure and felt qualities of experiences. The second question gets at the *objects* of experience, that is, the artifact or event out there in the world whose features or qualities stimulate, cause, and/or prompt experiences. The bulk of this chapter will summarize research approaches that took on these two questions, usually together, but often tending to emphasize one over the other. Either way, however, HCI and design researchers were turning to theory to help them work through it.

5.2   THE RE-THEORIZATION OF EXPERIENCE

It is important to acknowledge at the outset that the development of new theories and methods throughout this period in HCI was not limited to the humanities. In particular, there was also considerable work emerging out of both psychology-based and design-based perspectives. For example, the psychology-based work of Noam Tractinksy, Alistair Sutcliffe, Effie Law, Marc Hassenzahl, and (somewhat skeptically at first) Don Norman made huge strides in demonstrating the importance of a rich conceptual framework for the analysis of user experience, including psychological needs, aesthetics, as well as functional usability. They distinguished among experiential qualities at different temporal scales, for example, visceral responses that occur within milliseconds and reflective responses that can take hours or even years. This line of research meshed well with design, offering actionable implications for designers. That said, this psychology-based approach to user experience, while crucial to the story of experience design generally, is out of the scope of this book, so we encourage interested readers to see Alistair Sutcliffe's (2009) *Designing for User Engagement: Aesthetic and Attractive User Interfaces* and Marc Hassenzahl's (2010) *Experience Design: Technology for All the Right Reasons* in this *Synthesis Lectures on Human-Centered Informatics* series.

Similarly, designers were making important methodological contributions to user experience. One example is *experience prototyping* (Buchenau and Suri, 2000), a methodological approach coming out of IDEO, in which experiences, rather than artifacts, are prototyped as a means of helping interdisciplinary design teams come together to co-create (and experience) a shared vision for their design work that transcends each member's parochial concerns. Another example is *cultural probes*, which emerged out of the Royal College of Art and critical design in the late 1990s, which used designed artifacts to engage and even provoke users not to discover their existing preferences or needs, but to elicit surprising responses and stimulate design thinking (Gaver et al., 1999).

Beyond methodological contributions, design researchers have also contributed theoretical perspectives. For example, Forlizzi and Battarbee (2004) offer a critical synthesis of a number of theorizations of experience, including object-centered theories, subject-centered theories, and interaction-based theories. They link each of these theorizations to different types of experiences. They then develop an approach to applying these theorizations—in particular their preferred conceptualization, which is interaction-based co-experiences—to designing. It is this latter move that gives the paper its designerly feel. It does not offer a philosophical analysis of the concepts, develop it through examples, or otherwise dwell in the theory as such. Instead, it covers the theory just enough to set the authors up to explicate how these theories can serve as resources to support various specific activities undertaken by interdisciplinary design teams achieve their goals, e.g., to understand the fit of the product in its user's existing material ecologies and experiences, to trace the unfolding of experience with a product over time, to understand the sociality of product experiences, and to design prototypes and user studies that are optimized to shed light on these issues.

In parallel to all of this, HCI and design researchers were increasingly turning to philosophy, critical theory, literary theory, and more to reimagine user experience from a critical and humanistic perspective. As with the psychology-based perspective, this humanities-based perspective connected well with designers and design thinking; indeed, within the CHI community, the Design Subcommittee till this day features papers where humanistic and design thinking approaches are tightly coupled. Less positively, it appears that the psychology-based and humanities-based perspectives on user experience developed independent of, and occasionally even hostile to, one another, presumably due to deep and often tacit epistemological differences. Our position is that their epistemological diversity is precisely what makes them complementary and that a better sympathy across these perspectives would be salutary for the field. We will return to some of these issues in this chapter's conclusion

But first we turn to several key ideas in the humanistic formulation of user experience as it developed over the past 15 years or so. As noted in Chapter 3, humanistic approaches tend to tightly couple theoretical commitments and methodological tactics to the point that many humanists do not distinguish between the two but rather view research objectives, theoretical commitments, and methodologies holistically. This commitment to holistic thinking is readily apparent throughout the research on UX summarized in this chapter. The following quote, by way of example, constitutes the *entire* abstract of Bertelsen and Pold's (2002) paper, "Toward the Aesthetics of Human-Computer Interaction":

> We argue that the field of HCI needs a new aesthetic perspective to develop further, and to transcend current shortcomings. (p. 11)

Even compressed into a single sentence, this "new aesthetic perspective," with its goal of "develop[ing]" the field so that it can "transcend current shortcomings" suggests how ambitiously this project was formulated. A year later, in their introduction to the landmark book, *Funology* (Blythe et al., 2003), which castigated the field for its relentless utilitarianism and instead advocated for designing around values of fun and pleasure, Mark Blythe and Peter Wright write,

> Almost every philosopher who ever philosophised has speculated on how and why we enjoy, or take pleasure, in certain things. For Plato, pleasure was the absence of pain [...] For Aristotle, pleasure was caused by the stimulation of the senses through action [...] In the Confessions of St. Augustine pleasures are largely 'unlawful' or 'awful' unless they are pleasures in the contemplation of God. [...] Jeremy Bentham claimed that pleasures could be judged by intensity and duration [...] Freud famously argued for the existence of the pleasure principle (and later a death principle) as a motivating force for human action that could not necessarily be known by the conscious mind [...] Neurologists have discovered "pleasure centres" in the septal region of the brain which when electrically stimulated produce enjoyable feelings" (p. XIII–XIV).

This opening survey reminds its readers that the experience of pleasure is already thoroughly theorized and debated across millennia, suggesting that HCI also needs to take this seriously, but also that it need not reinvent any wheels. It also situates neuroscience within—but not against—that tradition.

Accompanying these calls for more humanistic approaches to user experience were a number of papers that undertook the task. For example, several researchers turned to critical practices in digital media studies, including new media writers Steven Johnson (1997), Lev Manovich (2002), Bolter and Grusin (1999), and more, seeking to extend them into HCI (e.g., Bertelsen and Pold, 2004; Udsen and Jorgensen, 2006; Bardzell, 2009, 2011). In what follows, we will focus on two major theoretical-methodological stances in user experience—a *pragmatist* stance and one based on the idea of *poetics*, beginning with the former.

5.3   PRAGMATISM AND USER EXPERIENCE

We have laid out some of the experiential qualities that researchers and practitioners alike were calling for: "surprise," "fulfillment of desire, pleasure and enhanced capability," and "fun," and a turn to experience is a unifying approach that could support designers in bringing about such values. It's also important to recognize that not all "good" experiences involve straightforwardly positive emotions: tragic plays, horror flicks, and even embarrassing but instructive experiences when we are young all might have predominantly negative emotional contours at the time and still be considered important and even "good" experiences when we think about them.

Accounting for product experiences requires a useful theorization of experience. "Although HCI research and practice is already moving toward experience as a response to the need to deal with technologies that we live with," McCarthy and Wright (2004) write, "there is now more than ever, a need for clarification on what we mean when we talk about experience of technology" (p. 5). This question helped motivate the turn to humanistic theory, and not just for McCarthy and Wright; for example, Petersen et al. (2004) developed a conceptualization of "aesthetic interaction," with aims to create "involvement, experience, surprise and serendipity in interaction when using interactive systems." This approach to interaction design "acknowledges man's ability to interpret and appropriate technology" and "promotes bodily experiences *as well as* complex symbolic representations when interacting with systems. It puts an emphasis on an actively engaged user with both cognitive skills, emotional values and bodily capabilities" (p. 274). Here we see experience theorized with the holism we mentioned earlier: it comprises a range of subjective qualities (surprise, serendipity, involvement), and it emphasizes the coordination of rational, emotional, and body faculties in the having and interpreting of experiences.

McCarthy and Wright (2004) had their own approach to the clarification of experience, also turning to aesthetic theory. They open their book *Technology as Experience* with a series of propositions, the first of which is: "we should try to interpret the relationships between people and technology in terms of the felt life and the felt or emotional quality of action and interaction" (p. 12). While the community has latched on to their conceptualization of "felt life," there is another, deeper, move that is worth pointing to: for McCarthy and Wright, experience is the sort of thing which has to be interpreted. They would use this foundational stance—to base interpretative inquiries about UX within felt experience—to try to take on "everyday raw aesthetic experiences that demand our attention and make us come *alive*" (p. 58, emphasis in the original). What was needed, then, was a theory of experience that could account for this sense of "coming alive": entailing all of those qualities that designers now wanted to incorporate into their designs: delight, enchantment, embodiment, attachment, and even emotional fulfillment.

Petersen et al. (2004) and McCarthy and Wright (2004) both turned to the pragmatist philosophy of John Dewey, whose 1934 *Art as Experience* offers a theory of aesthetic experience that is very appealing to designers. Dewey's theory of experience, which we summarize below, has the following key benefits for HCI and design.

- It is substantive yet easy to understand, apply, and teach.

- It conceives aesthetic experience as contiguous with and characteristic of everyday life, rather than as a special cognitive state separated from everyday life and limited to the contemplation of fine art.

- It gets at experiential qualities, such as involvement, delight, coming alive, pleasure, and embodiment, identified as important by interaction designers.

- It proposes that all of the objective and subjective qualities come together coherently as a whole, held together by emotion.

- It holds that experience is essentially interactive in nature.

As a result, Dewey's theory of experience applies very capably to interaction design. Before we explore that application, let us first summarize the theory itself.

5.3.1   DEWEY'S THEORY OF AESTHETIC EXPERIENCE

Dewey begins his analysis by distinguishing between the constant flow of experience that we all have all the time, and those experiences that we mark as "aesthetic." The former, the constant flow of experience, is inchoate and uncomposed: "There is distraction and dispersion; what we observe and what we think, what we desire and what we get, are at odds with each other" (Dewey, 2005 [1934], p. 36). In distinction to this is what Dewey describes as "an experience":

> we have *an* experience when the material experienced runs its course to fulfillment. Then and only then is it integrated within and demarcated in the general stream of experience from other experiences. [...] Such an experience is whole and carries with it its own individualizing quality and self-sufficiency. It is *an* experience. [...] In such experiences, every successive part flows freely, without seam and without unfulfilled blanks, into what ensues. [...] There are pauses, places of rest, but they punctuate and define the quality of movement. [...] An experience has a unity that gives it its name, *that* meal, that storm, that rupture of friendship. The existence of this unity if constituted by a single *quality* that pervades the entire experience in spite of the variation of its constituent parts. (36-8, emphases in the original)

Aesthetic experiences, in other words, are well formed; they are composed; they are complete; they are "demarcated" from the regular flow of experience; they are subjectively unified by a single overriding felt quality. Thus, whereas the act of listening to a favorite song, fixing a motorcycle, or playing a video game might be pleasurable while it is unfolding, it is not (yet) an aesthetic experience simply because it is not yet "*an* experience." To be "*an* experience," the experience in question has to be completed, and it has to be interpreted as such ("demarcated"), the way we say after some memorable event, "well, *that* was an experience!" We see this in games: to lose a game of Gin Rummy or Mah Jongg, or to die at the end of a boss fight in a video game, is often accompanied by a sense of interruption: "Aww, I was *soooo* close!"

Dewey's next step is to work out the components and the composition of such "an experiences." One element for Dewey is "a satisfying emotional quality because [the experience] possesses internal integration and fulfillment reached through ordered and organized movement" (pp. 39–40). Aesthetic experiences have *movement*—that is, they unfold over time—and when this unfolding has "internal integration" (e.g., the absence of distractions, loose ends, etc.) then it yields "a satisfying emotional quality." Again, it is easy to see how attending a pop concert, cooking a meal, solving a math problem, contemplating a painting, having sex, reading fiction, cleaning up a mess, praying, gardening, and any number of everyday activities can have these qualities.

But movement while necessary is not sufficient. Dewey notes that we engage in activities that have movement and which come to an end, but many of these do not rise to aesthetic experiences. Consider, for example, aimless activities, where we lack purpose and simply drift (e.g., when we arrive early for an appointment and have to kill time). Also consider having to send 1,000 letters in a single session, an activity characterized by repetitiveness and tediousness. There is little of the aesthetic in such experiences. Dewey explains:

> Thus, the non-esthetic lies within two limits. At one pole is the loose succession that does not begin at any particular place and that ends—in the sense of ceasing—at no particular place. At the other pole is arrest, constriction, proceeding from parts having only a mechanical connection to one another. (Dewey, 2005 [1934], p. 41)

Having ruled out purposeless activities with no outcome (the former case) and activities whose processes are merely connected to one another mechanically (the latter case), Dewey then turns his attention to the composition of the movement or process that does characterize aesthetic experience, two of which are key. The first is a *purposeful connection between elements*: for example, a special meal might be characterized in terms of washing and cutting vegetables, which leads to the combining of ingredients, which leads to the act of cooking, and then to serving, and then to an enjoyable meal with loved ones. It is easy to see how these same activities done by line cooks in a fast food restaurant typically are not aesthetic experiences. Second is the *interactive nature* of this: the experiencing subject interacts with her environment, both taking actions and undergoing their consequences: "A man does something; he lifts, let us say, a stone. In consequence, he undergoes, suffers, something: the weight, strain, texture of the surface of the thing lifted. The properties thus undergone determine further doing" (p. 45). This coupling of doing and undergoing, of doer and environment "continues until a mutual adaptation of the self and the object emerges and that particular experience comes to a close" (p. 45). He continues:

> The creature operating may be a thinker in his study and the environment with which he interacts may consist of ideas instead of a stone. But interaction of the two constitutes a total experience that is had, and the close which completes it is the institution of a felt harmony. An experience has pattern and structure, because it is not just doing and undergoing in alternation, but consists of them in relationshi (p. 45).

Dewey's Theory of Aesthetic Experience in a Nutshell

An aesthetic experience for Dewey is one where the flow of experience is bounded and composed; it is an experience. It has a beginning, a middle, and an end, and that end is a consummation (not merely a cessation). The process and outcome are related to one another; that is, the outcome is the purpose of the process. The process is highly interactive, a tightly coupled set of doings and undergoings whose alternations are composed, building on and enriching each other. All of this is subjectively experienced in relation to a single overriding felt quality. We visualize it in Figure 4.1.

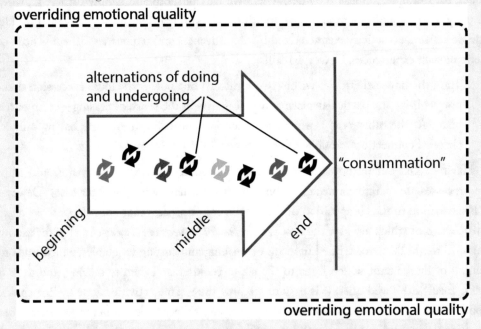

Figure 4.1: A visualization of Dewey's theory of aesthetic experience.

Dewey is keen to stress that this account of experience can apply equally well to the mathematician solving a problem as it can to a gardener weeding, and yet it still can apply to aesthetic experiences in the traditional sense of contemplating works of fine art. Some critics of Dewey see him as valorizing middle-brow values, and so even if he is quick to extend aesthetic experience beyond the fine arts to such experiences as gardening or mathematics, nonetheless the fine arts remain his paradigm case. That leaves open to question whether relatively "low brow" experiences can be aesthetic, say, watching an episode of *Married With Children* to pass the time. We tend to read Dewey as emphasizing the quality of the subjectively felt experience over the objective qualities of the activity, and thus one might very well have an aesthetic experience watching *Married With Children*, given the right circumstances (for that individual).

One can argue with any philosophical theory, often with the benefit of improving upon the theory in question. However, doing philosophy can also become overkill if our primary goal is to get a better handle on how and why people have the experiences that they do. Certainly, most of us can understand how a Hollywood summer blockbuster—experience designs through and through—are constructed to produce the sorts of good experiences that Dewey describes: the protagonist and antagonist do and undergo in a series of interactions that build on each other, rising in stakes, intensity, resonance, before resolving into a satisfying and usually appropriate consummation (e.g., the antagonist is often undone by his own machinations or undone in a way that symbolically reflects his crimes). Likewise, it is easy to apply this theory to the dialogical structure of human-computer interaction, whether it is at the level of the individual physically manipulating inputs and perceiving outputs (e.g., in a video game) or at the more social level of participating on Facebook or working in a nursing ward.

We stress again, as we have throughout this book, that any philosophical or critical theory aimed at supporting the interpretation of a complex phenomenon, such as an artistic work or a product experience, is typically viewed as a "way in," as a set of tools or concepts that support the original interpretative act of understanding that work or experience. Given that the work is understood as *sui generis*, so too is any reading of it. That means that Dewey's theory will always fall short of explaining a work or experience in question; instead, its role is to aid the interpreter in her act of constructing such an explanation.

5.3.2   DEWEYAN PRAGMATISM AND UX

For Petersen et al. (2004), a pragmatist view of aesthetics allows us to go far beyond aesthetics as mere surface decoration, to get at the purposiveness and holistic qualities of human-computer interaction: "aesthetics is not only an adhesive making things attractive, and it is part of the foundation for a purposeful system. Aesthetics cannot be sat aside as an 'added value'" (p. 271). As we've seen in Dewey, the aesthetic quality is that which renders coherent (or even: composed) everything from low-level interactions to the overall purposiveness and gestalt qualities of the activity. Udsen and Jorgensen (2006) summarize the pragmatist movement in HCI as seeking to replace the usability paradigm with an aesthetic one.

Other researchers such as Mark Blythe, Kees Overbeeke, Tom Djajadiningrat and Caroline Hummels encourage forgetting about usability, and instead discovering innovative aesthetic interactions (Blythe et al., 2003). Basically, the idea is to focus on how computers behave and engage users. Instead of studying users' perception, usability and issues of affordances, Blythe and colleagues suggest various ludic approaches to design. These address the users' senses and seek richer, more expressive forms of interaction in correspondence with the uniqueness of the actual socio-cultural use context. [...] The more critical constituents of this approach define themselves in direct opposition to the field of HCI and usability. Instead of searching for efficient, predictable and transparent interfaces, Anthony Dunne, Fiona Raby and William Gaver provide a new agenda for the design of interaction, aiming at creating varied, mysterious or even dysfunctional technologies. With design and use-qualities such as ambiguity (Gaver et al. 2003) and 'parafunctionality' (Dunne 1999), the idea is to experiment with digital designs, creating so-called 'post-optimal electronic objects', which minimise concerns of practicality and functionality to the advantage of expanding experiences and emotions with poetic dimensions. (pp. 209–210).

In their *Technology As Experience* (whose title references Dewey's book, *Art as Experience*), McCarthy and Wright (2004) develop a Deweyan perspective to HCI in two key ways. The first is that they use Dewey's account of experience to propose a framework by which user researchers and designers can analyze actual experiences. This framework can be used to answer the question: given the incredible complexity, range of inputs, and resonances of user experiences, *how should we look at experiences*? How do we separate the relevant from the irrelevant, or the idiosyncratic from the common? How can the different compositional elements of an experience be perceived and understood, without resorting to an overly reductive schema? How can we perceive what is most *alive* about experiences?

One of McCarthy and Wright's more enduring contributions is to propose an analysis of experience based on four "threads"—the sensual, emotional, compositional, and spatio-temporal—which we quote at length:

The sensual thread of experience therefore is concerned with our sensory engagement with the situation, which orients us to the concrete, palpable, and visceral character of experience. It draws attention to things being grasped pre-reflectively as the immediate sense of a situation in which the wonder of the material world is made actual for us in the quality of experience. (p. 80)

[On the emotional thread:] no emotion exists independent of the particular circumstances connected with it and the character of the experienced event permeates the emotion, whatever name we give it. The joy of solving a problem is not the same as the joy of required love [...] The emotions at work in an experience belong to a self engaged in a situation and concerned with the movement of events toward an outcome that is desired or disliked. It does not exist separate from the person, the situation, or the feelings of the person toward the situation. (p. 83)

The compositional thread is concerned with the relationships between the parts of the whole of an experience […] Faced with the potential arbitrariness of experience, a mean-ing-making creature or culture at try to bring a meaningful quality to experience […] We can also make decisions at the beginnings and ends of experiences, which would dissolve some of the arbitrariness. Jackson (1998) calls this 'framing experience' […] An important question with respect to the meaningfulness of experience is whether some technologies facilitate framing, or even whether different technologies facilitate framing in different ways for different people. (pp. 87–89)

All experience has a spatio-temporal component. […] Experiences of space and time are constructed through interaction. Time may speed up or slow down, pace may increase or decrease, spaces may open up or close down. Space and time may be connected or discon-nected. (p. 91)

In contrast to "subjective satisfaction," which could be measured using scales, McCarthy and Wright's "four threads" approach sees experience as something so dense and complex that instead of modeling and measuring it, we are better off interpreting it. McCarthy and Wright's framework supports the interpretation of user experiences akin to the way that critical theories support our interpretation of our experiences with art, film, or reading literature. To form an understanding of the character of such experiences, one must critically read the relationships between the design (or situation) in its concrete objectivity and the unfolding subjectively felt experience of someone engaging it. Such an analysis can begin by using each of the four threads as a lens to interpret a different aspect of user experience data. Indeed, in Bardzell and Bardzell (2007), we used McCa-rthy and Wright's "four threads" framework to analyze the user experience of an extreme sexual subculture in the virtual world Second Life, an analysis that helped us understand how members of this community constructed good experiences for themselves in this emerging technological environment (see Chapter 6).

The second way McCarthy and Wright develop their Deweyan perspective is to propose norms of design evaluation, which replace or at the very least significantly augment the thin cri-terion of "subjective satisfaction" in usability. Building on Dewey, McCarthy and Wright suggest questions that can help guide user engagement studies, such as the following.

- Do the technologies connect or fragment experience and life?

- Do the technologies help enrich our experience of what we already value, or do they impoverish it?

- Do the technologies facilitate unfolding potential, critical perception, and engagement?

- Specifically, does the Internet increase the potential for new relationships and new forms of communicating, or does it inhibit relating? (p. 66, bullet format in original)

Again, these questions should be read as generative prompts, as "ways in" to support the creative engagement with and insightful interpretation of one's data, or to support the design of acquiring good user experience data in the first place; these are not best used as literal prompts to put on questionnaires given to users.

Moving from very general HCI questions to more specific, yet common ones, McCarthy and Wright also envision how a Deweyan perspective could help guide the implementation of new technologies into an organization, asking the following.

- Does bringing technology into the organization help connect values, emotions, and physical activities, or does it fragment them?

- Is it respectful to tradition—the meanings already given to activities and artifacts by workers in the organization—while at the same time offering the kind of edginess that can release potential?

- Does the introduction of new technologies respect the stories we tell ourselves about what is important while also allowing us to create new stories? (p. 66, bullet format in original)

Bullet lists such as these serve two purposes. First, they can be useful in their own right, serving as a framework from which to design an empirical study, to formulate appropriate research questions, or to construct appropriate measures. Second, and perhaps more important, they exemplify a kind of thinking: if we take a reading such as Dewey on aesthetic experience seriously, how can we leverage that reading to innovate on our everyday HCI and design practice?

5.3.3   SOMAESTHETICS OR EMBODIED PRAGMATISM

The call for taking the body seriously in computing is not new (we saw it earlier, for example, in quotes from Petersen et al. (2004) and it was also heavily featured in Dourish's (2001) influential book *Where the Action Is*), and yet it is an agenda item that seems to progress all too slowly in HCI. As Höök et al. (2015) write:

> despite all the work we have seen on designing for embodiment, the actual corporeal, pulsating, live, felt body has been notably absent from both theory and practical design work. Most design work has taken a quite instrumental view on interaction: Our bodies are there to be trimmed, perfected, and kept free from illnesses and bad influences. (p. 27)

Pragmatic philosophy generally takes the body seriously—Dewey's philosophy frequently characterizes humans as "creatures" or "organisms" who are immersed in and interact with their environments as the normal activities of life, whether they are doing math or foraging for food. And yet, in spite of nods to emotion and similar concepts, Höök is right: HCI researchers using pragmatist perspectives do have surprisingly little to say about the "actual corporeal, pulsating, live" body, presumably revealing a bias we all have collectively toward the verbally articulable.

Yet Höök (2010) argues that we miss too much in this compromise. We fail to account for key qualities of experience sufficiently.

> Ways of knowing can arise from your bodily acts without any language translation in-between. The feel of the muscle tensions, the touch of the skin, the tonicities of the body, balance, posture, rhythm of movement, the symbiotic relationship to objects in our environment—these come together into a unique holistic experience. (p. 226)

And we similarly fail to take seriously that the direction of contemporary computing is becoming increasingly connected to our bodies and body experiences: "biosensors worn on your body, interactive clothes, or wearable computers such as mobiles equipped with accelerometers, a whole space of possibilities for body-based interaction is opened" (p. 226). Once again, we have a gap between an identified need and an existing practice, and once again, several researchers (e.g., Petersen et al., 2004; Schiphorst, 2009; Höök, 2010; Bardzell, 2012; Lee et al., 2014; Höök et al., 2015) turn to a philosopher of aesthetics to bridge that gap, in this case, Richard Shusterman and his conceptualization of somaesthetics.

Shusterman's Somaesthetic Theory

Somaesthetics is a pragmatist theory of aesthetics that seeks to do a much better job of situating the body in our understanding of aesthetic (or any other) experience. Shusterman (2000) offers the following definition of somaesthetics.

> Somaesthetics can be provisionally defined as the critical, meliorative study of the experience and use of one's body as a locus of sensory-aesthetic appreciation (*aisthesis*) and creative self-fashioning. It is, therefore, also devoted to the knowledge, discourses, practices, and bodily disciplines that structure such somatic care or can improve it. If we put aside traditional philosophical prejudice against the body and simply recall philosophy's central aims of knowledge, self-knowledge, right action, and its quest for the good life, then the philosophical value of somaesthetics should become clear in several ways. [...] The complementary route offered by somaesthetics is, instead, to correct the actual functional performance of our senses by an improved direction of one's body, since the senses belong to and are conditioned by the soma. (p. 267)

Shusterman shares the pragmatist goal of contributing to living, which is conceived as an embodied, interactive, skilled practice—a practice that has the potential, at least, to be artful. Like Dewey, he is more interested in artful living and aesthetic experience than he is in art itself. Somaesthetics is "meliorative," that is, aimed at improving life-practice; like other pragmatisms, it does not orient itself toward an austere and abstract pursuit of Truth but rather to the betterment of everyday life.

Somaesthetics

Somaesthetics combines the Greek word *soma* meaning "body" (e.g., in the English words "somatic" and "chromosome") and aesthetics (which characterizes the quality of our "lower cognition," including perception, imagination, insight, empathy etc.). For Shusterman, somaesthetics is "a life-improving cognitive discipline that extends far beyond questions of beauty and fine arts and that involves both theory and practical exercise," which seeks "to end the neglect of the body that [was] disastrously introduced into aesthetics," with the ultimate goal to "contribute significantly to … an art of living." (Shusterman, 2000, pp. 266–67).

Somaesthetics' key philosophical argument is that if we are to pursue knowledge, self-knowledge right action, and the good life, as the philosophers urge us to do, then we need to take seriously the locus and instrument in which those pursuits take place: our bodies.

> The body […] forms our primal perspective or mode of engagement with the world, determining (often unconsciously) our choice of ends and means by structuring the very needs, habits, interests, pleasures, and capacities on which those ends and means rely for their significance (Shusterman, 2008, pp. 2–3)

The capabilities of the body can be improved, as most of us know through sport or exercise in our own lives. But Shusterman—and with much to back him up here from philosophy, psychology, and sociology—points out that many of our social and intellectual capabilities—perception, imagination, empathy, social understanding, self-presentation, and so forth—depend upon body knowledge and body competence, and these same social capabilities shape how we engage the world, including our activities as scientists.

Similarly, our sense of self can be transfigured through transformative experiences (2008, p. 9). We hear about the self-transformative experiences had (and sought after) by yoga masters and body builders, and with tantric sex and even Timothy Leary's use of psychedelic drugs. Our neglect of the body—in science and philosophy alike—renders us less sensitive and perceptive than we could be about ourselves and others, and amounts to an abdication of our social and moral obligations. Shusterman's proposal to address this problem is threefold:

1. to offer an analytical or theoretical account of the significance of the body and the need for its cultivation (which is what we have summarized here);

2. to pursue the construction of somaesthetic disciplines and practices, such as dance, martial arts, yoga, aerobics, bodybuilding, erotic arts, and more; a discipline of "somaesthetic design" would certainly qualify; and

3. to engage in "practical somaesthetics," which means actually physically getting on the yoga mat (so to speak) and improving one's own body, so we're not just talking about it.

Shusterman's program has influenced HCI in two key ways. First, researchers have applied Shusterman's claim that body competence supports knowledge construction to design processes, methods, and education and begun to construct "somaesthetic design" as a subdiscipline. Second, researchers have sought to design somaesthetic experiences. We address each below.

Somaesthetic Design as a Disciplinary Practice

Bardzell (2012) explores the apparent fit between somaesthetic theory (the analytic part) and the sorts of intellectual qualities demanded of designers. He writes:

> somaesthetics occupies a unique theoretical position in our field, able to connect pragmatist approaches to HCI (design theory, experience design) and embodied approaches to HCI (affective computing; mobile, pervasive, and ubiquitous computing). This has implications both for users, and in particular, *norms for serving users in the deepest and most important ways possible*; and also for interaction designers, and in particular, *the cultivation of the professional self as an expert subject*. (section 21.10, emphasis in the original)

The first implication has to do with the goals for and evaluation of interactive systems: how a somaesthetic sensibility can help frame such goals. The second has to do with the designer as an expert subject, that is, someone who professionally develops subjective capabilities (including point of view, taste, imagination, sensitivity, empathy, perceptiveness, expressiveness) to support creative and insightful design thinking and processes (see Chapter 3). An expert subjectivity is needed in design because "design professionals require a cultivated ability to read socio-cultural signs and trends; a creative and reasoned ability to explore alternative futures; a verbal ability to articulate these activities; a receptiveness to alternative framings and a willingness to explore highly variable alternative directions; and above all a personal identity or coherence that holds all of these moving parts together through a given process" (Bardzell, 2012, Section 21.10.1).

Of Shusterman's three-part agenda for somaesthetics—analytic theory, the construction of somaesthetic disciplines and methods, and actually cultivating one's body on the mat (so to speak),

Bardzell (2012) stays primarily in the analytic while gesturing toward methods and practice. However, Hummels et al. (2007) argue that it's not enough for designers of movement-based interactions to understand movement analytically; they need body-expertise themselves. To cultivate such expertise, they provide a set of tools and methods. In two recent design research projects, one by Höök (2010) and the other by Lee et al. (2014), the authors have ambitiously incorporated all three parts of the somaesthetic agenda in their design research, contributing toward a somaesthetic design disciplinary practice.

In a paper that might seem eccentric, especially if one has not yet learned the lessons of somaesthetics—"Transferring Qualities from Horseback Riding to Design"—Kristina Höök (2010) argues that designers need good descriptions of embodied experiences to support the design of experience-oriented body technologies, such as wearable computing, interactive clothes, biosensors, mobiles, and so forth. But such descriptions are hard to find and difficult to achieve. Höök deploys Ljungblad and Homquist's notion of "transfer scenarios," which she summarizes as the idea "that we can learn from people's specific practices and use the qualities of those practices [by] transferring them into innovative design that can attract a more general audience" (p. 233). From there, she embarks on an autoethnography of her own experiences in horseback riding training, with a finely nuanced account of her body experiences throughout, described both analytically (as an athlete studies film of herself to observe posture, gait, and so forth) and experientially (as a subject capable of body pleasure, pain, clumsiness, tension, balance, and touch).

The payoff of this body autoethnography is a fine-grained description of body rhythm understood both interactively (as her body and the horse's learn to coordinate together) and aesthetically (when she achieves desired rhythms with the horse).

> I have kept coming back to rhythm, as it is an important aspect of riding. At the same time, it is an interaction quality we rarely talk about in our design processes even if we know that any interaction, be it bodily or a more traditional desktop system, reveals its dynamic gestalt over time and space [p. 17]. Any such interaction will have its rhythm – its ebbs and flows, intense or more slow reflective parts. But in the horseback riding, rhythm is a more intense experience, strongly intertwined with all the different parts of the riding activity. (p. 234)

The Deweyan qualities of this experience are quite clear: the "ebbs and flows" harken to Dewey's "doing and undergoing," the rhythm is the pleasing subjective quality that Dewey talks about, and the Deweyan consummation is Höök's surprising and powerful claim of becoming a "centaur"—again in Dewey's language, an intensity and clarification of experience characteristic of aesthetic "*an* experiences."

She also realizes that the mistake- and frustration-filled process of learning these rhythms contributed to her sense of accomplishment and therefore the overall pleasure; she would not want a special machine that perfected her posture and movements in a way that preempted such learnings. In Deweyan terms, such a move would sever process and consummation. Höök's sensibility for "wordless understanding" was also heightened and made her reflect on the ways that human-computer interactions also entail many types of wordless understandings between human and machine. But above all, it is clear that for Höök, the activity and eventual consummation of becoming rhythmic was the most powerful take-home.

Whereas Höök uses someaesthetics to support her ability to experience, analyze, and articulate her body experience, Lee et al. (2014) embed "somaesthetic reflection" into the early stages of a design process to support design ideation. Following Shusterman, himself synthesizing pragmatist William James' psychology and the Feldenkrais Method (a somatic educational system), Lee et al. deploy the following six strategies in their design team to "heighten attention and interest" to the body.

1. *Questions*: Asking questions about different aspects and relations of what we perceive.

2. *Division into parts*: Subdividing the body and directing our attention to each part, one by one.

3. *Contrasts of feeling*: Discriminating the different feelings in one part from those in another.

4. *Associative interests*: Making the noticing of what we are trying more precisely to feel a key to something we care about.

5. *Avoiding distracting interests*: Warding off competing interests to what we are trying to attend to and feel.

6. *Pre-perception*: Preparing our attention to notice what we are trying to discriminate in what we feel. (p. 1056, numbered list in the original)

They found that the use of this method helped the designers perceive unconscious movements and the coordination of movements, and that this in turn helped them identify design issues as well as a "more effective experience prototyping of interaction with moving products" (p. 1055). The authors elaborate:

> This study suggests a way to promote somatic empathy with a user in *a particular situation*. Our point is not simulating [a particular category of users] with additional equipment. It is about meticulously considering the somatic conditions that we usually blur in the name of 'situational, contextual factors', and directly experiencing those conditions: user's posture, attention, anticipation, and the physical interaction going on between the body and the surroundings. (p. 1062)

The Höök (2010) and Lee et al. (2014) studies don't so much *argue that* as they do literally *demonstrate how* somaesthetic body practices enrich design processes. The unavoidable implication of this—and this gets right at the heart of Shusterman's program—is that design practice is and has always been somaesthetic to begin with: the socio-physicality of team-based affinity diagramming, brainstorming, bodystorming, experience prototypes, sketching, crits, and so on become very obviously somaesthetic in nature; the challenge, then, is to heighten and enrich that nature, which somaesthetics is poised to do.

Somaesthetic Designs

We have summarized research showing how somaesthetics can support design practice—any design practice, but especially applicable to those involving movement or embodied interactions. But some design researchers have also sought to make designs that themselves embody somaesthetic theory. One example is Thecla Schiphorst's (2009) project *soft(n)*. Expressing a similar motivation as Höök's—that HCI needs better accounts of embodied experiences to support design for wearable, mobile, and ubiquitous technologies—Schiphorst introduces somaesthetics, but instead of verbally articulating its theoretical program, she instead argues for "a need for practice-based methods that can provide practical examples of these conceptually rich theories" (p. 2428).

Her first step is to rearticulate somaesthetics in terms of four generative design principles:

1. *Experience*, which frames questions of cultivating embodiment, sensory perception and links to techniques of somatics;

2. *Poetics of Interaction* including meaning-making and open interpretation, which explores perception and cross-modal relationships between touch [sic];

3. *Materiality*, which emphasizes the importance of the physical body as well as the physical material, texture, shape, and form that support experience within the installation; and

4. *Semantics of Caress*, investigating the meaning of touch as applied to tactile interaction (how can models of meaning be applied to a computational model for interaction) (pp. 2429–30).

From these she designed a collection of interactive pillow-like objects and set them up as a public installation in the Showroom style (Koskinen et al., 2011). She describes *soft(n)* as follows, and can be seen in Figure 4.2.

> The *soft(n)* installation is an intelligent tangible network comprised of soft physical objects that exhibit emergent behavior through interaction. soft(n) is a group of ten interactive soft objects, each containing a specially designed and custom-engineered multi-touch soft

input surface and motion detectors. Each soft object has an ability to actuate vibration, light and sound in response to its tactile induced state. Each soft object is able to communicate wirelessly to multiple others as a group (p. 2431).

Figure 4.2: *Soft(n)* by Thecla Schiphorst (images used with permission).

As with many research through design projects, it is not trivial to extract meanings or clearly formulated design implications from *soft(n)*. None of the technologies that Schiphorst uses are especially cutting edge, and individually none is used in any particularly radical ways. However, the gestalt, the overall effect of *soft(n)*, even with a couple of pictures and short textual description, is both estranging and inviting. *Soft(n)* pulls us into its world, inviting us to experience and perhaps reflect on the somaesthetic values it embodies, helping us to perceive how they contrast with the design-inscribed values in our own mundane reality (e.g., the hard, cold, minimalist designs of tablets and smart phones), revealing opportunities to enrich the somaesthetic qualities of future interaction design.

In "Somaesthetic Design" (2015), Höök and colleagues undertake a project that combines qualities of Lee et al. (2014) somaesthetic design process and Schiphorst's somaesthetic design practice-based research product; that is, using a somaesthetics-inspired design methodology, they set out to create somaesthetic designs. Their objective was no more and no less than "a return to the most basic pleasures in life: our own movements" (p. 28).

The role that somaesthetic methods and practice (Shusterman's second and third branches of somaesthetics) was substantial: the design team did Feldenkrais practices weekly for an entire year.

As with Lee et al.'s approach, Höök's team found that the somatic exercises were far more than new age touchy-feely activities, but that they significantly and positively influenced the design process.

> But what was even more interesting was how [the Feldenkrais] lessons influenced our brainstorming exercises. In a typical brainstorming session, ideas are aggressively put out there in rapid succession, one person taking up someone else's idea, changing it, turning it around, shifting perspectives. In the brainstorming sessions that followed a Feldenkrais exercise, we found that our ideas formed more slowly. They felt more honest, closer to our hearts and desires. The interactions we envisioned were delicate, sensitive to our bodily processes. (p. 29)

These qualities of delicacy, sensitivity, intimate honesty—all are properly aesthetic qualities according to most formulations of aesthetics—not merely pragmatist ones. The shifts away from aggression and speed toward slower idea formation are social qualities. Shusterman claims that "Feeling *bien dans sa peau* can make us more comfortably open in dealing with others" (2008, p. 41), and Höök et al. show here how the enhanced sociability of the team as a result of their somatic exercises was epistemically significant in the sense that it contributed to design knowledge.

In summary, HCI researchers turned to pragmatist philosophy because it helped them gain traction with an urgent but very difficult problem—how to understand experience in such a way that one can competently design for it. Pragmatist philosophy offers a theory of experience that can be used to interpret interaction in an incredibly diverse array of situations, whose key lessons can be easily taught and applied throughout the community regardless of disciplinary background, and that nonetheless captures something of the depth and seriousness of aesthetics (i.e., rejecting the notion that it describes surface decorations).

Someaesthetics is poised to build on pragmatist aesthetics, by theorizing the significance of the body in the processes, products, and reasons for knowledge activities, such as design. However, it is in an earlier phase in HCI and design. The Schiphorst, Lee et al., and Höök et al. projects cited in this section are early efforts to translate theory to designs and design methodologies. Much work is yet to be done before somaesthetic design theories and methods mature to the point that they widely influence practice, but we believe the potential is high enough to warrant further research and design.

5.4   INTERACTION DESIGN POETICS

Earier in this chapter we claimed that theories of aesthetic experience typically seek to account for the relation between works (such as artworks, performances, and designs) on the one hand and subjectively felt experiences of those works on the other. We also noted that most theories tended to prefer or start with one side over the other. The pragmatist theory is very strong on the subjective side of that equation: what experience is, how the body and our perceptual-intellectual apparatus is structured to process it, and how to articulate its parts in relation to its wholes. But it should also be clear that the pragmatist approach has less to say about the objects themselves. Dewey's picture of aesthetic experience is object-independent, and McCarthy and Wright's "four threads" characterize the felt qualities of experience but say nothing about the designs, artworks, events, or natural objects that contribute to or even cause them. Indeed, experiential qualities appear to cause other experiential qualities, for example, the way that the composedness of doing and undergoing contributes to a distinctive experiential tone. This limitation is not necessarily a problem: Höök's analysis of horseback riding would not have benefitted HCI readers had it gotten much more technical about the features of equine anatomy and kinesiology that contributed toward her experiences; her point was that HCI community needed descriptions of the type that her embodied felt experiences riding horses exemplified, not that the HCI community needs implications for saddle design.

Poetics

Poetics is a formal analysis of the elements and compositional techniques that constitute paradigmatic examples a given genre of work, as well as the ways that these elements as composed are expected to give rise to certain subjective effects, such as their social significances and experiential qualities.

As with most humanistic approaches to inquiry, poetics does not offer a scientific model that seeks to explain a phenomenon; instead, it offers conceptual structures that frame interpretative reasoning about a genre or form of human-made work.

That said, it is intuitively obvious that designers have far more control over choices concerning task sequences, layouts, color schemes, labels, inputs and outputs, functions, and so forth than they do over users' felt experiences. Gillian Crampton Smith offers such a position in her introduction to Moggridge's (2007) *Designing Interactions*, in which she offers a genealogy of ways that interaction design has borrowed "design languages" from poetry (first dimension), painting and typography (second dimension), sculpture and product design (third dimension), and sound, film, and animation (fourth dimension), before concluding the following.

> However, after twenty years of drawing upon existing expressive languages, we now need to develop an independent language of interaction with smart systems and devices, a language true to the medium of computation, networks, and telecommunication. In terms of perceptual psychology, we starting to understand the functional limits of interaction between people and devices or systems: speed of response, say, or the communicative capacity of a small screen. But *at the symbolic level of mood and meaning, of sociability and civility, we haven't quite achieved the breathtaking innovativeness, the subtlety and intuitive "rightness," of [Soviet film theorist Sergei] Eisenstein's language of montage.* (pp. xviii–xix, emphasis added)

Similarly, Lim et al. (2007) motivate their contribution—a theorization of what they call the "interaction gestalt"—by appealing to this sort of reasoning. They write that the problem with limiting our thinking to

> the user experience [is that it] cannot fully guide designers to explore a design space of possible aesthetic interactions in a concrete way. This means that designers should have knowledge of how to *shape* aesthetic interactions in a more visible, explicit, and designerly way. This is a kind of knowledge we are currently missing in HCI. [By analogy, we note that] visual designers know that they should be able to manipulate key attributes of visual products such as margins, shapes, typefaces, and spatial layouts in order to design the gestalt of the visual product. [...] [Accordingly,] we want to adopt and adapt certain ways of thinking through the use of a *design language*, similar to what can be found in established design disciplines. This language includes: (1) a good sense of what it is that is designed—i.e. a design target [...] (2) a good sense of what is possible for a designer to manipulate when designing the design target[...], and (3) a good sense of how to manipulate these attributes in order to shape a specific design (pp. 240–41, emphasis in the original).

How can designers shape design materials, signifying conventions, task/interaction flows, purposes, and so forth in such a way that leads to good experiences? They do not use the term explicitly, and in fact very few in HCI do, but what Crampton Smith and Lim et al. alike are calling for is a *poetics of interaction design*.

5.4.1   THE POETICS OF ARISTOTLE

> Let us discuss the art of poetry, itself, and its species, describing the character of each of them, and how it is necessary to construct plots if the poetic composition is to be successful, and furthermore the number and kind of parts to be found in the poetic work, and as many other matters as are relevant (Aristotle, *Poetics I*, 1447a, 1981).

So begins Aristotle in his *Poetics*, one of the most influential aesthetic treatises ever written (we're using the Leon Golden translation, used in Aristotle, 1981). The analytic focus is on "poetry, itself," which Aristotle then subdivides into species (e.g., tragedy, comedy, and epic), with each having a distinctive character, compositional strategy, and collection of parts or elements.

But a crucial part of Aristotle's program is to account for how these elements and the rules of composition that organize them into a whole yield experiential effects. Aristotle's classic definition of tragedy exemplifies this move from objective features of the work toward their subjective effects in experience.

> Tragedy is, then, an imitation of a noble and complete action, having the proper magnitude; it employs language that has been artistically enhanced by each of the kinds of

linguistic adornment, applied separately in the various parts of the play; it is presented in dramatic, not narrative form, and achieves, through the representation of pitiable and fearful incidents, the catharsis of such pitiable and fearful incidents (*Poetics VI*, p. 1449b).

Why are we talking about Aristotle and "poetics" when HCI and design researchers themselves don't use the term? Because the intellectual projects have striking similarity. Designers make decisions directly about objective features of products, working within and often innovating upon rules of composition. However, although designers want to create good experiences, they cannot directly design experiences. And thus any theory that can link individual design choices to experiential qualities has high practical value. Aristotle provides one of the first models of this approach, but that approach can still be seen today in HCI and design research. For example, let us compare Aristotle's project and recent work in HCI and design. Consider the texts in Table 4.1 side-by-side, which we have rearranged to create better syntactic parallels, but which are otherwise verbatim from their sources:

Table 4.1: A comparison from Aristotle's *Poetics* (top left) and Lim et al.'s (2007) description of their concept of "interaction gestalt" (top right), with comments on what these theories respectively set out to achieve (bottom left and right)	
Tragedy is, then, an imitation of a noble and complete action, having the proper magnitude; it employs language that has been artistically enhanced by each of the kinds of linguistic adornment, applied separately in the various parts of the play; it is presented in dramatic, not narrative form, and achieves, through the representation of pitiable and fearful incidents, the catharsis of such pitiable and fearful incidents (Poetics VI, 1449b)	interaction gestalt [is, then, understood] in relation to [an] interactive artifact, which can be described by artifact properties such as size, texture, weight, layout, arrangement, and structure [and] user experience, which can be described by user experience qualities such as pleasantness, fun, ease-of-use, and affect (assembled from Lim et al., 2007, pp. 245–6)
Aristotle's *Poetics* [offers] a detailed analysis of one literary genre, tragedy, outlining its constituent parts (plot, character, action, thought, diction) and the key concepts for describing its aims and effects (Lamarque, 2008, p. 1)	We believe that existing approaches without the notion of the interaction gestalt have a large gap between *use qualities* and *artifact properties* which designers need to bridge (Lim et al., 2007, p. 246)

Both Aristotle and Lim et al. offer an attempt to explicate a causal relationship between creative choices that give shape to the work in such a way that they also give shape to the experience of that work. This is not to claim in a literal way that these choices simply do cause these experiences— obviously people read and experience works in diverse ways. But it is a claim that specific design choices, guided by abstract concepts (e.g., the genre of tragedy as a species of poetry, the notion of "interaction gestalt" as a compositional theory for design), are likely also to shape common experiential qualities of the works as well. This is what the term "poetics" means in humanistic thought.

5.4.2 BRENDA LAUREL: COMPUTERS AS THEATER

Interestingly, all the way back in 1991 interaction designer and theorist Brenda Laurel (2003) developed a proposal for aesthetic computing, *Computers as Theater*, which was based on Aristotle's *Poetics*. One of her goals is to encourage and support the design of "human-computer activities that are—dare we say—*beautiful*" (p. 571). Laurel is known for being far-sighted, and she has here anticipated a movement in HCI that would only achieve critical a decade or more later (albeit shaped by her influence). Anyway, the criterion of beauty applied to computing is "aesthetic interaction" *par excellence*, and Laurel's choice to press Aristotle in service of this goal is significant.

> I present Aristotle's model [of tragedy] here for two reasons. First, I am continually amazed by the elegance and robustness of the categories and their causal relations [i.e., the elements of tragedy and how they are structurally composed]. Following the causal relations through as one creates or analyzes a drama seems to automagically reveal the ways in which things could work or exactly how they have gone awry. Second, Aristotle's model creates a disciplined way of thinking about the design of a play in both constructing and debugging activities. Because of its fundamental similarities to drama, human-computer activity can be described with a similar model, with equal utility in both design and analysis. (Laurel, 2003, p. 564)

It might seem odd that Laurel views HCI and drama as sharing "fundamental similarities," but actually she was standing on solid theoretical ground. Among the very origins of HCI as a discipline is the concept of interaction as a *dialogue*:

> the key notion [of our proposed new discipline of applied information processing psychology] is that the user and the computer engage in a communicative dialogue whose purpose is the accomplishment of some task. (Card et al., 1983, p. 4)

We can see the minimal contours of a simple Deweyan "an experience" in Card, Moran, and Newell's formulation of HCI as "dialogue": the dialogue constitutes the "doings and undergoings" and the completion of the task constitutes the "consummation." But it is also easy to imagine that interaction to complete a task is not itself aesthetic. Laurel's move is to take the dialogue metaphor to the next level, by seeking a paradigm example of beautiful dialogue as a model for her thinking. Not surprisingly, she arrives at theater, and once there she turns to one of the most seminal theoretical accounts of theater ever written. Aristotle's *Poetics* becomes a resource to envision the dialogue that is human-computer interaction elevated to theater.

Laurel's project entails a systematic synthesis of Aristotle's *Poetics* in order to apply it to interaction design. For example, she explicates six hierarchically structured elements of drama, according to Aristotle: action, character, thought, language, melody/pattern, spectacle/enactment. The play constitutes a single action, which is undertaken by a small number of coherent characters, who have thoughts and intentions, which are expressed in their language, which itself is melodic and rhythmic, all of which is part of the spectacle. She then applies each of these to computing, beginning by mapping "action" onto "an interactive session," in which the "characters" are the human and the computer, each of whom has thoughts/internal representations, which are expressed via language (I/O), etc. She also applies various Aristotelian points and distinctions to different specific forms of computing, e.g., observing that good plots have beginnings, middles, and endings, and when computers crash and applications quit, it is equivalent to a play with a beginning and a middle but not ending.

5.4.3   READING LAUREL—AND ARISTOTLE—TODAY

Aristotle's *Poetics* offers a detailed analysis of Ancient Greek epic and theatrical poetry, forms of writing and of life that are no longer with us today. Therefore, the *Poetics'* implications for contemporary playwriting, let alone human-computer interaction design, are doubtful (see Aristotle commentator Ross, 1995 [1923]). Indeed, as widely documented in literary theory and history, Aristotle was misread during the Renaissance as offering universal rules of theatrical writing and production, and was followed slavishly by playwrights and critics alike, to the detriment of the art. One might reasonably ask whether Laurel might also have too literally tried to apply Aristotle, and indeed we suspect that design practitioners today would find her use of Aristotle long on technical theory and comparatively short on actionable advice.

But we would argue instead that Laurel's work enduring significance lies less in her specific applications of the *Poetics* to video games and electronic spreadsheets, and more in the fact that she sought to construe interactive sessions as aesthetic wholes, which could both be theorized and analyzed as such and intentionally designed for. By implication, instead of reading Aristotle for actionable recommendations for interaction design, we would argue that HCI and design should read Aristotle for modeling a certain style of criticism, that is, a methodological approach having the following characteristics.

- It presents a formal analysis of a corpus of works taken to be exemplary in some way (for Aristotle, the best works of Greek epic, tragedy, and comedy).

- That analysis is multilevel, in that it accounts for the relatedness of small components, compositional rules, and wholes (e.g., from individual lines' diction and poetic meter to the work's overall organizing principles).

- That analysis also describes and *explains* subjective effects of the type of work, including significance (e.g., what tragedy is for, what it does in or means for society) and experiential qualities (e.g., its emotional trajectories, experiential effects).

In HCI, *interaction criticism* is the closest analogue to this type of analysis, as developed in Bertelsen and Pold (2004), Löwgren (2009), and Bardzell (2011) (see Chapter 3). Going a step further, we believe that this style of design criticism can help the community identify and analyze "strong concepts" (Höök and Löwgren, 2012). For Höök and Löwgren, a "strong concept"

> is generative and carries a core design idea, cutting across particular use situations and even application domains; concerned with interactive behavior, not static appearance; is a design element and a part of an artifact and, at the same time, speaks of a use practice and behavior over time; and finally, resides on an abstraction level above particular instances.

Examples of strong concepts that they cite include "social navigation" and "seamfulness."

We have seen in this chapter that Schiphorst (2009), Höök (2010), Bardzell (2012), Lee et al. (2014), and Höök et al. (2015) all contribute toward an emerging notion of "somaesthetic design." There are different ways one might be tempted to frame somaesthetic design from a research perspective. One way is to read it as a disciplinary practice in Shusterman's sense (i.e., the development of any discipline that contributes to somaesthetic practices). In such a view, somaesthetic design is a design methodology that is significantly imbued by somaesthetics—we saw glimpses of such a project in Lee et al. (2014) and Höök et al. (2015). Another way to read it is as a "strong concept" in Höök and Löwgren's (2012) sense. In this view, somaesthetic design supports design ideation by foregrounding a collection of interrelated concepts, design values, interactional behaviors, and experiential qualities—the body, movement, tactuality, self-cultivation, physical pleasure, sensitivity, insight, imagination, intimacy, and empathy. We read Schiphorst's *soft(n)* (2009) as an attempt to use somaesthetics as a strong concept.

At any rate, we imagine that a poetics-based critical approach can contribute to theory about somaesthetic design on broadly Aristotelian terms. Doing so would have two benefits. First, we begin by recognizing that designers, like artists, learn from prior works, but such learnings are predicated on an ability to perceive the value and disvalue of such works. Literary critic and theorist M.H. Abrams (1991) credits Aristotle's *Poetics* for "providing terms and analytic devices that enable us to experience [tragedies] in a discriminating rather than crude way, through directing our attention to their important features and the ways these features are ordered according to distinctively artistic reasons for order" (p. 45). Designers learn best from other designs when they are discriminating, rather than crude in their responses, and so a somaesthetic design poetics would support such an objective. Second, an analytic vocabulary built around intermediate concepts can be generative of design ideation and decisionmaking, because the intermediate level is the glue between the concrete and particular choices that designers must make and the meaningful and significant wholes that these particular choices eventually constitute. Aristotle's *Poetics* can be read as one of the West's earliest treatises on intermediate knowledge in the context of the arts.

5.5 CONCLUSION: A CRITICAL TAKE ON USER EXPERIENCE CONCEPT SYSTEMS

In this chapter, we summarized the turn to experience as an alternative paradigm to the usability movement. We recognized that it has been re-theorized throughout HCI, including in psychology-based, design-methods-based, and humanities-based approaches. Within the humanities-based approaches, we summarized two major movements: a pragmatist movement that focuses on subjective experience, and a poetics movement that focuses on form and composition. We also mentioned some conflict—expressed via mutual neglect and/or confrontation—between psychology-based and humanities-based approaches, in spite of the evidence suggesting that both can and have contributed to HCI design practice in significant and positive ways.

One of the intellectual services commonly provided by philosophy is a critical assessment of thought systems. This analysis often reveals the blind spots and unintended consequences of such systems. For example, St. Augustine's belief in an omnipotent, omnipresent, and omniscient god carries with it a pressure to deny the existence of evil. Now, there is more than one way Augustine might choose to respond to such a pressure, e.g., by offering an account of why such a god and evil could co-exist, or by claiming that evil in fact does not exist and is just an illusion, so the pressure is not sufficient to *determine* the theory, but the pressure is there and a successful theory should address it somehow.

All of the theories of experience that we have covered in this chapter (and every other one, ever) also have blind spots, unintended consequences, and pressures. For example, we have noted that the theory of pragmatism offers many tools to help us analyze subjective experiences, but relatively few tools to account for the significance of actual works—be they artworks, designs, performances, etc.—in the formation of those aesthetic experiences. Thus, on its surface, a pragmatist approach would seem to support the interpretation of user experiences of designs from an aesthetic perspective (including the designer's own experiences, as in Höök's (2010) horseback riding article), but not to offer effective tools to support the analysis of the designs themselves. Now, a pragmatist could counter, offering an argument that actually it does support such an analysis, e.g., of the putative experience of the implied user, but it is easy to see that such a counter would take more work than the more obvious use of pragmatism. In philosophical circles, it has been noted that Dewey's theory fails to explain aesthetic experiences of works widely recognized as significant works of art, e.g., of (near-) contemporary artists Mark Rothko, John Cage, and Robert Morris; and if Dewey's "aesthetic experience" can't even cover aesthetic experiences of art, it is dubious in its application beyond art (Carroll, 2001). Again, there are ways a Deweyan might respond to this, but the point is that every concept system has strengths and limits, and we are better able to use them well if we understand them.

We can offer a similar analysis for poetics. Poetics offers tools to support the analysis of a corpus or group of designs, linking very specific design choices to organizing wholes and from there to anticipated experiences. We argued that poetics might actually work very well with the construction and elaboration of "strong concepts" as a form of "intermediate knowledge" for design. Now, a pragmatist might point out that a formalistic analysis of an artifact doesn't tell one much about actual user experiences (nor the sociocultural and institutional contexts of those experiences). Aristotle writes about the effects of pity and fear, but there is little evidence that he did any empirical work, and most of us have experienced tragedies ourselves—did we actually experience *katharsis*? Given the Renaissance fiasco of literal-mindedly applying Aristotelian "rules" to French drama, how are we to know which parts of the Poetics remain generally applicable, and which parts reflect the historical contingencies in which the work was produced? Again, there are ways to counter such concerns, but it seems reasonable to say that poetics-based approaches are comparatively weak on supporting the analysis of actual experiences and provide little basis to imagine that their implications are transferable across time and, significantly for a globalized field such as HCI, other cultures.

Let us now step back and reflect on humanities-based approaches to user experience more generally. Their clear and obvious strength is that they are non-reductive, at least in comparison to the scales used in traditional usability, and in so doing they render experiences available to our analytical consciousness in a way comparable to how we experience them ourselves. This means that they take the subjective qualities of experience seriously, and similarly they take seriously the possibility for such experiences to be aesthetic—or nightmarish (e.g., the monotony of standing on the assembly line hour after hour, day after day, do the same simple task over and over again). They frame our thinking in such a way that a non-reductionist approach is cognitively tractable: we can consider user experience socially, economically, politically, materially, stylistically, historically, spatiotemporally, morally, emotionally, and so on, *all at once*, without losing our bearings. They allow us to approximate experiential extremes—bliss, joy, despair, as well as conflicted feelings (e.g., feeling relief and guilt at the same time because of the misfortune of a rival)—in their particularity. They allow us to explicate connections across many scales, from the macro to the micro, and significantly right in the middle: intermediate concepts. They support us in our quest to understand not what is typical, but what is atypical in an important way (e.g., the way that the "Will It Blend?" iPhone video dwarfed the thousands of other iPhone-related videos that appeared on YouTube with the iPhone 1's release, as we saw in Blythe and Cairns, 2009).

But it is important to recognize that the humanist framing has inscribed assumptions within it, which merit critical scrutiny. Above all is the notion that *experience is the sort of thing that is best interpreted*. As noted in Chapter 4, humans turn to interpretation when something is puzzling, unclear, hard to understand, resistant to other methodologies (Taylor, 1971). In a pragmatic field such as HCI and design, where we are not necessarily concerned with the Truth of User Experience but more concerned in learning just what we need to know to make good design choices, it is possible that this assumption—that experience is so complex and nuanced that it can only be interpreted— is overkill. In some cases, even usability's thin notion of "subjective satisfaction" can be sufficient, without invoking a notion of experience that *a priori* defies comprehension (and therefore requires interpretation). Further, the view that experience is the sort of thing that must be interpreted has some costly implications. Any interpretation of experience depends on the critical-hermeneutic skills of the analyst, and this is an ability that is not easy to teach or learn. Neither are its outcomes easy to validate. Kind of like design itself!

In such a context, we return to the question of psychology-based approaches to user experience. The goal of doing so is (again) to contextualize for our readers what the strengths, blindspots, and pressure points of the different theoretical and methodological options are. We begin by turning to a criticism of the humanistic approach, offered in Hassenzahl et al. (2010), who write the following.

> With their emphasis on "values, needs, desires and goals," McCarthy and Wright (2004) are in line with accepted psychological theories […] The question at hand, however, is what these "values, needs, desires" are. In fact, McCarthy and Wright (2004) seem to explicitly avoid any commentary on the content of "needs." This is due to a critical view of attempts to reduce, what they call "felt experience", to a set of generalized concepts. Due to experiences' highly situated, unique and inseparable character – their "perpetual novelty" as Schmitt (1999, p. 61) calls it – they lend themselves to description, but not to any type of categorization or reduction to a set of underlying principles. "Perpetual novelty" implies that experiences can be described in retrospect. However, in the moment of description, they are gone and will never occur again. This actually would be the end of story for experience in HCI, because designing for bygone and unrepeatable experiences is futile. (p. 354)

The gist of the argument is that McCarthy and Wright's account says nothing about the content of experience, because doing so presupposes an operationalization of "experience" into parts that the non-reductive impulse in McCarthy and Wright categorically rejects; that as a consequence of this move they can offer descriptions (but, by implication, cannot offer scientific explanations); and that each one becomes unique and particular, and therefore not generalizable and so impossible to derive any knowledge from.

In contrast, Hassenzahl et al. (2010) use psychological research to construct a sophisticated model of experience, comprising need fulfillment, affect, and product perception/evaluation, each of which is similarly broken down into components. For example, need fulfillment includes competence, relatedness, popularity, stimulation, meaning, security, and autonomy. Using a questionnaire format, the authors asked nearly 700 people to describe in their own words a positive experience and to fill in scales on these three dimensions of experience. The results include data about how each of these aspects of experience were present in their experience, and further statistical analysis yielded correlations across the categories to reveal how they clustered together, influenced one another, etc. In such a way, Hassenzahl and colleagues claimed to offer a contribution about the "content" of experience, to explain that content, and to do all of this in a generalizable way.

We basically accept Hassenzahl et al.'s account and agree that it is a significant contribution to user experience research. On the terms that they offer, they do indeed offer a scientifically compelling sense of the "content" of users' experience in a way that McCarthy and Wright do not. They also reveal relationships among the fine details of user experiences that are virtually impossible to see without this type of analysis. This account is explanatory in nature and generalizable. And it is pragmatically useful to many instances of design.

However, Hassenzahl and colleagues also make certain epistemological commitments that introduce blind spots and pressures. One of these is the assumption that *experience can be analytically broken down into smaller and smaller sub-units*, and that measures for each of these sub-units do, in fact, truthfully represent what they say that they do. Again, HCI and design are pragmatic fields. It is easy to imagine design scenarios where such an analytic approach provides the information needed to support good design decisions. But it is harder to argue that this is *universally* so, that is, that every experience can be accounted for in this way. Trained in comparative literature as we were, we are doubtful that any reader could render the most important literary or aesthetic experiences of her life—those which, like Jeffrey's high school reading of James Joyce's *A Portrait of the Artist as a Young Man*, are utterly life-changing—in an adequate way using Hassenzahl et al.'s questionnaire. This is not to assert that the questionnaire would reveal nothing, just to express doubt that it would capture what matters most in that experience. In other words, to break down the experience into such a model, one has to understand that type of experience in the first place; *the model itself is an interpretation.*

Further, the model assumes that certain qualities generalize. Let us say that "joy" is a part of a model (e.g., in a measure of affective response). But as we cited earlier, McCarthy and Wright point out that "The joy of solving a problem is not the same as the joy of requited love." Again, there are ways to respond to this objection, e.g., by claiming that the model captures all the relevant variations of "joy" or by claiming that for the pragmatic purposes of this project, there is no need to further analyze "joy."

Another assumption of Hassenzahl et al.'s work is that *knowing the content of experience in an explanatory and generalizable way is sufficient to guide experience design.* Again, this is likely to be true much of the time, but unlikely to be true all of the time. Consider, for example, Brenda Laurel's 1991 problem: how to construe for herself and her colleagues a form of "human-computer activity" that is "beautiful." We suspect that it would have at the time been very difficult for her to find 700 computer users who had had "beautiful" computer experiences, and likewise very difficult for her to elicit those experiences meaningfully using the questionnaire that Hassenzahl et al. developed (not to mention that psychology-based approaches in the early 1990s were nothing like Hassenzahl and colleagues' in their 2010 paper). Laurel's turn to Aristotle scaffolded her as she constructed an image of beautiful human-computer interaction—an image that is both rationally defensible and also practical in its applicability.

What we hope is becoming clear in this analysis is that humanistic and psychology-based approaches to user experience make different epistemological commitments (for better and worse in both cases) and pursue different intellectual ends. Hassenzahl and colleagues are correct that McCarthy and Wright's approach fails to offer a sense of the content of experience in the way that their approach does. But McCarthy and Wright could reasonably respond that Hassenzahl et al.'s approach works best when the experience is already fairly well understood, but that their own approach thrives when important aspects of the user experience are not yet well understood. When we consider, for example, Höök's account of her experiences training to ride horses, again, we are frankly skeptical that Hassenzahl et al.'s approach would have yielded the same sort of descriptive richness that Höök was able to achieve by blending her expert subjectivities as both design researcher and horseback rider. Höök's interpretativist approach is a flashlight in a cave, helping us get a sense for the space but by no means yielding a defensible and generalizable model of it. For some of her readers, Höök's analysis helped us (to use a phrase of McCarthy and Wright that is also common throughout aesthetics) "become alive to" the experiential qualities that she was discussing.

Psychology- vs. Humanities-Based Methodologies

We do not believe that either a psychology-based approach or a humanities-based approach is more "correct" than the other. The question is pragmatic, that is, having to do with what we already know and what we need to know to do design. The following table reflects the sorts of applications for which we intuit the respective approaches would excel; it is intended as an illustrative brainstorm, and should not be taken too literally as a guide.

UX research issues that would likely be a better fit for...	
A psychology-based approach	**A humanities-based approach**
The experience is already relatively well understood, and what's needed are fine-grained details to guide concrete design decisions	The intent is to explore the role of design in relation to new, or as yet poorly understood, types of experiences
The UX questions are of the sort that regular users are well equipped to answer	The UX questions are of the sort that users may not be able to articulate and instead require an expert/critical perspective
People have had, or can be given, the types of experiences that are under question	The desired experience is aspirational and speculative ("what would it be like if...") and no such experience or close analogue is available to study empirically
The research contribution is to the improved understanding, theorization, and/or modeling of user perceptions and judgments	The research contribution is to contribute to the theorization of interaction criticism and/or its teaching and practice
The research objective is to discover and analyze what is typical or representative of a population	The research objective is to understand standouts and apparently important exceptions

In short, we are inclined to believe there are two very different sorts of research question being asked in UX research.

- What do *actual* users like about, and how do they feel about, given experiences involving actual interactive products or prototypes of near-future products?

- How can user experience researchers and designers perceive *what is most worthy* of perceiving in an experience? What are the qualities of the most aesthetic experiences humans can have, and how might they be transferred to design?

Bardzell (2014) summarizes what's at stake in these two sorts of research questions.

> The first question is fundamentally empirical in nature: the desired information is "out there" (i.e. users do have preferences, feelings and perspectives about their experiences), and the job of the UX researcher or designer is to discover that information in the best way possible. The second question is about distinguishing among relevant elements of an experience to perceive and to clarify their significances and meanings [...] an interaction designer should be able to "read" relationships among the visual languages of an interaction, its functionality, and the most important use qualities that contribute to its experience.

> Is there any doubt that competence in answering both questions would support the design of better interactive experiences? (p. 134)

In short, our position is that both approaches, broadly construed, are legitimate "ways in" to the complex problem of designing for aesthetic user experiences. Epistemologically, they do not compete with each other, and indeed there is opportunity for them to support one another. A critical approach could reveal experiential issues that could subsequently be instrumented. Is it possible to measure the somaesthetic qualities of an interaction? If so, what might we learn from such measures? Conversely, instrumented studies can often reveal fine-grained empirical nuggets that aesthetic philosophers and critics were unaware of, which ought to inform subsequent theorizing (indeed, analytic aesthetics has begun to incorporate findings from cognitive science, e.g., about the role of visceral judgments). But such a positive objective is unlikely if researchers and designers with an arts and humanities orientation view researchers and designers with a psychology-based orientation as bad copies of themselves, and vice-versa.

One hope of this chapter, and indeed this book, is to help all researchers and practitioners of HCI and interaction design understand what a humanistic perspective on user experience and aesthetics really is—where it is coming from, what its values are, its forms of rigor, as well as its limitations, etc.—and in seeing that perspective, come to understand where it might *fit* in a robustly interdisciplinary practice, avoiding the twin extremes of fetishizing it above other approaches and of rejecting it as irrelevant.

CHAPTER 6

Social Change and Emancipation

6.1 INTRODUCTION

And still the computer reaches out. We saw in Chapter 5 how computing came to take user experience and aesthetics seriously, how this made us focus on computing in more intimate ways: as it joined up with our bodies, as it transitioned from individual interfaces to a new—and culturally dominant—communications medium. In this chapter, we consider how computing becomes implicated in sociopolitical issues. These include digital divides, including gender and computing, and computing in non-Western regions. It also includes hot-button political issues, including labor issues, environmental sustainability, poverty, online sex, and racism.

Within HCI, research and design projects that confront sociopolitical issues have roots in design traditions that preceded and subsequently fed into HCI, including participatory design (PD) and politically conscious design movements such as Italian Radical Design. We witnessed a drastic uptick of emancipatory HCI since the early 2000s, and much, though not all, of this work has embraced humanistic theories and tactics. The turn to humanistic thought is no coincidence, since as we will sketch out in the following pages, emancipatory theory in service of sociocultural activism has been a major thread of the humanities for over a century.

Emancipation and Emancipatory HCI

Emancipation refers to deliverance from various forms of restriction and bondage. The ending of slavery in the U.S. is emancipation in its most literal and important sense. But the introduction of labor rules as a result of the Industrial Revolution—rules that limited the number of hours workers could work, established minimum wage laws, prevented children from entering the workforce, and so forth—were also emancipatory. So too was the suffrage movement, intending to ensure that women, racial and religious minorities, and so forth had the right to vote. Still more subtle is emancipation from unconscious or hidden ideologies, e.g., the reluctance to hire well qualified women because of the suspicion that their family is more likely to come between them and their jobs than it is for similarly qualified men.

Emancipatory HCI refers to any HCI research or practice oriented toward exposing and eradicating one or more forms of bondage and oppression, including structural racism, poverty, sexual repression, colonialism, and other forces/effects of the hegemonic status quo.

We begin this chapter with a survey of emancipatory critique in the humanities, in particular four of its major formulations: Marxism, psychoanalysis, feminism, and postcolonialism. We survey them up front and together because, in addition to sketching out each one's key features, we also want to focus on what they share, that is, what makes them emancipatory and what makes them humanistic. We also briefly survey the impressive and diverse emancipatory agendas already in HCI that are predominantly non-humanistic, being instead either social scientific and/or design-based in nature. The main part of the chapter is devoted to surveying emancipatory humanistic HCI.

6.2   EMANCIPATORY CRITIQUE IN THE HUMANITIES

We noted in earlier chapters that departments of literature studies emerged in the late 19th century to provide access to models of cultivated thinking to the masses through education. So-called "Great Books"—at the time comprising what was then considered the best of national literature—were seen to provide formative materials out of which good citizens were to be made; the great tradition of British literature (or French, or German) could help cultivate the population to be good British (or French or German) citizens. Even today, the National Endowment for the Humanities in the United States asserts the role of the humanities in bringing about public wisdom, essential to the functioning of democracy: "Because democracy demands wisdom, NEH serves and strengthens our republic by promoting excellence in the humanities and conveying the lessons of history to all Americans" (http://www.neh.gov/about, accessed 16 August 2014).

With the social and political upheavals of the 19th and early 20th centuries, which saw the intensification of the Industrial Revolution, factory labor, and the Gilded Age; as well as violent government overthrows, intercontinental wars, and radical new models of government, including fascism and communism—the humanistic notion of citizens reading classic poems to shape their national sensibilities was not enough. Philosophy, the sciences, and the arts, sometimes in opposition to and sometimes in collusion with forces of change, had to do more than cultivate citizens; they had to emancipate them.

Today, emancipatory social science, philosophy, cultural studies, and so forth, are "guided by a reflexive interest [in enabling] human beings to have greater autonomy and self-determination" (How, 2003, p. 117). These approaches offer expositions and analyses of social injustices, including their mechanisms of reproduction, and seek to disrupt those mechanisms and to introduce the possibility of bringing into being more just systems—legal, political, aesthetic, and so forth.

6.2.1   MARXISM, PSYCHOANALYSIS, FEMINISM, AND POSTCOLONIALISM

Four threads of thought from the humanities have been especially influential throughout 20th-century emancipatory thinking: Marxism, psychoanalysis, feminism, and post-colonialism. We refer to each as a "meta-approach," intending to bring under a single umbrella each thread's core concept system, methodological predispositions, and favored domains of inquiry.

Marxism is a meta-approach that seeks to confront the ways that the dominant economic system—capitalism—plays out *materially* in the world. That is, rather than viewing capitalism as an abstract system that regulates the circulation of money, Marxism focuses on the materiality of economic production and distribution: the bodies of factory workers, the physical environments in which they labor, their labor practices, and of course the distribution of wealth that is made possible as a result of this labor. Marxism commonly seeks to reveal the difference between who produces value (e.g., crops in the fields, cars in factories, childrearing in the home, computer code in IT offices) and who controls the system of production, including the distribution of its wealth (e.g., entrepreneurs, managers, accountants, lawyers). One of Marxism's key concepts is *ideology*, which refers to a human-made system of beliefs and values, which explains and justifies a view of society (including what is good and just), and which perpetuates itself through diverse mechanisms, including powerful symbols (e.g., national flags, the cross or Star of David), myths (e.g., that the United States is a great "melting pot" of ethnicities and races), and habits (e.g., singing the national anthem before sports events). Through these constant perpetuations throughout and across all levels of society, the ideology comes to seem natural and good and therefore unchangeable, while, from a Marxist standpoint, effectively solidifying the control over material production and capital by the very few. A Marxist approach, broadly speaking, seeks to call attention to such systems of belief, to denaturalize them, reveal their mechanisms of perpetuation, demonstrate their inequalities, and intervene upon them. Beyond Marx, the Frankfurt School of Critical Theory, including Adorno, Marcuse, Horkheimer, and later Habermas, and cultural critics such as Stuart Hall, Frederic Jameson, and Terry Eagleton have all embraced various forms of Marxism.

Psychoanalysis is a meta-approach that examines the conflicts between individuals (comprising primordial desires, body functions, and needs) and the social world (comprising behavioral rules and norms), conflicts that often find their locus in language. "Through language, desire becomes subject to rules, and yet this language cannot define the body's experience accurately [… and especially it cannot define] that aspect of experience which has been ignored or prohibited by the rules of language" (Wright, 1984, p. 1). For example, our bodies often feel sexual desires that when put into language take on powerful and often shameful social meanings: leering, frigid, slut, creep, horny, rape fantasy, porn, incest, hooker and john, wet dreams, boner, exhibitionist. To be verbally described by one of these terms is also to be socially accountable to it. One of psychoanalysis' key concepts is that of *the subject*, which is a structural understanding of a socialized individual, which includes both conscious and unconscious drives that are in many ways defined by, and must act within, social and linguistic rule systems. The excess, that is, those aspects of the self that are experienced but ignored or prohibited in the social world (e.g., the need to use the toilet), manifests itself in unconscious words and deeds, in anxiety, depression, neuroses, and so forth. Broadly speaking, a psychoanalytic approach is therapeutic, seeking to help the subject consciously explain and understand the nature of its own conflicts. Psychoanalysis as we understand it today owes much to the work of Sigmund Freud, and his thought was further developed in the humanities by Jacques Lacan, Julia Kristeva, Gilles Deleuze, and Félix Guattari, and most recently Slavoj Žižek. Significantly, the psychology community has largely (if not completely) rejected psychoanalysis, and psychoanalysis' greatest legacy is arguably in aesthetics and literary theory. (We will return to the benefits of psychoanalysis for aesthetics shortly.) Anyway, psychoanalysis' disciplinary history explains why HCI—a discipline with psychology in its earliest and arguably most far-reaching roots—has been little influenced by psychoanalysis, and also why, with the increasing influence of humanistic HCI, that might change.

Feminism is a meta-approach that confronts unjust social systems as they are gendered, commonly seen as the result of the ideological conflation of biological sex and socially constructed gender, naturalizing women as inferior to men; this is known as the gender-sex system. Of it, feminist philosopher Seyla Benhabib (1992) writes:

> for feminist theory the gender-sex system is not a contingent but an essential way in which social reality is organized, symbolically divided and lived through experientially. By the 'gender-sex' system, I understand the social-historical, symbolic constitution, and interpretation of the anatomical differences of the sexes. The gender-sex system is the grid through which the self develops an *embodied* identity, a certain mode of being in one's body and of living the body….. The gender-sex system is the grid through which societies and cultures reproduce embodied individuals…. [T]he historically known gender-sex systems have contributed to the oppression and exploitation of women. The task of feminist critical theory is to uncover this fact, and to develop a theory that is emancipatory and reflective, and which can aid women in their struggles to overcome oppression and exploitation. (p. 152, emphasis in original)

Early feminism rallied around women's suffrage, before moving onto other forms of injustice, including gender violence (e.g., rape), workplace inequality (e.g., in wages and opportunities for promotion), and media representation (e.g., media stereotypes). One of its key concepts is *patriarchy*, which refers to a societal organization in which men hold more power than women (e.g., a male-only managerial class, male inheritance, male-dominated goverance). Broadly speaking, a feminist approach seeks to expose gendered injustice and to propose alternative policies, rights, ways of life, practices, etc., to bring about a more just society. Key figures of feminism include early suffragists, such as Emmeline Parkhurst in Britain, who focused on changing laws hostile to women; later, the movement took a more theoretical and academic turn, e.g., with Simone de Beauvoir's 1949 book *The Second Sex* fusing feminism with Marxist and existentialist themes. More recent feminist theorists include Helen Longino, Sandra Harding, and Judith Butler.

Postcolonialism is a comparatively recent meta-approach that examines the nature, consequences, and mechanisms of Western colonial powers over the nations and peoples that they have colonized, and how this experience shaped both Western and non-Western peoples (Boehmer, 2006). One of its key concepts is *Orientalism*, which refers to "a way of coming to terms with the Orient that is based on the Orient's special place in European Western experience" (Said, 1979, p. 1). (The "Orient" in question here refers to what is in North America called the "Middle East," as opposed to the Far East, including Iraq, Iran, Syria, Saudi Arabia, etc.). For Said, Orientalism works as an epistemological binary. The binary is between Orient and Occident, and it is epistemological because much European thinking and action that depends on it rests on this binary.

> Thus a very large mass of writers, among whom are poets, novelists, philosophers, political theorists, economists, and imperial administrators, have accepted the basic distinction between East and West as the starting point for elaborate theories, epics, novels, social descriptions, and political accounts concerning the Orient, its people, customs, "mind," destiny, and so on. This Orientalism can accommodate Aeschylus, say, and Victor Hugo, Dante, and Karl Marx. (Said, 1979, pp. 2–3, emphases in original)

What Said is getting at is that the West has constructed a comprehensive vision of "the Orient"—from the facts of its social life to its "destiny"—based on a Western perspective, which includes the historical perspective of how the West colonized (in its view, "brought civilization to") these peoples, as well as the intellectual bedrock of Western thought (from the ancient Greek tragedian Aeschylus through to Marx). The diverse peoples of "the Orient" (who do not even see themselves as belonging to such a homogeneous group) have no way of contributing to this vision. The intellectual bedrocks upon which their cultures, thinking, and ways of life rest are not accounted for. And these are no mere disputes among Cultural Studies departments in France vs. Syria; for Orientalism shapes how Europeans intervene politically, economically, and militarily in this region. Postcolonialism is an emancipatory perspective that seeks critically to reveal and to problematize the Euro-centrism, framed as a kind of intellectual colonialism that underlies political colonialism and continues to guide the relationships between West and Orient after the fall of traditional colonialism; it seeks to deconstruct the binary between West and Orient (revealing that binary to be a Western construction); and it attempts to recover and reassert the histories, visions, and intellectual bedrocks of the peoples and nations previously understood (and controlled) as "Oriental." Key thinkers have included Edward Said, Gayatri Spivak, and Frantz Fanon.

6.2.2 "THE HERMENEUTICS OF SUSPICION"

Even in these brief sketches, several commonalties across Marxism, psychoanalysis, feminism, and postcolonialism of these come into view.

Historically, all have roots in late 19th-century social and intellectual upheavals, and four of them became potent critical theories between 1920 and 1960 (postcolonial theory emerged a generation later), each deeply influencing the humanities ever since.

Epistemologically, all concern themselves with social forces that both determine our social reality and do so hidden from view (making it hard to intervene upon). For Marxism, that force is the machinations of ideology, which maintain a status quo in which the few extract surplus capital from, and at the expense of, the many. For psychoanalysis, it is the deeply conflicted structure of the individual as subject (psychoanalysis), which produces anxiety, depression, and similar maladies. For feminism, it is patriarchy, which binds women to subordinate societal roles. For postcolonialism, it is the West's construction of the Oriental Other that subjects to diverse peoples to exploitative Western policies.

Because these determinative social forces are hidden from view, they threaten the Enlightenment rationalist project, since the individual cannot rationally understand and act rightly with a substantially flawed view of the world. A methodological first step for all four, then, is to develop conceptual resources that make it possible to bring these hidden forces into view (e.g., the systems of concepts that form around ideology, the subject, patriarchy, and orientalism), and to use these concept systems as resources to practice a "hermeneutics of suspicion."

Hermeneutics of Suspicion

The "hermeneutics of suspicion" (the term is Paul Ricoeur's) refers to an interpretative stance that suspects that things are not as they seem and to seek evidence (often at the repressed seams, that is, what journalists and academics alike tend not to talk about) of the social force in question. Once the source cause (capitalist ideology, unconscious conflict, patriarchy, orientalism) and its symptomatic cases are exposed, intervention into those cases becomes more tractable.

It is worth stressing that Marxism, psychoanalysis, feminism, and postcolonialism are all thoroughly political and emancipatory. That is, they see formal and informal, explicit and implicit social structures as impeding human freedom and self-actualization. This is overt in Marxism, feminism, and postcolonialism, but it is also unavoidable in psychoanalysis, e.g., in the case of anxiety or neurosis caused by one's sexual non-conformity. Moreover, power on this view is pervasive; these issues concern everyone in all parts of life, and these issues cannot be cordoned off as a domain of inquiry, in the way that, e.g., early reading acquisition is a specialty domain of the pedagogical sciences, or computer vision is a specialty domain of computer science.

Power

Intuitively, most of us think of power in terms of individuals who have it using it to exert control over individuals who do not. A manager, sergeant, parent, teacher, or priest has this kind of power.

However, while not disputing that this form of power exists, the notion of power operative within the hermeneutics of suspicion is more subtle, more distributed, and more systemic. For example, according to Marxism, the capitalist system is not unjust because the business owners are individually morally evil (as if we could put some morally upright business owners in place and everything would suddenly work out). Instead, society itself is structured in a way that creates roles for each of us to inhabit—roles that include business owners, managers, and workers—and individually we are disempowered from changing that role. Some billionaires are philanthropists and others are not; neither disturbs capitalism, however.

There is a further point. According to Marxism, psychoanalysis, feminism, and postcolonialism, any social or cultural analysis that does not engage politics is almost certainly ideological itself. On such a view, the scientific value of objectivity becomes suspect, because it makes it difficult for science to critically assess its own ideological underpinnings and contributions. From such a perspective, the following questions about science emerge: Who controls research agendas, who pays for, and who materially benefits from scientific outcomes? What does science *not* talk about or take seriously? In what ways does science reinforce or resist the gender-sex system? Asking these questions does not imply that science is evil; it does imply that science is a constituent (for better and worse) of contemporary systems of power, be they capitalism, patriarchy, etc.

Summary: The Humanistic View of Emancipation

The humanistic view of emancipation is that one way or another, virtually every social group is subjected to forces of bondage, literal or figurative, some greater than others; that the underlying causes of this bondage are systemic and hidden, so people often do not perceive that they are bound and/or feel powerless to enact change; that instead of autonomous rational individuals, humans are better seen as "subjects," who are subjected to and constituted by the hidden social forces that they must navigate; that these causes, although hidden, remain discoverable; that the explication of these underlying causes is foundational to the possibility of real change, i.e., by revealing bonds as such and by suggesting ways to remove them.

As a practice, emancipatory humanistic thinking is distinguished by two separate impulses:

- the *hermeneutic impulse* is to expose or reveal a hidden force or mechanism that inhibits people's freedom and

- the *speculative impulse* is to imagine a society, including its structures, policies, and practices, where that hidden force has been eradicated.

And it is specifically this speculative practice that most often looks dubious from a scientific standpoint, because by definition it is not cautiously and painstakingly derived from accepted facts and is therefore difficult to justify using scientific standards. This is why psychoanalysis was not destroyed as a practice by its eventual rejection from the field of psychology; even if it is repudiated as an explanatory theory of human psychology, psychoanalysis nonetheless continues to support a *speculative* practice that thinks deeply about the interrelatedness of subjecthood, sexuality, desire, fetish, and anxiety on the one hand, and social norms, policies, and practices on the other, often as explored in the arts. For example, feminist psychoanalyst film theorist Laura Mulvey (1975) argues that cinematic pleasure derives from the "male gaze" of directors, who present female actors as objects of erotic contemplation, who in turn help male characters fully realize their own identities, reinforcing through the pleasure of identifying with the protagonist the subjugation of women to men. As a result of this analysis, Mulvey was able to imagine (i.e., speculatively construct) a new aesthetics of cinematic pleasure, which she and other feminist directors pursued and which, although experimental and relatively short-lived, nonetheless influenced mainstream cinema.

6.3   EMANCIPATION IN HCI

It is important to recognize that there has been plenty of research in HCI that has emancipatory objectives. However, we observe that the majority of such work is better described as social scientific or design-based, rather than humanistic in nature. Social scientific emancipatory HCI focuses on improving our understandings of the domain of inquiry, clarifying present opportunities, needs, obstacles, and so forth. Design-based emancipatory HCI typically uses design methodologies to speculate about alternative futures that critique the present and offer aspirational images to work toward (e.g., in critical design) and/or reconfigures design methodologies themselves to better position design as an emancipatory practice (e.g., in participatory design and value-sensitive design). Again, what would typically distinguish a humanistic approach from these would be an emphasis on holistic interpretation taking a suspicious stance, often focusing on a relatively small number of highly resonant or exemplary works (as outlined in Section 6.2).

Obviously, as we have stressed throughout this book, these disciplinary approaches are all compatible with one another and are often used in concert. The hermeneutics of suspicion could raise a question best answered empirically—this dynamic is quite common in sociology, for example. Similarly, we have already shown how Dunne and Raby's critical design practice relies on (and also departs from) Frankfurt School Marxism (Bardzell and Bardzell, 2013). Practices such as participatory design and participatory action research so deeply intertwine social scientific, design, and critical sensibilities and practices that it seems a fool's errand to even attempt to analyze them separately.

All of this is to emphasize that the humanities do not have a monopoly on emancipatory research and practice. Indeed, when Max Horkheimer took over the directorship of the Frankfurt Institute for Social Research in 1930, he envisioned a collaboration between philosophy and empirical social science, blending rather than separating critical and empirical approaches (How, 2003). We envision the possibility of HCI being a field where such a blending could be fruitful, and indeed it already is, though for now we see plenty more opportunity (and need!) to improve this blending, and we hope resources such as this book further that agenda.

The following list provides an illustrative overview of emancipatory HCI; it is out of the scope of this book to offer a more comprehensive survey. We offer this overview both because we want to acknowledge that emancipatory HCI has been in full swing for quite some time, and also because we also believe that this active research agenda provides plenty of hooks for humanistic emancipatory critique to participate along the lines of Horkheimer's vision, as a collaboration between social science, design, and the critical humanities.

Action research (AR) is a form of inquiry that is performed by or with insiders in a community, but not on them, often in the domains such as public health, sustainable livelihood, and civic engagements, among others. It is often reflective and collaborative in nature and is oriented to action and change, rather than to traditional scientific description and explanation. Hayes (2011) argues that there are rigorous practices of conducting and assessing AR projects and identifies ways AR might be meaningfully applied to HCI research.

Participatory Design is an approach that democratizes design by involving those with a stake in its implications, especially end-users (Nygaard, 1990; Simonsen and Robertson, 2013). The term "PD" first came into use as a shorthand for "user participation in system development," an important aspect of the approach to computing developed in the Nordic countries in the 1970s, something still referred to as "the Scandinavian approach to system development." Today, PD is a global methodology, practiced diversely in American corporate IT design, in what is known as "participatory culture," and in IT projects within the Global South (e.g., in HCI4D).

Value-Sensitive Design (VSD) seeks to account for human values in the design of information systems, pioneered by Friedman (2004). VSD emphasizes values with moral import, such as trust, privacy, informed consent, human rights, accountability, and democracy. A related concept, "Values in Design," focuses on operationalizing, discovering, and analyzing values in the design of socio-technical systems (Nissenbaum, 1998).

Critical Design is a design research methodology that creates design artifacts that reflect counterfactual and even dystopian values. These designs are intended not for actual use, but rather to provoke. Their goal is to make consumers more critical about how their lives are mediated by assumptions, values, ideologies, and behavioral norms inscribed in everyday designs, and thereby to create consumer demand for designs that reflect better assumptions, values, or ideologies (Dunne and Raby, 2002; Dunne, 2008; Mazé and Redström, 2007; Lee and Lee, 2010; Malpass, 2010; Bardzell and Bardzell, 2013).

Sustainable HCI is a research agenda in HCI that focuses on environmental sustainability and the linkage between interactive technologies and the use of resources. Blevis coined the term "Sustainable Interaction Design (SID)" in 2007 (Blevis, 2007) and argued that principles such as linking invention and disposal, renewal and reuse can guide interaction design to contribute toward an ecologically viable future. Since then, this line of research has been extended to focus on the power relationships with regard to energy use in low-income communities (Dillahunt and Mankoff, 2014) and the study and design of sociotechnical systems in the abundant present for use in a future of scarcity, namely "collapse informatics" (Tomlinson et al., 2012).

Poverty in HCI is a line of research that focuses on democratizing and broadening the scope of participation in technology use at the margins of society. This includes designing for urban homeless (Le Dantec, 2008), hunger and food systems (Dombrowski et al., 2013), and non-profits (Voida, 2014), among others. Collectively, this research pushes back on the tendency of IT invention to focus on the middle and upper classes that can afford its products, thereby scoping out, and ultimately leaving behind, the poor and other groups from the benefits of IT to society.

HCI4D, also known as ICT4D (Information and Communications Technologies for Development), is a subdomain in HCI that focuses on understanding the role of technology in development (Toyama, 2010). "Development" here refers to economically developing regions, and HCI4D research encompasses diverse topics such as rural and urban community development, conflict zones, and designing for disenfranchised groups or resource-constrained populations (Ho et al., 2009).

Again, while none of the above works is predominantly humanistic, there is no doubt of an affinity between them and humanistic approaches. As with emancipatory humanist approaches, all of the social science and design approaches feature the double-move we have seen throughout the chapter so far: a theory-supported hermeneutic move to expose or to reveal a state of affairs that is undesirable, and a speculative move intended to reveal and to propose alternative, and more desirable, futures.

6.4   HUMANISTIC EMANCIPATORY HCI

We now turn to a survey HCI research contributions that are both emancipatory and also strongly reflect humanistic epistemologies and methodologies. We order it as follows: Reflective HCI introduces one of the foundational HCI papers on emancipation, foundational because it expresses the most basic positions about criticality in an emancipatory sense; after, we go through HCI research reflecting each of the four emancipatory traditions introduced earlier, Marxism, feminism, psychoanalysis, and postcolonialism.

6.4.1   REFLECTIVE HCI

An early humanist contribution to emancipatory HCI is Sengers et al.'s (2005) "Reflective Design," which develops Agre's (1997) notion of a "critical-technical practice" in the context of HCI. The paper outlines the project of critical theory, citing (as we have here) the historical roles of Marxism, psychoanalysis, and feminism in this project, summarizing critical reflection as follows:

> bringing unconscious aspects of experience to conscious awareness, thereby making them available for conscious choice. This critical reflection is crucial to both individual freedom and our quality of life in society as a whole, since without it, we unthinkingly adopt attitudes, practices, values, and identities we might not consciously espouse. (p. 50)

Their basic argument, then, is that "reflection itself should be a core technology design outcome for HCI" (p. 50), which they define as extending in two directions: to designers (to support critical thinking about the values inscribed in designs) and to users (to support critical thinking about how they use and experience interactive technologies). They flesh out a number of design practices from the perspective of their support for reflectiveness along these two dimensions, including Scandinavian participatory design, value-sensitive design (Friedman, 2004), critical design (Dunne and Raby, 2002), ludic design (Gaver et al., 2004), critical-technical practice (Agre, 1997), and reflection-in-action (Schön, 1983); they offer two case studies of their own design work; and they derive several principles of reflective design and several reflective design strategies.

We argue that this is humanistic HCI because it explicitly engages critical theory; it critically reinterprets a range of design practices insofar as they manifest qualities of critical reflectiveness; the authors present their own design work in a form of design criticism; and their outcome is to derive a synthesis of concepts/ideas that equally reflects the underlying critical theory and the design practices in the field.

We argue that this is emancipatory, because it explicitly engages the efficacy of hidden regressive structures (e.g., patriarchy and ideological oppression), it stresses the need to focus on marginal values and practices, and it extends the power to determine what technology can or should be beyond designers to users. The article also provides accessible heuristic criteria (i.e., its "principles of reflective design") and also generative design approaches (i.e., its "reflective design strategies") that help empower designers by moving the key insights of critical theory out of a technical and specialist practice in literary theory and cultural studies into the everyday toolbox of both designers and users.

6.4.2   POLITICAL (MARXIST?) HCI

Another emancipatory contribution of humanistic HCI is the critique against the tacit de-politicization of HCI. Deploying both prongs of emancipatory critique—the hermeneutic/expository analysis of hidden forces against progressive change and the speculative analysis of a better future—this research observes that HCI as a science is always already political, and that its tendency not to disclose or engage the significance of this fact is both epistemically and politically problematic. It is epistemically problematic, because it forecloses whole categories of inquiry, and it is politically problematic because by doing so, it forecloses whole categories of action.

One characteristic work is Dourish's (2010) article, "HCI and Environmental Sustainability: The Politics of Design and the Design of Politics." In this article, he begins by exploring the mechanisms that allow HCI to become connected to sustainability. In the most common model, he argues, the connection is "information technology as a persuasive force in behavior change." A secondary model is "environmental sustainability as a site of technologically mediated 'citizen science.'" In both models, the burden of sustainable change is placed upon the shoulders of the "moral individual," either the energy/resource consumer who is persuaded to consume less, or the mobile user who lends his or her phone's sensors to a citizen science project. (Online satire site *The Onion* recently had a headline, "New Report Finds Climate Change Caused By 7 Billion Key Individuals," which humorously captures the spirit of Dourish's critique.) Both of these mechanisms for connecting HCI to sustainability, by focusing only on the moral individual as sustainable actor, systematically direct our attention away from a very different category of sustainable actor: massive-scale industry and the potential roles of government regulation.

Dourish's critical-emancipatory contribution is thus to shine a light on this epistemological-political gap (for the regressive political efficacy of sustainability in HCI is made possible by its epistemological blind spots), and then to leverage theories from outside of HCI (including postcolonial and critical geography theory) to help him "move from a position of critique to one of more constructive engagement." Although Dourish does not assert that his analysis is Marxist, psychoanalytic, or feminist in its underpinnings, it is easy enough to see that they—Marxism in particular—provide much of the theoretical and methodological vocabulary underlying his analysis. With sections called "The Market as Natural Fact" and "Nature as a Social Fact," and by using phrases like "anti-politics machine" and Lukacs' notion of "reification," Dourish is activating the Marxist notion of contingent and regressive social forces that disappear through mechanisms of naturalization, which can be exposed via critical analysis, which in turn enables his "move from a position of critique to one of more constructive engagement." His (speculative) solution is to envision HCI exploring a design space of change at scale, rather than change at the level of the individual actor, which of course would imply sociopolitical change of the sort that is commonly resisted by the status quo. His work is emancipatory, because is pursuing the potential for a more sustainable future not dependent on individual sacrifices alongside industrial and political status quo, but rather changes in the industrial and political status quo that make it easier for individuals to live sustainably.

A less grandiose and more grounded in practice view can be found in Light's (2010) "The Unit of Analysis in Understanding the Politics of Participatory Design." This paper highlights the political complexity of participatory design (PD), demonstrating that the general fact of participation in a design process is not sufficient to address the political aspects and consequences of design. Light asks who owns the design problem, observing that the owner has the power to reframe the problem as the problem space is better understood. She observes a potential conflict between inquiry objectives (of the participatory designer as researcher) and sustainability objectives (of the stakeholders of the project, broadly construed). She references the notion of "benign imposition," which is the power of the outsider, in and through the act of inviting to participate, to unilaterally establish "how values, ambitions, tools and methods may be unilaterally introduced by outsiders to the design context" (p. 184). Such benign imposition is hard to avoid, given that "much ICT research that seeks to advance social change starts out as submissions for funding by professional researchers and subject to the terms of that funding" (p. 184).

Light calls for a methodological stance for PD, one that is critical of the roles of participants at different moments of the process and at different scales of analysis, and one specifically that seeks to account for agency and power at each of these moments and scales. One might characterize Light's position as an emancipatory critique, because it critically interrogates several soft spots of PD as a methodology, demonstrating where the methodology, as currently practice, fails, or is at least pressured to fail, on its own terms. Like Sengers et al.'s work on reflective design, Light offers no methodological "fix," nor even the possibility of one, but rather seeks to render these problems visible, to hold them up to our critical view, and to encourage designers to incorporate this more nuanced reflexivity into their future work. As with Dourish's paper, Light focuses on exposing and intervening upon hidden structures of power and hegemony, without explicitly invoking a Marxist framework in her analysis.

Although researchers have availed themselves of Marxist-like critiques, few have explicitly characterized their work as "Marxist." In fact, some, like critical designers Dunne and Raby, who clearly rely on Marxist theories, go so far as to disavow their Marxism. This decision to play down one's Marxist influences and objectives could be read negatively or positively; negatively, because it might seem to be a form of (self-)censorship, arguably even an unscholarly failure to acknowledge one's intellectual resources; positively, because perhaps the currency of Marxist concepts and methods is so wide, and because Marxism has woven itself so deeply through thought disciplines, that one simply doesn't need to explicate the role of Marx—any more than one acknowledges Plato or any other figure who has deeply shaped our intellectual culture. The positive and negative interpretations need not be exclusive.

6.4.3   FEMINISM, QUEER THEORY, AND/IN HCI

Just as some politically oriented forms of HCI have not openly avowed any connection to Marxism, so has much research taking on the issue of gender and HCI not directly engaged feminism (e.g., Bødker and Greenbaum, 1988; Beckwith and Burnett, 2004; Cassell, 2002). Research on gender and HCI has often reflected psychology-based disciplinary approaches that tend to avoid overtly political stances and objectives. Gender HCI asks questions such as how do women's uses of technology differ from men's? What design implications can be derived from these differences, to make technology use more inclusive for all?

Gender HCI vs. Feminist HCI

The primary difference between gender HCI and feminist HCI is the question of what causes the differences among gender-specific computing practices (and non-practices). Gender HCI tends to bracket the cause question aside, focusing on the specifics of behavioral and attitudinal differences and deriving actionable design implications from them. Its strength is to contribute toward technologies now that are more inclusive.

Feminist HCI views such questions and their answers as enmeshed in broader hegemonic social structures. That is, gendered technology differences reflect ways that women are subordinated and/or face injustices as women. Computing is viewed as the latest domain in which these dynamics play out, and HCI is suspected of complicity in the perpetuation of structural sexism. As Rode puts it, feminist HCI's "question is not 'do women and men display different aptitudes for technological tasks?' but rather, 'how are beliefs and use of technology embedded in the production and ongoing management of gender in daily life?' (Rode, 2011, p. 393). Its strength is in its challenge to the field to reframe gender-related HCI questions in generative new ways.

Although gender HCI and feminist HCI are distinguishable in the abstract, several researchers have contributed to both agendas and there is evidence of mutual influence in recently published papers as well.

Feminist HCI

One of the earliest and most direct linkages between HCI and feminism was Shaowen Bardzell's (2010) "Feminist HCI: Taking Stock and Outlining and Agenda." We outline its key arguments below, but we note here that one of its claims was that feminism had influenced HCI for decades, both directly and indirectly, only that this linkage had not been acknowledged. By making this argument, Bardzell encouraged readers to perceive a diverse collection of papers in HCI as feminist, to engage that research as such, and to build on that underlying feminism in future research. We are appropriating this argument on a more general scale in this chapter and book, that is, to suggest that in addition to recognizing feminism's under-acknowledged influence on HCI, it is worth surfacing how other emancipatory humanistic theories, methodologies, and perspectives have shaped our field, and building more deliberately on those contributions.

Bardzell (2010) lays out a broad argument in favor of a feminist HCI, defining it as the reflective integration of feminist strategies as a resource for interaction design, deferring its definition of "feminism" to the intellectual movement that defines itself as such. She argues for two central motivations for a feminist HCI: First, the reaching out of the computer into everyday life means that computing becomes caught up in the same social structures and struggles that define the rest of everyday life; there is no reason to believe that computing is exempt from them. Second, as we have already noted above, Bardzell argues that much of HCI already implicitly reflects key elements feminist thinking and goals, which she frames in terms of individual fulfillment, agency, identity, equality, reflection, empowerment, and social justice. Thus, because computing is already entangled in issues of concern to feminists, and because HCI as a discipline is already reflecting feminist ideals and perspectives, it makes sense to name this already existing agenda and to consider it more deliberately.

After surveying diverse hooks that could or already do link HCI to feminism, e.g., by tracing the role of feminism in fields similar to HCI, including science and technology studies, architecture, and industrial design, Bardzell proposes six "feminist design qualities," following Löwgren and Stolterman's (2004) definition of design qualities as ways to articulate a holistic and pervasive trait characterizing a design. The qualities she identifies are pluralism, participation, advocacy, ecology, embodiment, self-disclosure, which she synthesized from feminist sources and exemplifies with interaction designs.

In a follow-up to the 2010 paper, Bardzell and Bardzell (2011) collaborated to develop links between feminist social science methodology and HCI user research methods, entitled "Toward a Feminist HCI Methodology: Social Science, Feminism, and HCI." Central to the paper is the conflict between "knowing truth" and "doing good." Knowing truth refers to the scientific epistemology that cherishes researcher objectivity as a central aspect of methodological rigor. Doing good is the human impulse to contribute positively to the world. The challenge is that the latter seems to be strategically bracketed off by the former, and as we have seen throughout this chapter, any time a practice is advanced as "apolitical," it is likely to be regressively political. The paper turns to feminist philosophy of science and feminist social science to explore ways to pursue the good while remaining scientifically rigorous, and offers several guiding qualities of a feminist HCI methodology, including epistemological links to feminist theory and methodology, an empathic and participatory stance toward research subjects, researcher/practitioner self-disclosure, and methodological dialogism to avoid monological information gathering or knowledge production.

An alternative vision of feminist HCI is offered in Jennifer Rode's (2011) "A Theoretical Agenda for Feminist HCI." She argues that beyond supporting HCI researchers and practitioners directly with design-critical and design-generative resources, as Bardzell argues for feminist HCI, that there is also a need "to build the foundation for a socio-technical theory of gender" (p. 394). To pursue this objective, she offers two side-by-side critical surveys of gender and technology. The first is from within HCI, in which she considers three common framings of gender within HCI: liberal feminism, which she argues provides an intellectual framework for gender-blind notions of the user; the parameterization of gender for interface design, which takes gender seriously, but which both essentializes it and fails to engage with its sociopolitical causes; and finally, ethnomethodological treatments of gender, which offer what amounts to a principled stance against dealing with it.

Finding HCI's liberal feminist and ethnomethodological treatments of gender deficient, Rode then turns outside of HCI for potentially useful views, surveying technology as masculine culture (i.e., the view that women's lack of involvement in technology design yields designs that reflect men's values and marginalize women's), gender positionality (i.e., a view that deconstructs the male/female binary and instead considers women in relation to society), and lived body experience (i.e., another non-binary approach to gender that situates gender alongside of factors such as race, class, disability, etc., as they are experienced *in situ*). In addition to presenting each of these positions, Rode also critically analyzes each as a candidate for uptake in HCI, laying out obstacles, strategies, and heuristics for successful uptake.

Although diverse in their particulars, there are several deep similarities in Bardzell's and Rode's formulations of feminist HCI. Above all, both researchers seek to develop momentum and technical vocabulary to support the uptake of a feminist conceptualization of gender more systematically in HCI. That is, both view gender in terms of the socio-political history of gender, including the history of gender-based repression and feminist activism; neither accepts gender as a neutral descriptive category. Both seriously treat the role of gender and feminism in HCI today, although they vary in the general tone. Bardzell's assessment of feminism in HCI to date is more optimistic, while Rode's is more critical. However, the tone in each case reflects the rhetorical objectives of each piece: Bardzell is arguing for the underlying compatibility of feminist and HCI values and methods as a way to legitimate feminist HCI; Rode is critiquing the limitations of gender in HCI in order to demonstrate the need for a more solid theoretical footing, which she then seeks to contribute. Finally, both frame feminist HCI as an open project into which they invite the community to participate; neither seeks to provide closure in the sense of a comprehensive or final theory of feminist HCI.

Queer Theory

Arguably an offshoot of third-wave feminism, Queer Theory focuses on the way that the gender-sex system shapes human identity, in particular through binaristic thinking. Queer theory seeks to "queer" such binaries and thereby emancipate us from its oppressive consequences.

Queer Theory

Queer theory traces the emergence of the heterosexual/homosexual binary and its epistemic and political consequences as an example of non-essentialist thinking about identity. Like other forms of emancipatory critique, it reveals how sexual orientation and all socially constructed categories, such as gender and color, harden into norms that fix people's identities and in doing so also fix those identities beyond the present into the future. Queer Theory adopts the concept of *performativity* to explain how we enact our identity as a result of the social formations we are born into.

For example, science fiction critic Wendy Pearson (2003) notes that in spite of massive cultural changes explored in science fiction—faster than the speed of light space travel, intelligent machines, and interplanetary colonization—gender and sexual orientation roles tend to remain as they are in the present. It is easy to find, for example, futuristic novels taking place tens of thousands of years in the future, with fantastic robots and space vehicles, where women still do all the cooking! Thus, the critic deploys queer theory to expose such ideological failures of the imagination and open up speculative space to imagine otherwise. The "real aim of queer theory," Pearson writes, "is to make possible a future in which society is radically restructured in order to invalidate fixed identities and deconstruct the Cartesian binarisms which automatically value white over black, male over female and straight over gay" (p. 157).

In "HCI as Heterodoxy: Technologies of Identity and the Queering of Interaction with Computers," Ann Light (2011) extends queer theory into the domain of social computing. Her critical focal point is how computers formalize identity, which perpetuates the status quo through apolitical design. She argues that queer theory provides conceptual tools that can resist these processes and enable a more negotiated stance toward identity in computer systems. Specifically, she identifies a range of tactics that can be ported from queer theory generally into the domain of HCI, observing that

> to *queer* something [...] is to treat it obliquely, to cross it, to go in an adverse or opposite direction. It has movement and flex in it. Queering is problematizing apparently structural and foundational relationships with critical intent, and it may involve mischief and clowning as much as serious critique (p. 432)

The focal point here is that queering is not merely adversarial, not merely a contrarian impulse. Instead, it is playful, mischievous, even "clowning." What's behind this is a theory of how to engage binarism. It's goal is not to advocate for the feminine or the homosexual against the masculine or the heterosexual in hopes of bringing about parity between them; it is to deconstruct the binarism itself, to creatively reveal an infinite number of third ways that are outside of that binary. SF critic Pearson notes that "almost all cultural discourses naturalize the idea that humans come in only two sexes, despite the known incidence—about 1.7 %—of intersex births" (p. 154). The queer theorist, rather than suppressing that third option, wants to use it as a lever to open up new possibilities that ultimately invalidate the binarisms.

Light spends much of her essay explicating queer tactics applied to HCI. These queer design tactics include the following.

- *Making trouble* applies queer practices such as drag are to HCI, e.g., in the critical design work of Dunne and Raby.

- *Thinking obliquely* refers to designing for unintended uses and/or designing for plurality and heterodoxy to open up spaces for divergent identities .

- *Forgetting* is the tactic of enabling systems to remember very little, using data minimalization techniques.

- *Obscuring* gives users more control over which of their use data is shared, recorded, or made available to others.

- *Cheating* is a tactic modeled on the widespread use of cheat codes in video games, which are built-in features that allow users to escape the standard rules and procedures built into a system.

- *Eluding* is a tactic in which the introduction of random and absurd relations are entered into computational hierarchies to change combinational possibilities.

Light's work is similar to Bardzell's and Rode's work on feminist HCI, in that by using politicized gender issues as a lever to reveal hegemony, she introduces techniques to open up alternative design practices that can think and do otherwise. Situated in third-wave feminism, queer theory focuses less on second wave feminist issues of individual agency, equality, and empowerment, and instead places its emphasis on a form of postmodern play that doesn't target patriarchy so much as the underlying binarisms of which patriarchy is but one symptom.

Summary: Feminism, Queer Theory, and HCI

Perhaps one way to organize these ideas is to consider second vs. third wave feminism from the perspective of their potential uptakes and limitations for HCI. We summarize the pros and cons of different formulations of feminist HCI in Table 6.1.

Table 6.1: Second- vs. third-wave feminism

	Second Wave Feminism	Third Wave Feminism
Emancipatory Commitments	Equality of access, individual fulfillment, democratic participation, empowerment	Gender as performance, queering binaries, rich theories of identity, extending of feminism to all marginalized peoples
Applicability to HCI	Highly compatible with existing themes and values widely expressed throughout HCI; easy to justify as contributing to HCI	Connects well to social computing and virtual worlds, links feminism to other political HCI discourses including STS and HCI4D
Disadvantages for HCI	Limited by its tacit commitments to gender essentialism; misses out on the insights of third wave feminism; emancipatory impulse limited to gender	Its radical postmodernism likely alienating to some in HCI, linking to mainstream HCI research methods likely difficult

From our point of view, one of the most exciting aspects of feminist HCI is that its emancipatory agenda, and its reliance on feminist theory (in all of its diversity), is all explicit, rather than tacit. This is important because any given research project or paper is part of a group, and dialogue becomes possible across the group. For example, the extent to which a given work reflects second vs. third wave feminism is most visible when a work acknowledges its links to feminism. It also supports a research dialogue, where one researcher can respond to another on her or his interpretation of feminism.

6.4.4   SEX AND THE SUBJECT (PSYCHOANALYTIC HCI?)

There is very little humanistic HCI research that openly calls itself "psychoanalytic." However, as a major hermeneutic and emancipatory theory of the 20th century, psychoanalysis deeply shaped humanistic thought, with some of its key concepts—the notion of the subject in particular—spreading throughout humanistic inquiry, from feminism to film studies. It is not surprising, then, that the concept has also appeared in HCI.

What is the subject? As a radical departure from Enlightenment notions of the self as unified and autonomous entity, thinkers since Marx and Freud have proposed *the subject* as an alternative model. This view considers an individual human's identity/consciousness not as foundational and unified, but as emergent, relational, and fractured. For example, Freud proposed a three-part relation between the ego, the id, and the superego. Feminists view the subject as a relation between biological sex and socially constructed gender. Social philosophers, such as Althusser and Foucault, view the subject within structures of power (e.g., police-citizen, doctor-patient, teacher-student). In each case, the individual is thrust into predefined "subject positions," and any response (e.g., behavior, attitude, self-perception, intention) is at least partly determined by those structures. In subjectivity theory, the structural determinants that result in our selves can grouped into four categories: psychic, social, libidinal, and biological (Kennedy, 2002).

The Subject

Subjectivity theory posits that individual selfhood is outcome of, rather than source of, a human's positioning within diverse structures. The theory relies on an ambiguity in the word "subject" itself: that one can be *subjected* to a system, power, or authority, and one can be the *subject* of one's experience and response to that subjection. The concept of a "subject position" gets at the first of these notions, to be subjected to a structural role (e.g., mother-daughter, manager-worker, police-citizen), given that such roles carry with them systems, institutional practices, policies, norms, prohibitions, etc. Conversely, the concept of "subjectivity" refers to the second half: the phenomenologically felt experience of subjecthood, including one's agency in choosing how to respond. The subject position provides a template and the subjectivity provides the agency to act in accordance with the template, to stylize and individuate one's responses, or even to resist and transgress it.

One of the most obvious ways that this theory applies to HCI is through the concept of "the user." The user has structural relationships to us, as designers, user researchers, theorists—whatever. The user is also inscribed in the computer system as someone with a given set of understandings, skills, and needs; permissible operations within the system; and someone with some sort of stake in that interactive practice. In certain design practices, including research through design and critical design, where the design is not really intended for actual consumers, the user shifts to whoever engages the design and for whatever purpose—entertainment and enlightenment in a museum or even the HCI research community being subtly called out by a design for tacit ageism.

Using philosopher and sociologist Michel Foucault's theory of subjectivity, Cooper and Bowers (1995) analyze "the user" in HCI as a subject (though they don't actually use that word). They argue that "the user" is a discursive construct created by HCI to establish a need for, and to confer legitimacy on, HCI as a field. That is: HCI is the field whose area of expertise is the user. HCI now "represents" in two distinct ways. In the first way, the user is modeled with cognitive representations, for example, in the case of the Model Human Processor of Card et al. (1983). This type of representation is useful to HCI practice because it represents humans and computers as the same sort of thing—modeled information processors—which greatly simplifies the concept of "interaction" as the structured flow of information between these two information processing models. The second way of representation is that the HCI practitioner advocates for (like a lawyer to a client) this user: the HCI practitioner can speak up for the needs and requirements of the user and make sure that any system design satisfies them.

Actual flesh-and-blood users of systems become *subjected* to these discursive moves, e.g., to have an HCI expert speak on their behalf, to have cognitive models represent their interactions. But we also know that users are *subjects* of this discursive move as well, which comes through in the ways that they comply with, resist, transform, and even reject the models we impose on them. This last case is explored in Satchell and Dourish's (2009) "Beyond The User: Use And Non-Use in HCI," in which they point out that HCI leaves little room for non-users. These include lagging adopters, active resisters, the disenchanted, the disenfranchised, the displaced, and the disinterested. "The user" does not accommodate any of these particularly well, although it is manifestly obvious that all are important and relevant to HCI practice.

More recently, this discursive notion of the user has acquired a name: it is a *subjectivity of information*; the term was coined by Paul Dourish in the context of the Intel Science and Technology Center for Social Computing. In the context of that center, we built on prior work to develop this concept, in part by proposing a definition: "We understand subjectivity of information to refer to any combination of (structural) subject positions and (felt and performed) subjectivities relevant to the context of information technology use" (Bardzell and Bardzell, 2015, p. 2). We considered two positive implications for the intentional use of this construct. First (Bardzell and Bardzell, 2014) is the case where users don't yet exist, as is the case in speculative designs or designs that are projected into the proximate future (as is the case in a lot of ubiquitous computing research). Although the users don't exist, we can approximate them based on the structures that we can reasonably anticipate that they will be subjected to (including but not limited to the design or technology in question). In this way, we can offer some basis to support our speculations about this imagined future. Second is the case where structures are viewed not as constraining the self, so much as enabling new forms of identity exploration and play, including pushing oneself to extremes, as we saw in our ethnographic research in Second Life's sexual communities (Bardzell et al., 2014).

As is well known, psychoanalysis had a special emphasis on sexuality. The reason of course is that our sexual needs and experiences are extremely powerful, as are the social structures (legal and normative) that seek to control them. This conflict both served as a powerful explanation for psychological maladies (e.g., anxiety and depression), and also as a hermeneutic "way in" to interpret the nature of human consciousness itself. Applied to computing, psychoanalysis would seem to be well positioned to contribute the relationships among technology, identity, and intimacy. This is precisely the argument made by Sherry Turkle (2004) in her "Wither Psychoanalysis in Computer Culture?" in which she argues that anthropomorphic robots, affective computing, and virtual worlds are increasingly "intimate machines." She doesn't mention the swiftly innovating field of online pornography, but certainly it has a role to play here as well. Machines do much more than serve our intentions or augment our intelligence; they become intimately bound up with our own identities and desires. Echoing the language of subjectivity theory, Turkle writes, "The instrumental computer, the computer that does things *for* us, has another side," she writes: "It is also a subjective computer that does things *to* us—to our view of our relationships, to our ways of looking at our minds and ourselves." As a result, she argues:

> We must cultivate the richest possible language and methodologies for talking about our increasingly emotional relationships with artifacts. We need far closer examination of how artifacts enter the development of self and mediate between self and other. Psychoanalysis provides a rich language for distinguishing between need (something that artifacts may have) and desire (which resides in the conjunction of language and flesh). It provides a rich language for exploring the specificity of human meanings in their connections to the body. (p. 29)

Like many others before and since, Turkle criticizes the notion of computation as merely instrumental, that is, as serving human needs without in any way transforming them. She argues that our relationships to (and through) computers is intimate, constituting and therefore shaping, even transforming, our relationships with others, our desires, even our very identities. Psychoanalysis offers sophisticated theories about these issues, and for that reason, Turkle forcefully argues, "I shall argue the renewed relevance of a psychoanalytic discourse in digital culture. Indeed, I shall argue that this relevance is so profound as to suggest an occasion for a revitalization and renewal of psychoanalytic thinking" (p. 17).

Unaware of Turkle's paper, but influenced by many of the same thinkers (French philosophers such as Foucault in particular), our research group has been pursuing a similar line of inquiry in a number of studies of online intimacy and sexuality. Although this research has entailed a number of empirical methods, including virtual ethnography, interview studies, and questionnaires, overall our research on sexual and intimate interaction has largely been a critical and humanistic practice for us. Specifically, our goal has been less about discovering what online sexual practices are social scientifically, and more about leveraging such understandings to investigate extremes of user experience, to help us think beyond more pedestrian applications of the term.

In 2006, we noticed that the virtual world Second Life seemed to have unexpectedly large, and unexpectedly public, BDSM (bondage, discipline, and sadomasochism) communities—one could hardly go to a party or go shopping in those days without seeing a near-naked avatar on his/

her knees, chained to a master, and very public online figures seen as thought leaders of Second Life and virtual worlds were often open members of such communities. We felt that the theories of experience prevalent in HCI at the time could not adequately account for intimate and sexual online experiences in general, nor BDSM in particular. In Bardzell and Bardzell (2007), we built off McCarthy and Wright's (2004) reworking of Dewey's conceptualization of experience, supplementing that with Foucault's writings about sexual experience (as noted in Chapter 5, Foucault not only offered a major philosophical contribution to the study of sexuality, but he also was an openly gay BDSM practitioner and in his interviews spoke frankly about how his sex life and philosophical practice mutually illuminated one another). At any rate, we argued that virtual BDSM can be understood as a broad aesthetic (including color palettes, common imagery, common props, a technical vocabulary, a public code of ethics, and highly dramaturgical sex scenes, among others), and that engaging this aesthetic online enabled participants to push themselves to uncomfortable extremes and thereby to experience intense pleasures.

In later work we continued to explore the nature of designing for dark pleasures (Bardzell and Odom, 2008). In Bardzell and Bardzell (2011), we studied designers of high-end sex toys (e.g., Jimmyjane, Lelo) and argued for an epistemic role of the sexualized body in their design processes (and by extension all experience- or intimacy-oriented design processes). We also studied the role of intimacy in online play, looking at friendships, romance, and cybersex in World of Warcraft (Pace et al., 2010). More recently, we offered critical-empirical studies of the design of new sexual desires in the context of sexual geo-mapping applications (Kannabiran et al., 2011) and contributed to the development of the notion of a subjectivity of information in the context of intimate experiences in virtual worlds (Bardzell et al., 2014).

Reflecting back on this work, it seems clear now to us that part of what we were interested in was understanding user experience at the extreme, in particular, what are the most intense pleasures that users experience? This work was emancipatory, because it confronted a silence in HCI—the constitutive role of sexuality in human experience—and asserted that individuals are not "perverts" or "losers" for finding intimacy online or even having sexual experiences online, and that HCI researchers therefore ought to take sexuality seriously as a component of human experience—points well established in psychology and health sciences research on human sexuality. And by implication, we have argued that HCI's disengagement with sexuality is itself a form of repression.

But in what sense is this sexuality research psychoanalytic? We never invoke psychoanalysis in this research (neither in the publications nor at any point during the research activities themselves), so the influence is indirect. Psychoanalytic concepts are part of people's everyday vocabulary and also very influential in humanistic research in the latter part of the twentieth century—the unconscious, the subconscious, repression, anxiety, the id, the ego, the Oedipus Complex, Freudian slips, the subject, latent sexuality, and so on. Our research points to a form of repression—HCI's repression of sexuality and desire in its analysis of user experience. Going further, we argued that sexuality is more than merely relevant to experience-oriented HCI.

> If third-wave HCI is about experience, pleasure, embodiment, intimacy, social activism, aesthetics, wellness, and lifestyle, then sexual interaction is arguably the paradigmatic example of third-wave HCI. (from a slide at our CHI 2011 presentation of "'Pleasure is Your Birthright': Digitally Enabled Designer Sex Toys as a Case of Third-Wave HCI" (2011))

This position—that sexual experience can be seen as paradigmatic of all experience—owes itself to psychoanalysis, as does our reliance on the concept of "the subject" throughout this work.

Most of the work described in this section is "edgy"—taking on taboo themes like sexuality or challenging HCI's most fundamental claims (that it serves users) to argue that the opposite may be the case (the user serves us)—the latter also explaining why the field "forgot" to talk about non-users until 2009. This edginess is the strength and weakness of psychoanalytic-like HCI. Positively, it helps push boundaries and thereby reveal them; it helps us make sense of extreme or otherwise highly atypical examples so we can learn from them; it makes us take the marginal—e.g., those dismissed as perverts—seriously; and it helps us reflect on the conditions of possibility of our own knowledge practice by making us confront our blind spots. Negatively, its uptake if often slow to non-existent. That subjectivities of information is only gaining steam twenty years after Cooper and Bowers (and see also Bannon and Bødker, 1991) basically proposed the concept is evidence of that, as is the ghettoizing of all sexuality-related HCI research into a specialty domain whose implications for the field as a whole can be safely bracketed aside (Kannabiran et al., 2011).

6.4.5 POSTCOLONIAL HCI

Earlier in this chapter we characterized postcolonialism as the systematic tendency of the West to define itself in binary opposition to an eastern "other," based on its own histories with the East, and without regard for how peoples and nations in the East understand themselves or their own history. Following postcolonial theorist Edward Saïd, we wrote that this tendency covered virtually all Western knowledge disciplines, from poets to statesmen, from social scientists to historians.

One might reasonably imagine that IT design and development, too, would assert and build upon this binary opposition, and indeed, such an argument is explored in Irani et al.'s (2010) "Postcolonial Computing: A Lens on Design and Development." In it, the authors confront the challenges of technology design and development in diverse cultural contexts, arguing that postcolonial computing can serve as an "analytic orientation" that introduces questions and concerns inspired by the conditions of postcoloniality, and manifested in binary distinctions between West and East, developed and developing, civilized and uncivilized, enlightened and un-enlightened—which underlie Western IT design briefs, design methods, and evaluation criteria for cultural others.

As an example, the authors reveal some of the subtlety at play in HCI4D. They note that postcolonialism can operate at the level of methodology as well. For example, user-centered design is a tried and true HCI method that happens to reflect Western ideals of individualism; but these notions of individualism are not universal, and so user-centered design as a method can perpetuate postcolonial conditions. Their point is not that HCI4D practitioners are a bunch of naïve racists—quite the opposite—but that rather the problems HCI4D practitioners face are enmeshed in historical, political, and ethical complexities that are nearly intractable. Postcolonial computing, then, is introduced not to "correct" what is "wrong," nor to offer any actual solutions, but rather to inject a vocabulary and a sensibility that can support designers and developers as they navigate these issues on the ground.

The authors conclude by moving beyond critique into the speculative role of proposing new methodological meta-process.

> Traditional design processes, in HCI as well as related disciplines, break down into a familiar range of steps and procedures, from the identification of potential user communities, the analysis of their activities, the formulation of design requirements, ideation and iteration, and so forth. We suggest an alternate formulation of design work – *engagement, articulation*, and *translation*. (p. 6)

At a high level, "engagement" means little more than connecting with users in their application domains and material spaces. But the authors are keen to assert a distinction between extractive methods (i.e., where researchers extract knowledge from participations seen as data providers) and mutual encounters, where parties come together in staged bidirectional exchanges. "Articulation" refers to how the design situation and problem space is represented, e.g., as user requirements, opportunities, or constraints. Here again the authors assert a distinction between knowledge as captured vs. knowledge as performed or enacted. "Translation" also gets at how statements about technology are represented, and once again the authors assert a distinction between a static notion of translation and a more dynamic and situated one. In short, the authors advocate against a classificatory notion of culture (this person is Indian, that person is Chinese) and instead for a more generative and enacted notion of culture (i.e., where this person acts in a specific way, performing and perpetuating an Indian or Chinese way of being or doing), and they criticize a recipe-based, step-by-step, one size fits all notion of design, in favor of a design methodology committed to emergent performance, enactments, and engagement.

The following year, Taylor (2011) published an essay called "Out There" in which he offers a critical discourse analysis (see Chapter 3 for more on that methodology) on "HCI's disciplinary turn 'out there.'" The criticality of the essay is announced on its first page: "I want to try to turn our interpretative frame inside out so that we might somehow catch sight of ourselves, looking out there" (p. 686), seeking to respond to three issues: "how it is we are configuring the world out there";

"the analytical resources we assemble to do so"; and "our own roles in the processes of configuring 'out there'" (p. 686).

In analyzing ways that HCI looks "out there," he identifies three themes or tropes: the network, difference, and complexity. As for the first, he observes that HCI uses the metaphor of the network to express the idea of social groups and how they link to transnationalism and globalism, and from there to establish a link between (and hence to reify) here and there. He then turns to prior work in anthropology to critically examine the network as a "framing device," to problematize the linkages the device too easily provides. (Significantly, in this context, Taylor uses the Irani et al. (2010) paper that we just summarized to exemplify and work through his critique.) The concepts of difference and complexity operate in similar ways, i.e., as "framing devices" that tacitly facilitate the construction of "here" vs. "there" reasoning.

Having worked through his critical analysis, and following the formula that we've talked about through this chapter, he then offers his emancipatory-speculative move, in this case, to propose "three orienting frames," all of which nonetheless fall short of "a concrete approach or method." His first frame is "right there," which is proposed to be a turning inside-out of network, "so that it is not just our ways of ordering we rehearse, but we attend to the orderings as they are achieved 'right there' on the ground" (p. 692). The second is "collective configurations of technology," which combines Suchman and Latour "to imagine human-computer systems that enrich the locally organising practices of emergent assemblies, rather than reasserting the lines between in here and out there" (p. 692). The third is "instabilities," which references Wittgenstein's famous aversion to yet another theory, and instead "to be more comfortable with our own pauses and moments of going on," a stance he offers as a means of resisting the ordering impulse that is triggered when we view a situation as "complex."

6.5   CONCLUSION: A CRITICAL TAKE ON EMANCIPATORY HCI

At the beginning of this chapter, we argued that the humanistic conceptualization of emancipation runs the gamut from the literal (i.e., the freeing of slaves) to the metaphorical (e.g., resistance toward invisible lines of power, the insidious machinations of patriarchy, and to crude oversimplifications of entire ways of life mobilized as military and economic policy). Emancipatory HCI—which again comprises social scientific, design-based, as well as humanistic approaches—has taken up these issues in many of the ways that HCI is implicated in them.

We argued that one of the distinguishing features of humanistic approaches to emancipation its theory-supported deployment of the hermeneutics of suspicion, the view that all is not as it seems, and that malignant and contingent forces often pass as natural and inevitable features of the world given to us. For example, the recognition that poverty is human-made, not natural, and that it can (and can only be) fixed by humans, as Nelson Mandela reminds us, goes to show just how much we must have "forgotten" in order to need that reminder. The hermeneutics of suspicion in its various forms—Marxism, psychoanalysis, feminism, and postcolonialism—offers a powerful set of tools to pull those forces out of hiding, to remind ourselves that, though it will be difficult, we have some agency to effect real change.

These points bring into view several strengths of emancipatory humanistic HCI. It implies— correctly in our view—that HCI is not merely about discovering needs and requirements the better to support the design of buttons and task sequences, but that it is a cultural force in its own right. As the novel dominated the nineteenth century, the film dominated the twentieth century, now many of us agree with Gillian Crampton Smith when she says that interaction design will dominate the twenty-first century. This move is empowering—it certainly increases the scope of the field well beyond designing task sequences, and it invites us to think big, to think about the kind of world we want to live in and the kind of world we want our children to inherit from us. But this move is also a moment of accountability. Are we creating such a world? Has HCI emancipated anyone? Given our close ties to global multinationals, how do we know that we are not merely handmaidens to a capitalist status quo? The hermeneutics of suspicion provide at least some tools to take on such questions.

Another strength of emancipatory humanistic HCI is that it promises to help HCI practice stop chasing the computer as it reaches out and start pushing it—pushing the computer toward preferred futures. We are speaking, of course, of the speculative capabilities of emancipatory humanistic HCI, which includes the world opened up, the forms of life revealed when emancipatory critique has disclosed the contingency of our problematic present. It allows us to ask whether HCI can support sustainability beyond trying to persuade individuals to unplug their computer speakers. It helps us see that who we invite to the design table deeply shapes the values inscribed in the result and that changing these values means bringing new voices to the conversation. It forces us to ask whether those observable differences in the ways that women vs. men use computers might constitute more than immediate design implications for HCI practitioners, but might instead give those same practitioners a way in to disclose and to resist the patriarchal influence widely and (sometimes) subtly interwoven in computing cultures. It makes us reflect on whether our best scientific methods in fact embody just another example of postcolonial speaking-over and speaking-for the marginal groups we are "representing."

But we also see two concerns that have emerged in this chapter. Recall earlier that we said that emancipatory activism typically involved two moves, the first hermeneutic, critical, and diagnostic, and the second speculative, activist, engaged. Even within the humanities, the accusation has surfaced that humanistic modes are far more effective at the former than they are at the latter. Perhaps that dynamic is replicating itself in HCI. To what extents have the sorts of critiques raised in this chapter actually altered the course of HCI research and computing itself? HCI research, at least, does appear to have changed, given the rise of emancipation-oriented projects and papers in the field since the early 2000s. As for computing itself, it seems less clear. In contrast, there is no question that UX has influenced not just HCI discourse and practice, but computing itself in the same time period. Then we wonder: the profit motive for improving user experiences was drastically higher for industry than it was for emancipatory designs. Perhaps we in HCI are just tools of industry after all (at least we must ask ourselves).

Another concern that we have raised in this chapter—one for which we have been guilty ourselves—is the tendency of emancipatory HCI research to make use of, without owning up to, specific emancipatory theories. Feminist HCI and postcolonial HCI have been positive exceptions in this regard, but Marxist and psychoanalytic influences are not well acknowledged by HCI practitioners and therefore it is difficult for the community to build on them. Again, contrast this with the explicit use of Dewey and Bakhtin in McCarthy and Wright, or the use of Shusterman's somaesthetics by researchers in East Asia, North America, and Europe as outlined in Chapter 5. In both cases, a research agenda gained traction and coherence in part because there was a shared commitment to disclosing the underlying theory, including the researchers' own struggles to make use of that theory in HCI. This concern at least has an action item: HCI researchers making use of and benefitting from emancipatory theories (Marxism and psychoanalysis in particular) should at least reflect on whether they are adequately articulating the significances of these theories in their thinking, and especially the places where they are struggling or being especially creative about how to appropriate them.

CHAPTER 7

Conclusion

We conclude the book by looking forward. What comes next for humanistic HCI? What should HCI do about/with humanistic HCI? As we brainstormed and wrote down all the implications and recommendations and agenda items we could, we discovered that really there was one overriding agenda item that we wanted to highlight for humanistic HCI.

Agenda for Humanistic HCI

Improve humanistic HCI's "fit" with social science, engineering, and design in HCI research and practice.

Our concern based on our experiences doing humanistic HCI—characterized by the usual mix of triumphs and screw-ups—is that humanistic HCI remains a little bit mysterious, inchoate, undetermined. How, for example, can we mesh social scientific and humanistic methodologies? How do we write about such projects? This is not to say that humanistic HCI has been oppressed: if nothing else, this book should have demonstrated that humanistic HCI has had an impact in, and has been welcomed to, the broader interdisciplinary field of HCI.

The challenge, rather, is to improve our collective sense of how humanistic HCI researchers can best contribute to broader HCI, how to participate robustly in its interdisciplinary conversations—and that means both speaking and listening. It means understanding and being able to speak to what HCI's diverse constituencies—engineers, designers, and social scientists—recognize as research, as generative, as a contribution. It means articulating one's methods or tactics or approaches in ways that are recognizable as such. It means introducing theories at the right level of detail—neither becoming a pedantic historian of philosophy nor, at the other extreme, becoming piecemeal. It means being able to judge when tacit knowledge in the humanities must be made explicit in order to make work legible to an interdisciplinary readership. It includes the ability to speak academically and pragmatically, in the right ways, to the right audiences, in the right moments. We two have struggled at times with all of these issues—as the first round of reviews of this book made clear enough—and we know we're not alone in this struggle.

We also believe that as an interdisciplinary community, HCI as a whole also has a stake in understanding humanistic practice—both in processes and methods and also in research products and results. Designers working with an emancipatory agenda should be able to turn to humanistic HCI for resources. Similarly, a social scientist might design a user research study in a way that reflects humanistic thinking, say, to do empirical research to improve our ability to design for aesthetic experiences. Humanistic researchers in HCI want to welcome all of these researchers, not scare them away by being too parochial. Years ago, after we gave a talk, Hiroshi Ishii came up to us afterwards and said that he loved what we were doing, but that short of going back and getting a literature degree himself, he didn't see how he could incorporate anything like it into his practice. That comment has haunted both of us ever since: it made us realize that it is incumbent on us to build those bridges.

These are not easy challenges to address. But now we are in the Conclusion, now is the time to leave it all on the road, as the cyclists say. We'll give it a go.

Speaking generally, when we blend two things, the elements we start with are each distinct. We don't make peanut butter and undefined substance sandwiches. We make peanut butter and jelly sandwiches. It will be hard for everyone in HCI if we try to mix social science and humanistic thinking, or design and humanistic thinking, if we as a community don't yet have much sense of what humanistic thinking is. Our point is not that HCI needs to change so it better understands humanistic HCI research and practice. Our point is rather that humanistic HCI researchers and practitioners need to continue to work to bring about the shared understanding we want to have.

We want (obviously) a peer reviewing process that can handle humanistic contributions (see Chapter 4 for our specific suggestions in that regard). Among other things, that means we need to train junior reviewers to be able to recognize different types of contribution and invoke appropriate reviewing criteria and reviewers. We want HCI to appreciate the epistemic role of writing, of the essay, in humanistic contributions; just as the scientific report is a fit for the epistemic needs of its readers (and writers), so too is the essay for its readers and writers. We need to talk—loudly—about what the essay means to us, and we need to train Ph.D. students in the craft of writing—especially if we are to support humanistic blending in HCI.

More deeply, we want to create better "hooks" that allow social scientists, designers, and engineers to find humanistic work interesting and valuable—on their own terms. Just as everyone needs facts and information, not just scientists; and just as everyone intentionally intervenes upon their surroundings to improve them, not just designers: so everyone wants to be made alive to new issues and to acquire new perspectives on the familiar, not just humanists. What are the tactics by which humanists cultivate their perceptiveness, imaginations, insights? How does a reader or viewer come alive to an object or issue of interest? How does one help another reader or viewer come alive to an object or matter of interest?

We'll approach these questions by anecdote. When we were in Comparative Literature classes as graduate students, we would sit in a seminar room discussing a play or lyric poem we had read. The professor would often pick a student and ask her what a given passage or symbol meant. More often than not, the student did not offer a propositional response; she did not say "the rose symbolizes love." Instead, the more common response was to offer an account of how she would *approach* responding to such a question: "well, I was noticing this tendency across several of his poems where he…," she might begin, or: "Roland Barthes has this concept of 'hinge points,' and I thought if I were to apply that as a way of distinguishing between individual actions in this scene that it might…." In Chapter 4, we quoted essayist Philip Lopate's notion of the essay as "enacting the struggle for truth in full view." The Comparative Literature student who doesn't answer the question but talks aloud about the resources she would marshal in order to approach such an answer is doing just that. The reason, of course, is that what is of interest is the *effort after meaning itself*, the marshaling of resources to give us new ways in, to improve understanding or appreciation of a challenging work or situation—and not on the specifics of any given solution. As her auditors in class, we were following along, integrating her approach into our own efforts after meaning. The process would have been short-circuited, and frankly rather boring, had she just propositionally declared what the symbol meant (and we wouldn't have accepted such an answer, anyway).

As we prepared to write this book, we saw that dynamic time and again in humanistic HCI. McCarthy and Wright (2004) spend a significant portion of their book working through Dewey's and Bakhtin's theories (see especially Chapter 3); that chapter's unusual structure and surprising moves back and forth among philosophy, literary criticism, and HCI concerns all suggest that that chapter was a struggle for them. Yet it was the struggle of two experts—trained psychologists with decades of experience in HCI who had additionally spent years reading philosophy and literary theory together and with colleagues—mustering all those resources to take on the hardest question they knew: how should HCI think about experience? As we argued earlier, that chapter's value may be less in its propositional claims about experience than in the ways that it "enacts that struggle for truth" before our eyes—challenging us not so much to accept its results as a finished model of experience, but rather to try out its project for ourselves, augmented and guided by its leads.

Thecla Schiphorst (2009), in the *soft(n)* project (see Chapter 5), makes no bones about her uncertainty about how to translate someasthetic theory into HCI and design; her design is her enactment of that struggle, and *soft(n)* is as important for that reason as it is for any implications for future tangible user interfaces (TUIs) one might derive from it. Laurel's *Computing as Theater* (2003) did not have the impact it had because of her solution (i.e., to use Aristotle's "rules" to guide interaction design), but rather because she posed what was at the time a surprising and ambitious challenge—to conceive of beautiful interaction—and then she experimentally tried what was then a radical solution (i.e., to turn to an ancient text on aesthetics)—opening up whole new vistas on how we might pursue computing. When Light (2011) proposes six ways to "queer" a design process, or Satchell and Dourish (2009) suggest six kinds of non-use, or Blythe and Cairns (2009) do side-by-side grounded theory and psychoanalytic readings of YouTube comments—all are struggling with issues not yet in their control, in front of our eyes, inviting us to test our own mettle beside them.

What we infer from all of this is that HCI needs to build a community of humanistic prac-tice, that is, a community with sufficient critical mass that we can understand and build on each other in a constructive way. We don't all have to agree with each other, of course, but like any community of practice, there must be some underlying coherence to our practice. By way of conclusion, we propose that that coherence looks something like this.

- Mastery of the key **concepts** we've been discussing throughout this book: interpretation, subjectivity and the expert subject, judgment, aesthetics, poetics, holism, emancipation, reflexivity, canons, ideology, discourse, forms of life, false pleasures, the hermeneutics of suspicion, etc.

- Facility with key humanistic **methodologies** or inquiry practices: critique, genealogy, conceptual analysis, discourse analysis, hermeneutics of suspicion, speculation, *explication de texte*—all guided but not determined by an intelligent and judicious use of critical theory.

- Cultivated **sensibility** for objects and ideas: sensitivity, insight, provocativeness, originality, perceptiveness, empathy, taste, the generous yet critical reading of others, domain mastery, and a developed capacity for appreciation.

- Excellence in humanistic **expression**: crafted and shapely writing, honesty (especially with regard to the struggle for truth or meaning), a coherent and distinctive voice, and positionality (i.e., not speaking with the voice from nowhere).

Each of these excellences is teachable and learnable. It is reasonable to expect that HCI researchers and practitioners without advanced training in the humanities can learn and use humanistic ideas and approaches in their work. It is also reasonable to expect that in reading each other's work—as peer reviewers, while pursuing a research project, or merely as intellectually curious human beings—readers from wide interdisciplinary backgrounds can understand and appreciate humanistic writings in relation to their own interests.

If we can improve humanistic HCI's fit with other disciplinary agendas in HCI, we expect that humanistic approaches will improve its ability to partner with all of HCI to take on problems or opportunities of an ambitious scale; to reframe or revitalize stale research and design agendas; to keep the field honest and reflective; and to help all of us imagine better futures and better forms of life that are worthy of the whole field's tremendous collective gifts and energies, and more importantly worthy of our "users" (who is pretty much everyone now) and their children's children.

Such, anyway, is our hope.

Bibliography

Abowd, G.D. (2012) What Next, Ubicomp? In the *2012 ACM Conference on Ubiquitous Computing*. NY, USA. ACM, 31–40. DOI: 10.1145/2370216.2370222. 70

Abowd, G.D. and Mynatt, E.D. (2000) Charting Past, Present, and Future Research in Ubiquitous Computing. *ACM Trans. Comput.-Hum. Interact.* 7 (1), 29–58. DOI: 10.1145/344949.344988. 50, 63

Abrams, M.H. (1991) *Doing Things with Texts*. W. W. Norton and Company. 106

Agre, P. (1997) Toward a Critical Technical Practice: Lessons learned in trying to reform AI. In *Social Science, Technical Systems and Cooperative Work*. ed. by Bowker, G.C., Star, S.L., Turner, W., and Gasser, Les. Mahwah, N.J.: Lawrence Erlbaum Associates. 125

Akah, B. and Bardzell, S. (2010) Empowering Products. In *CHI '10 Extended Abstracts on Human Factors in Computing Systems*. New York: ACM, 4021–4026. DOI: 10.1145/1753846.1754096. 20

Andersen, C.U. and Pold, S.B. (2011) *Interface Criticism*. Aarhus University Press. 40, 41

Aristotle, Golden, L., and Hardison, O.B. (1981) *Aristotle's Poetics: a Translation and Commentary for Students of Literature*. Tallahassee: University Presses of Florida. 102, 103

Arnold, M. (2010) The Function of Criticism at the Present Time. In *The Norton Anthology of Theory and Criticism*. W. W. Norton, 806–825. 14, 50

Arnold, M. (1865) The Function of Criticism at the Present Time. In *Essays in Criticism*, Macmillan & Co. London, U.K. 14, 50

Bannon, L.J. and Bødker, S. (1991) Beyond the Interface: Encountering Artifacts in Use. In *Designing Interaction Psychology at the Human-Computer Interface*. ed. by Carroll, J.M. New York: Cambridge University Press, 227–253. 3, 17, 138

Bardzell, J. (2009) Interaction Criticism and Aesthetics. In *Proceedings of the SIGCHI Conference on Human Factors in Computing Systems*. New York: ACM, 2357–2366. DOI: 10.1145/1518701.1519063. 28, 40, 84

Bardzell, J. (2011) Interaction Criticism: an Introduction to the Practice. *Interacting with Computers* 23 (6), 604–621. DOI: 10.1016/j.intcom.2011.07.001. 20, 40, 41, 84, 106

Bardzell, J. (2012) Commentary on: Shusterman, Richard (2014): Somaesthetics. In *The Encyclopedia of Human-Computer Interaction, 2nd Ed.* [online] ed. by Soegaard, M. and Dam, R.F. Aarhus, Denmark: The Interaction Design Foundation. available from <https://www.interaction-design.org/encyclopedia/somaesthetics.html>. 39, 93, 95, 96, 106

Bardzell, J. (2014) Critical and Cultural Approaches to HCI. In *The SAGE Handbook of Digital Technology Research*. ed. by Price, S., Jewitt, C., and Brown, B. London: SAGE Publications Ltd, 130–143. DOI: 10.4135/9781446282229. 113

Bardzell, J. and Bardzell, S. (2008) Interaction Criticism: a Proposal and Framework for a New Discipline of Hci. In *CHI '08 Extended Abstracts on Human Factors in Computing Systems*. New York: ACM, 2463–2472. DOI: 10.1145/1358628.1358703. 41

Bardzell, J. and Bardzell, S. (2011) Pleasure Is Your Birthright: Digitally Enabled Designer Sex Toys as a Case of Third-Wave HCI. In *Proceedings of the SIGCHI Conference on Human Factors in Computing Systems*. New York: ACM, 257–266. DOI: 10.1145/1978942.1978979. 129, 137, 138

Bardzell, J. and Bardzell, S. (2013) What Is 'Critical' About Critical Design? In *Proceedings of the SIGCHI Conference on Human Factors in Computing Systems*. New York: ACM, 3297–3306. DOI: 10.1145/2470654.2466451. 39, 70, 123, 124

Bardzell, J. and Bardzell, S. (2014) "A Great and Troubling Beauty": Cognitive Speculation and Ubiquitous Computing. *Personal and Ubiquitous Computing* 18 (4), 779–794. DOI: 10.1007/s00779-013-0677-8. 20, 58, 60, 135

Bardzell, J. and Bardzell, S. (2015) The User Reconfigured: on Subjectivities of Information. In *Proceedings of Aarhus on Critical Alternatives*. 135

Bardzell, J., Bardzell, S., DiSalvo, C., Gaver, W., and Sengers, P. (2012) The Humanities and/in HCI. In *CHI '12 Extended Abstracts on Human Factors in Computing Systems*. New York: ACM, 1135–1138. DOI: 10.1145/2212776.2212405. 5

Bardzell, J., Bardzell, S., Zhang, G., and Pace, T. (2014) The Lonely Raccoon at the Ball: Designing for Intimacy, Sociability, and Selfhood. In *Proceedings of the SIGCHI Conference on Human Factors in Computing Systems*. New York: ACM, 3943–3952. DOI: 10.1145/2556288.2557127. 54, 63, 135, 137

Bardzell, S. (2010) Feminist HCI: Taking Stock and Outlining an Agenda for Design. In *Proceedings of the SIGCHI Conference on Human Factors in Computing Systems*. New York: ACM, 1301–1310. DOI: 10.1145/1753326.1753521. 128, 129

Bardzell, S. and Bardzell, J. (2007) Docile Avatars: Aesthetics, Experience, and Sexual Interaction in Second Life. In *Proceedings of the 21st British HCI Group Annual Conference on People and Computers HCI...but not as we know it - Volume 1.* Swinton, UK: British Computer Society, 3–12. 91, 137

Bardzell, S. and Bardzell, J. (2011) Toward a Feminist HCI Methodology: Social Science, Feminism, and HCI. In *Proceedings of the SIGCHI Conference on Human Factors in Computing Systems.* New York: ACM, 675–684. DOI: 10.1145/1978942.1979041.

Bardzell, S., Light, A., Bardzell, J., and Blythe, M. (2011) *Proceedings of The Second International Symposium on Culture, Creativity, and Interaction Design.* Northumbria University, Newcastle, UK. 5

Bardzell, S. and Odom, W. (2008) The Experience of Embodied Space in Virtual Worlds. *Space and Culture* 11 (3), 239–259. DOI: 10.1177/1206331208319148. 137

Barry, P. (2002) *Beginning Theory.* Manchester, UK: Manchester University Press. 14

Beardsley, M.C. (1981) *Aesthetics, Problems in the Philosophy of Criticism.* Hackett Publishing. 38, 62

Beckwith, L. and Burnett, M. (2004) Gender: an Important Factor in End-User Programming Environments? In *2004 IEEE Symposium on Visual Languages - Human Centric Computing.* IEEE, 107–114. DOI: 10.1109/vlhcc.2004.28. 128

Bell, S. (2010) *Fast Feminism.* Brooklyn, NY: Autonomedia.

Bell, G. and Dourish, P. (2007) Yesterday's Tomorrows: Notes on Ubiquitous Computing's Dominant Vision. *Personal and Ubiquitous Computing* 11 (2), 133–143. DOI: 10.1007/s00779-006-0071-x. 20, 57

Bell, G., Blythe, M., and Sengers, P. (2005) Making by Making Strange: Defamiliarization and the Design of Domestic Technologies. *Transactions on Computer-Human Interaction* (TOCHI '12) (2), 149–173. DOI: 10.1145/1067860.1067862. 56

Benhabib, S. (1992) *Situating the Self: Gender, Community and Postmodernism in Contemporary Ethics.* NY: Routlegde. DOI: 10.2307/2956405. 118

Berry, D.M. (ed.) (2012) *Understanding Digital Humanities.* Palgrave Macmillan. DOI: 10.1057/9780230371934. 32

Bertelsen, O.W. and Pold, S. (2002) Toward the Aesthetics of Human Computer Interaction. In *Proceedings of the Second HCI Research Symposium.* 11–12. 4, 84

Bertelsen, O.W. and Pold, S. (2004) Criticism as an Approach to Interface Aesthetics. In *Proceedings of the Third Nordic Conference on Human-Computer Interaction.* New York: ACM, 23–32. DOI: 10.1145/1028014.1028018. 20, 40, 41, 84, 106

Bleeker, J. (2009) *Design Fiction: a Short Essay on Design, Science, Fact and Fiction.* Los Angelas, CA: Near Future Laboratory. 59, 60

Blevis, E. (2007) Sustainable Interaction Design: Invention and Disposal, Renewal and Reuse. In *Proceedings of the SIGCHI Conference on Human Factors in Computing Systems*. New York: ACM, 503–512. DOI: 10.1145/1240624.1240705. 124

Blevis, E. (2012) The PRInCiPleS Design Framework. In *Creativity and Rationale*. ed. by Carroll, J.M. London: Springer London, 143–169. 40

Bloom, H. (1994) *The Western Canon: the Books and School of the Ages*. 1st edn. New York: Harcourt Brace. 16, 26

Bloom, H. (2000) *How to Read and Why*. New York: Scribner. 16

Bloom, H. (2004) *Where Shall Wisdom Be Found?* New York: Riverhead Books. 16

Blythe, M. (2014) The Hitchhiker's Guide to Ubicomp: Using Techniques From Literary and Critical Theory to Reframe Scientific Agendas. *Personal and Ubiquitous Computing* 18 (4), 795–808. DOI: 10.1007/s00779-013-0679-6. 20, 58, 60

Blythe, M. and Cairns, P. (2009) Critical Methods and User Generated Content: the iPhone on YouTube. In *Proceedings of the SIGCHI Conference on Human Factors in Computing Systems*. New York: ACM, 1467–1476. DOI: 10.1145/1518701.1518923. 52, 53, 75, 108, 145

Blythe, M., Bardzell, J., Bardzell, S., and Blackwell, A. (2008) Critical Issues in Interaction Design. In *Proceedings of the 22nd British HCI Group Annual Conference on People and Computers: Culture, Creativity, Interaction - Volume 2*. British Computer Society, UK, UK. DOI: 10.1145/1531826.1531880. 5

Blythe, M., Light, A., and Wright, P. (2006) *Proceedings of the First International Symposium on Culture, Creativity and Interaction Design*. Queen Mary's, London. 5

Blythe, M., McCarthy, J., Light, A., Bardzell, S., Wright, P., Bardzell, J., and Blackwell, A. (2010) Critical Dialogue: Interaction, Experience and Cultural Theory. In *CHI '10 Extended Abstracts on Human Factors in Computing Systems*. New York: ACM, 4521–4524. DOI: 10.1145/1753846.1754189. 5

Blythe, M.A. and Wright, P.C. (2006) Pastiche Scenarios: Fiction as a Resource for User Centred Design. *Interacting with Computers* 18 (5), 1139–1164. DOI: 10.1016/j.intcom.2006.02.001. 58, 60

Blythe, M.A., Overbeeke, K., Monk, A.F., and Wright, P.C. (eds.) (2003) *Funology: From Usabilty to Enjoyment*. vol. 3. Dordrecht: Springer Netherlands. DOI: 10.1007/1-4020-2967-5. 4, 20, 84

Boehmer, E. (2006) Postcolonialism. In *Literary Theory and Criticism: an Oxford Guide*. ed. by Waugh, P. New York: Oxford University Press, 340–361. 119

Boehner, K., DePaula, R., Dourish, P., and Sengers, P. (2005) Affect: From Information to Inter-action. In *Proceedings of the 4th Decennial Conference on Critical Computing: Between Sense and Sensibility.* New York: ACM, 59–68. DOI: 10.1145/1094562.1094570. 17, 63

Boehner, K., Vertesi, J., Sengers, P., and Dourish, P. (2007) How HCI Interprets the Probes. In *Proceedings of the SIGCHI Conference on Human Factors in Computing Systems.* New York: ACM, 1077–1086. DOI: 10.1145/1240624.1240789. 50, 63

Bolter, J.D. and Gromala, D. (2006) Transparency and Reflectivity. In *Aesthetic Computing. Digital Art and the Aesthetics of Interface Design.* Cambridge, MA: MIT Press, 369–382. 43, 44

Bolter, J.D. and Grusin, R.A. (1999) *Remediation: Understanding New Media.* Cambridge, MA: MIT Press. 84

Buchenau, M. and Suri, J.F. (2000) Experience Prototyping. In *Proceedings of the 3rd Conference on Designing Interactive Systems: Processes, Practices, Methods, and Techniques.* New York: ACM, 424–433. DOI: 10.1145/347642.347802. 83

Buxton, B. (2007) *Sketching User Experiences.* San Diego: Elsevier.

Bødker, S. (2006) When Second Wave HCI Meets Third Wave Challenges. In *Proceedings of the 4th Nordic Conference on Human-Computer Interaction: Changing Roles.* New York: ACM, 1–8. DOI: 10.1145/1182475.1182476. xv, 18

Bødker, S. and Greenbaum, J. (1988) A Feeling for Systems Development Work. In *Women, Work, and Computerization.* North Holland, 161–170. 128

Card, S.K., Newell, A., and Moran, T.P. (1983) *The Psychology of Human-Computer Interaction.* Hillsdale, NJ: L. Erlbaum Associates Inc. 104, 135

Carroll, N. (2001) Four Concepts of Aesthetic Experience. In *Beyond Aesthetics: Philosoph-ical Essays.* Cambridge, UK: Cambridge University Press, 41–62. DOI: 10.1017/CBO9780511605970.005. 107

Carroll, N. (2009) *On Criticism.* New York: Routledge. 19, 40

Cassell, J. (2002) Genderizing Human-Computer Interaction. In *The Human-Computer Interac-tion Handbook.* ed. by Jacko, J.A. and Sears, A. Hillsdale, NJ: L. Erlbaum Associates Inc, 401–412. 128

Cavell, S. (2002) *Must We Mean What We Say?* Cambridge, UK: Cambridge University Press. DOI: 10.1017/CBO9780511811753. 30, 37, 72

Cavell, S. (1969) *Must We Mean What We Say?* Cambridge, UK: Cambridge University Press. 30, 37, 72

Cockton, G., Bardzell, S., Blythe, M., and Bardzell, J. (2010) Can We All Stand Under Our Umbrella: the Arts and Design Research in HCI. In *CHI '10 Extended Abstracts on Human Factors in Computing Systems*. New York: ACM, 3163–3166. DOI: 10.1145/1753846.1753944. 5

Cooper, G. and Bowers, J. (1995) Representing the User: Notes on the Disciplinary Rhetoric of Human-Computer Interaction. In *The Social and Interactional Dimensions of Human-Computer Interfaces*. ed. by Thomas, P.J. NY: Cambridge University Press, 48–66. 3, 17, 23, 134

Crampton Smith, G. (2007) Foreword: What Is Interaction Design?. In *Designing Interactions*. Cambridge, MA: MIT Press.

Dewey, J. (2005) *Art as Experience*. NY: Perigree Books. 86, 87

Dewey, J. (1934) *Art as Experience*. NY: Minton, Balch and Co. 86, 87

Dillahunt, T.R. and Mankoff, J. (2014) Understanding Factors of Successful Engagement Around Energy Consumption Between and Among Households. In *Proceedings of the 17th ACM Conference on Computer Supported Cooperative Work and Social Computing*. New York: ACM, 1246–1257. DOI: 10.1145/2531602.2531626. 124

Dindler, C. and Iversen, O.S. (2007) Fictional Inquiry—Design Collaboration in a Shared Narrative Space. *CoDesign: International Journal of CoCreation in Design and the Arts* 3 (4), 213–234. DOI: 10.1080/15710880701500187.

DiSalvo, C., Sengers, P., and Brynjarsdóttir, H. (2010) Mapping the Landscape of Sustainable HCI. In *Proceedings of the SIGCHI Conference on Human Factors in Computing Systems*. New York: ACM, 1975–1984. DOI: 10.1145/1753326.1753625. 50, 63

Djajadiningrat, J.P., Gaver, W.W., and Fres, J.W. (2000) Interaction Relabelling and Extreme Characters: Methods for Exploring Aesthetic Interactions. In *Proceedings of the 3rd Conference on Designing Interactive Systems: Processes, Practices, Methods, and Techniques*. New York: ACM, 66–71. DOI: 10.1145/347642.347664. 56, 60

Dombrowski, L., Brubaker, J.R., H Hirano, Sen, Mazmanian, M., and Hayes, G.R. (2013) It Takes a Network to Get Dinner: Designing Location-Based Systems to Address Local Food Needs. In *Proceedings of the 2013 ACM International Joint Conference on Pervasive and Ubiquitous Computing*. New York: ACM, 519–528. DOI: 10.1145/2493432.2493493. 124

Dourish, P. (2001) *Where the Action Is: the Foundations of Embodied Interaction*. Cambridge, MA: The MIT Press. DOI: 10.1007/s10606-004-1193-1. xix, 92

Dourish, P. (2006) Implications for Design. In *Proceedings of the SIGCHI Conference on Human Factors in Computing Systems*. New York: ACM, 541–550. DOI: 10.1145/1124772.1124855. 49

Dourish, P. (2010) HCI and Environmental Sustainability: the Politics of Design and the Design of Politics. In *Proceedings of the 8th ACM Conference on Designing Interactive Systems*. New York: ACM, 1–10. DOI: 10.1145/1858171.1858173. 27, 126

Dourish, P. and Bell, G. (2014) "Resistance Is Futile": Reading Science Fiction Alongside Ubiquitous Computing. *Personal and Ubiquitous Computing* 18 (4), 769–778. DOI: 10.1007/s00779-013-0678-7. 58, 59

Dourish, P., Finlay, J., Sengers, P., and Wright, P. (2004) Reflective HCI: Toward a Critical Technical Practice. *CHI '04 Extended Abstracts on Human Factors in Computing Systems* 1727–1728. DOI: 10.1145/985921.986203. 4

Dunne, A. (2008) *Hertzian Tales: Electronic Products, Aesthetic Experience, and Critical Design*. Cambridge, MA: MIT Press. 46, 124

Dunne, A. and Raby, F. (2002) *Design Noir*. Springer Science and Business Media. 124, 125

Dunne, A. and Raby, F. (2013) *Speculative Everything*. Cambridge, MA: MIT Press. 57, 60, 63

Eagleton, T. (2004) *After Theory*. NY: Basic Books. 27

Erickson, T. and McDonald, D.W. (2008) *HCI Remixed: Essays on Works That Have Influenced the HCI Community*. Cambridge, MA: MIT Press. 17

Fairclough, N. (1995) *Critical Discourse Analysis: the Critical Study of Language*. NY: Longman. 48, 51

Fernaeus, Y. (2012) *Plei-Plei!* Hong Kong: PPP Ltd. 20

Forlizzi, J. and Battarbee, K. (2004) Understanding Experience in Interactive Systems. In *Proceedings of the 5th Conference on Designing Interactive Systems: Processes, Practices, Methods, and Techniques*. New York: ACM, 261–268. DOI: 10.1145/1013115.1013152. 83

Foucault, M. (1970) *The Order of Things: an Archaeology of the Human Sciences*. London: Tavistock Publications. 51

Foucault, M. (1972) *The Archaeology of Knowledge*. NY: Pantheon Books. 51

Foucault, M. (1977) 'Nietzsche, Genealogy, History'. NY: Cornell University Press. 51

Foucault, M. (1998) 'Nietzsche, Genealogy, History'. In *Michel Foucault: Aesthetics, Method, and Epistemology*. ed. by Faubion, J.D. The New Press, 369–391. 51

Freedman, C. (2000) *Critical Theory and Science Fiction*. Wesleyan University Press. 24

Friedman, B. (2004) 'Value Sensitive Design'. In *Berkshire Encyclopedia of Human-Computer Interaction*. ed. by Bainbridge, W.S. Great Barrington, MA: Berkshire Pub. Group, 769–774. DOI: 10.1145/242485.242493. 123, 125

Friedman, B. and Nathan, L.P. (2010) Multi-Lifespan Information System Design: a Research Initiative for the Hci Community. In *Proceedings of the SIGCHI Conference on Human Factors in Computing Systems*. New York: ACM, 2243–2246. DOI: 10.1145/1753326.1753665.

Gadamer, H.-G. (1975) *Truth and Method*. London: Sheed and Ward. 30

Gaver, B., Dunne, T., and Pacenti, E. (1999) Design: Cultural Probes. *interactions* 6 (1), 21–29. DOI: 10.1145/291224.291235. 83

Gaver, W., Boucher, A., Pennington, S., and Walker, B. (2005) Cultural probes and the value of uncertainty. In *interactions* 11 (5), 53-56. ACM. DOI: 10.1145/1015530.1015555. 4

Gaver, W.W., Bowers, J., Boucher, A., Gellerson, H., Pennington, S., Schmidt, A., Steed, A., Villars, N., and Walker, B. (2004) The Drift Table: Designing for Ludic Engagement. In *CHI '04 Extended Abstracts on Human Factors in Computing Systems*. New York: ACM, 885–900. DOI: 10.1145/985921.985947. 4, 125

Glock, H.-J. (2008) *What Is Analytic Philosophy?* Cambridge, UK: Cambridge University Press. DOI: 10.1017/CBO9780511841125. 22, 23

Greenberg, S. and Buxton, B. (2008) Usability Evaluation Considered Harmful (Some of the Time). In *Proceedings of the SIGCHI Conference on Human Factors in Computing Systems*. New York: ACM, 111–120. DOI: 10.1145/1357054.1357074. 30, 49, 79

Grudin, J. (1989) *The Computer Reaches Out*. Aarhus University, Computer Science Department. DOI: 10.1145/97243.97284. 2, 80

Guillory, J. (1995) *Canon. In Critical Terms for Literary Study*. 2nd edn. ed. by Lentricchia, F. and McLaughlin, T. Chicago: University of Chicago Press, 233–249. 25

Hanfling, O. (2000) *Philosophy and Ordinary Language: The Bent and Genius of Our Tongue*. NY: Routledge. 48

Harrison, S. and Dourish, P. (1996) Re-Place-Ing Space: the Roles of Place and Space in Collaborative Systems. In *Proceedings of the 1996 ACM Conference on Computer Supported Cooperative Work*. New York: ACM, 67–76. DOI: 10.1145/240080.240193. 3, 17, 23

Harrison, S., Tatar, D., and Sengers, P. (2007) The Three Paradigms of HCI. *Proceedings of the Conference on Human Factors in Computing Systems*, alt.chi. New York: ACM. xv, 18

Hassenzahl, M. (2010) *Experience Design*. Morgan and Claypool Publishers. DOI: 10.2200/S00261ED1V01Y201003HCI008. 30

Hassenzahl, M., Diefenbach, S., and Göritz, A. (2010) Needs, Affect, and Interactive Products - Facets of User Experience. *Interacting with Computers* 22 (5), 353–362. DOI: 10.1016/j.intcom.2010.04.002. 109

Hayes, G.R. (2011) The Relationship of Action Research to Human-Computer Interaction. *Transactions on Computer-Human Interaction* (TOCHI 18 (3), 1–20. DOI: 10.1145/1993060.1993065.

Ho, M.R., Smyth, T.N., Kam, M., and Dearden, A. (2009) Human-Computer Interaction for Development: the Past, Present, and Future. *Information Technologies and International Development* 5 (4), 1–18. 124

How, A. (2003) *Critical Theory*. New York: Palgrave MacMillan. 24, 116, 123

Höök, K. (2004) Active Co-Construction of Meaningful Experiences: But What is the Designer's Role? In *Proceedings of the 3rd Nordic Conference on Human-Computer Interaction: Extending Boundaries*. New York: ACM. DOI: 10.1145/1028014.1028015. 4

Höök, K. (2010) Transferring Qualities From Horseback Riding to Design. In *Proceedings of the 6th Nordic Conference on Human-Computer Interaction: Extending Boundaries*. New York: ACM, 226–235. DOI: 10.1145/1868914.1868943. 20, 93, 96, 98, 106, 107

Höök, K. and Löwgren, J. (2012) Strong Concepts: Intermediate-Level Knowledge in Interaction Design Research. *Transactions on Computer-Human Interaction* (TOCHI 19 (3), 1–18. DOI: 10.1145/2362364.2362371. 47, 106

Höök, K., Ståhl, A., Jonsson, M., Mercurio, J., Karlsson, A., and Johnson, E.-C.B. (2015) Somaesthetic Design. *interactions* 22 (4), 26–33. DOI: 10.1145/2770888. 39, 92, 93, 99, 106

Hummels, C., Overbeeke, K.C., and Klooster, S. (2007) Move to Get Moved: a Search for Methods, Tools and Knowledge to Design for Expressive and Rich Movement-Based Interaction. *Personal and Ubiquitous Computing* 11 (8), 677–690. DOI: 10.1007/s00779-006-0135-y. 96

Irani, L., Vertesi, J., Dourish, P., Philip, K., and Grinter, R.E. (2010) Postcolonial Computing: a Lens on Design and Development. In *Proceedings of the SIGCHI Conference on Human Factors in Computing Systems*. New York: ACM, 1311–1320. DOI: /10.1145/1753326.1753522. 20, 138, 140

Johnson, S. (1997) *Interface Culture: How New Technology Transforms the Way We Create and Communicate*. San Francisco: HarperEdge. 84

Kannabiran, G., Bardzell, J., and Bardzell, S. (2011) How HCI Talks About Sexuality: Discursive Strategies, Blind Spots, and Opportunities for Future Research. In *Proceedings of the SIGCHI Conference on Human Factors in Computing Systems*. New York: ACM, 695–704. DOI: 10.1007/s00779-014-0773-4. 51, 52, 137, 138

Kaye, J. and Dourish, P. (2014) Editorial: Special Issue on Science Fiction and Ubiquitous Computing. *Personal and Ubiquitous Computing* 18 (4), 765–766. DOI: 10.1007/s00779-014-0773-4. 58

Kennedy, B.M. (2002) *Deleuze and Cinema*. Edinburgh Univ Press. 134

Kincaid, H. (1996) *Philosophical Foundation of the Social Sciences: Analyzing Controversies in Social Research*. Cambridge: Cambridge University Press. 48, 66

Koskinen, I., Zimmerman, J., Binder, T., Redstrom, J., and Wensveen, S. (2011) *Design Research Through Practice: From the Lab, Field, and Showroom*. 1st edn. San Francisco, CA: Morgan Kaufmann Publishers Inc. 98

Krippendorff, K. (2013) *Content Analysis: an Introduction to Its Methodology*. 3rd edn. Thousand Oaks: SAGE Publications, Inc. 48

Kristeller, P.O. (2008) 'Part I: Classical Sources: Introduction'. In *Aesthetics: a Comprehensive Anthology*. ed. by Chan, S.M. and Meskin, A. Malden, MA: Malden, MA: Blackwell Pub, 3–15. 14

Kuhn, T.S. (1996) *The Structure of Scientific Revolutions*. 3rd edn. Chicago: The University of Chicago Press. DOI: 10.7208/chicago/9780226458106.001.0001. xv

Kuniavsky, M. (2003) *Observing the User Experience: a Practitioner's Guide to User Research*. San Francisco, CA: Morgan Kaufmann Publishers. 80

Kuutti, K. (2009) 'HCI and Design: Uncomfortable Bedfellows'. In *Researching the Digital Bauhaus*. ed. by Binder, T., Löwgren, J., and Malmborg, L. London: Binder. 79

Lamarque, P. (2008) *The Philosophy of Literature*. Wiley-Blackwell. DOI: 10.1002/9780470756645. ch11. 25, 61, 64, 103

Latour, B. (2004) 'Why Has Critique Run Out of Steam? From Matters of Fact to Matters of Concern'. *Critical Inquiry* 30 (2), 225–248. DOI: 10.1086/421123.

Laurel, B. (2003) 'Two Selection by Brenda Laurel'. In *The New Media Reader*. Cambridge, MA: Cambridge, MA: MIT Press, 563–573. 145

Laurel, B. (1991) 'Two Selection by Brenda Laurel'. 145

Le Dantec, C.A. (2008) 'Life at the Margins: Assessing the Role of Technology for the Urban Homeless'. *interactions* 15 (5), 24–27. DOI: 10.1145/1390085.1390090. 124

Leavis, F.R. (1975) *The Living Principle: English as a Discipline of Thought*. London: Chatto and Windus. 36

Lee, W. (2014) Pragmatic and Practical Somaesthetics for Interactive Product Design. In *Proceedings of the 2014 Companion Publication on Designing Interactive Systems*. New York: ACM, 167–171. DOI: 10.1145/2598784.2598790.

Lee, Y.-K. and Lee, K.-P. (2010) Design Research and the Complexity Encountered in People's Critical Thoughts. In *Proceedings of DRS'10*. held 2010. 124

Lee, W., Lim, Y.-K., and Shusterman, R. 2014. Practicing somaesthetics: exploring its impact on interactive product design ideation. In Proceedings of the 2014 conference on Designing interactive systems (DIS '14). ACM, NY, USA, 1055-1064. DOI: 10.1145/2598510.2598561. 39, 93, 97, 98, 99, 106

Leitch, V.B. (2001) *The Norton Anthology of Theory and Criticism*. New York: Norton. 14

Light, A. (2010) The Unit of Analysis in Understanding the Politics of Participatory Practice. In *Proceedings of the 11th Biennial Participatory Design Conference*. New York: ACM, 183–186. DOI: 10.1145/1900441.1900473. 127

Light, A. (2011) 'HCI as Heterodoxy: Technologies of Identity and the Queering of Interaction with Computers'. *Interacting with Computers* 23 (5), 430–438. DOI: 10.1016/j.intcom.2011.02.002. 39, 59, 60, 131, 145

Light, A., Cahour, B., and Otero, N. (2010) Reflections on Reflection: How Critical Thinking Relates to Collecting Accounts of Experience Using Explication Techniques. In *Critical Dialogue Interaction, Experience and Cultural Theory workshop in association with ACM CHI*. NY. 55

Lim, Y.-K., Stolterman, E., Jung, H., and Donaldson, J. (2007) Interaction Gestalt and the Design of Aesthetic Interactions. In *DPPI '07: Proceedings of the 2007 Conference on Designing Pleasurable Products and Interfaces*. New York: ACM, 239–254. DOI: 10.1145/1314161.1314183. 102, 103

Lopate, P. (1995) *The Art of the Personal Essay: an Anthology From the Classical Era to the Present*. New York: Anchor Books. 67, 69, 72

Lopate, P. (1998) *Totally, Tenderly, Tragically: Essays and Criticism From a Lifelong Love Affair with the Movies*. New York: Anchor Books/Doubleday. 67

Löwgren, J. (2006) 'Articulating the Use Qualities of Digital Designs'. In *Aesthetic Computing*. ed. by Fishwick, P.A. Cambridge, MA: MIT Press, 383–404. 20

Löwgren, J. (2009) 'Toward an Articulation of Interaction Esthetics'. *The New Review of Hypermedia and Multimedia* 15 (2), 129–146. DOI: http://dx.doi.org/10.1080/13614560903117822. 46, 106

Löwgren, J. and Stolterman, E. (2004) *Thoughtful Interaction Design: a Design Perspective on Information Technology*. Cambridge, MA: The MIT Press. 129

Malpass, M. (2010) Perspectives on Critical Design: a Conversation with Ralph Ball and Maxine Naylor. In *Design and Complexity proceedings of Design Research Society conference 10*. 124

Manovich, L. (2002) *The Language of New Media*. Cambridge, MA: MIT Press. 84

Mazé, R. and Redstrom, J. (2007) Difficult Forms: Critical Practices of Design and Research. In *IASDR International Association of Societies of Design Research - Emerging Trends in Design Research*. The Hong Kong Polytechnic University, School of Design. 124

McCarthy, J. and Wright, P. (2004) *Technology as Experience*. Cambridge, MA: MIT Press. DOI: 10.1145/1015530.1015549. 20, 24, 30, 37, 38, 55, 80, 85, 90, 109, 137, 145

McCarthy, J. and Wright, P. (2005) 'Putting "Felt-Life" at the Centre of Human–Computer Interaction (HCI)'. *Cognition, Technology and Work* 7 (4), 262–271. DOI: 10.1007/s10111-005-0011-y.

McLaren, M.A. (2002) *Feminism, Foucault, and Embodied Subjectivity*. Albany, NY: State University of New York Press. 27

Mills, S. (1997) *Discourse*. New York: Routledge. 51

Moggridge, B. (2007) *Designing Interactions*. Cambridge, MA: MIT Press. 17, 100

Monk, A., Hassenzahl, M., Blythe, M., and Reed, D. (2002) 'Funology: Designing Enjoyment'. *CHI '02 Extended Abstracts on Human Factors in Computing Systems* 924–925. DOI: 10.1145/506443.506661. 4

Mulvey, L. (1975) 'Visual Pleasure and Narrative Cinema'. *Screen* 16 (3). DOI: 10.1093/screen/16.3.6. 122

Nardi, B.A. (2010) *My Life as a Night Elf Priest: an Anthropological Account of World of Warcraft*. Ann Arbor: University of Michigan Press. DOI: 10.3998/toi.8008655.0001.001. 20

Nielsen, J. (1995) *10 Usability Heuristics for User Interface Design* [online] available from <http://www.nngroup.com/articles/ten-usability-heuristics/> [5 August 2015]. 42, 43

Nissenbaum, H. (1998) Values in Computer System Design: Bias and Autonomy. In *Proceedings of the Conference on Computer Ethics*. Delhi. 35–42. 123

Norman, D.A. (1988) *The Design of Everyday Things*. New York: Basic Books. 42

Nygaard, K. (1990) The Origins of the Scandinavian School, Why and How? In *Participatory Design Conference 1990*. Seattle. 123

Pace, T., Bardzell, S., and Bardzell, J. (2010) The Rogue in the Lovely Black Dress: Intimacy in World of Warcraft. In *Proceedings of the SIGCHI Conference on Human Factors in Computing Systems*. New York: ACM, 233–242. DOI: 10.1145/1753326.1753361. 20, 54, 137

Pearson, W.G. (2003) 'Science Fiction and Queer Theory'. In *The Cambridge Companion to Science Fiction*. ed. by James, E. and Mendlesohn, F. 149–160. DOI: 10.1017/ CCOL0521816262.011. 131

Petersen, M.G., Iversen, O.S., Krogh, P.G., and Ludvigsen, M. (2004) Aesthetic Interaction: a Pragmatist's Aesthetics of Interactive Systems. In *Proceedings of the 5th Conference on Designing Interactive Systems: Processes, Practices, Methods, and Techniques*. New York: ACM, 269–276. DOI: 10.1145/1013115.1013153. 85, 89, 92, 93

Quine, W.V.O. (1951) Two Dogmas of Empiricism. *The Philosophical Review* 60(1), pp.20-43. 24

Rode, J.A. (2011) 'A Theoretical Agenda for Feminist HCI'. *Interacting with Computers* 23 (5), 393–400. DOI: 10.1016/j.intcom.2011.04.005. 128, 130

Rogers, R. (2004) *An Introduction to Critical Discourse Analysis in Education*. Lawrence Erlbaum Associates.

Rogers, Y. (2004) New Theoretical Approaches for human-computer interaction. *Annual Review of Information Science and Technology* 38, 87-143. DOI: 10.1002/aris.1440380103. 49, 51, 63

Rogers, Y. (2006) 'Moving on From Weiser's Vision of Calm Computing: Engaging UbiComp Experiences'. In *UbiComp 2006: Ubiquitous Computing*. Heidelberg: Springer, 404–421. DOI: 10.1007/11853565_24. 20

Rogers, Y. (2012) *HCI Theory: Classical, Modern, and Contemporary*. ed. by Carroll, J.M. Morgan & Claypool Publishers. DOI: 10.2200/S00418ED1V01Y201205HCI014. xv, 18, 27, 50

Ross, D. (1923) *Aristotle*. London: Methuen's Publications. 105

Ross, D. (1995) *Aristotle*. Sixth Edition. Routledge. 105

Said, E.W. (1979) *Orientalism*. Vintage Books. 119

Satchell, C. (2008) Cultural theory and real world design: Dystopian and Utopian Outcomes. In *Proceedings of the SIGCHI Conference on Human Factors in Computing Systems (CHI '08)*. ACM, New York, NY, USA, 1593-1602. DOI=10.1145/1357054.1357303.

Satchell, C. and Dourish, P. (2009) Beyond the User: Use and Non-Use in HCI. In *Proceedings of the 21st Annual Conference of the Australian Computer-Human Interaction Special Interest Group: Design: Open 24/7*. New York: ACM, 9–16. DOI: 10.1145/1738826.1738829. 135, 145

Schifferstein, H. and Hekkert, P. (2008a) 'Introduction'. In *Product Experience*. San Diego, CA: San Diego, CA : Elsevier. 81

Schifferstein, H. and Hekkert, P. (2008b) *Product Experience*. San Diego, CA: Elsevier.

Schiphorst, T. (2009) 'Soft(N): Toward a Somaesthetics of Touch'. *CHI EA '09: CHI '09 Extended Abstracts on Human Factors in Computing Systems* 2427–2438. DOI: 10.1145/1520340.1520345. 39, 75, 93, 98, 106, 145

Schön, D.A. (1983) *The Reflective Practitioner: How Professionals Think in Action*. New York: Basic Books. DOI: 10.1016/0738-3991(84)90022-3. 125

Sengers, P. and Gaver, B. (2006) Staying Open to Interpretation: Engaging Multiple Meanings in Design and Evaluation. In *Proceedings of the 6th Conference on Designing Interactive Systems*. New York: ACM, 99–108. DOI: 10.1145/1142405.1142422. 20, 45

Sengers, P., Boehner, K., Gay, G., Kaye, J., Mateas, M., Gaver, B. and Höök, K. (2004) "Experience as Interpretation." *CHI 2004 Workshop on Cross-Dressing and Boundary Crossing: Exploring Experience Methods Across the Disciplines*. Vienna, Austria, April 2004. 4

Sengers, P., Boehner, K., David, S., and Kaye, J. (2005) Reflective Design. In *Proceedings of the 4th Decennial Conference on Critical Computing: Between Sense and Sensibility*. New York: ACM, 49–58. DOI: 10.1145/1094562.1094569. 125

Shedroff, N. (2003) 'Research Methods for Designing Effective Experiences'. In *Design Research: Methods and Perspectives*. ed. by Laurel, B. Cambridge, MA: MIT Press, 155–163. 81

Shneiderman, B. and Plaisant, C. (2010) *Designing the User Interface: Strategies for Effective Human-Computer Interaction*. 5 ed. Boston: Addison-Wesley. DOI: 10.1002/(SICI)1097-4571(198801)39:1<22::AID-ASI5>3.0.CO;2-#. xv, 79, 80

Shusterman, R. (2000) *Pragmatist Aesthetics: Living Beauty, Rethinking Art*. Lanham, MD: Rowman and Littlefield. DOI: 10.1093/ml/85.4.677. 39, 93, 94

Shusterman, R. (2008) *Body Consciousness: A Philosophy of Mindfulness and Somaesthetics*. Cambridge; New York: Cambridge University Press. DOI: 10.1017/CBO9780511802829. 39, 94, 100

Simonsen, J. and Robertson, T. (2013) *Routledge International Handbook of Participatory Design*. New York: Routledge. DOI: 10.4324/9780203108543. 123

Sterling, B. (2014) 'Futility and Resistance'. *Personal and Ubiquitous Computing* 18 (4), 767–768. DOI: 10.1007/s00779-013-0676-9. 59

Sternberg, R.J. (ed.) (1999) *Handbook of Creativity*. ed. by Sternberg, R.J. Cambridge; New York: Cambridge University Press. 49

Stroll, A. (2000) *Twentieth-Century Analytic Philosophy.* New York: Columbia University Press. DOI: 10.17161/AJP.1808.9494. 23

Suchman, L.A. (1987) *Plans and Situated Actions: the Problem of Human-Machine Communication.* New York: Cambridge University Press. 2, 3

Sutcliffe, A. (2009) *Designing for User Engagement: Aesthetic and Attractive User Interfaces.* ed. by Carroll, J.M. Morgan & Claypool Publishers. DOI: 10.2200/S00210ED1V01Y-200910HCI005. 82

Tanenbaum, J., Tanenbaum, K., and Wakkary, R. (2012) Steampunk as Design Fiction. In '*Proceedings of the SIGCHI Conference on Human Factors in Computing Systems*'. New York: ACM, 1583–1592. DOI: 10.1145/2207676.2208279. 20

Taylor, A.S. (2011) Out There. In '*Proceedings of the SIGCHI Conference on Human Factors in Computing Systems*'. New York: ACM, 685–694. DOI: 10.1145/1978942.1979042. 139

Taylor, C. (1971) *Interpretation and the Sciences of Man.* Review of Metaphysics. 19, 37, 53, 70, 108

Tomlinson, B., Silberman, M.S., Patterson, D., Pan, Y., and Blevis, E. (2012) Collapse Informatics: Augmenting the Sustainability and ICT4D Discourse in HCI. In *Proceedings of the SIGCHI Conference on Human Factors in Computing Systems.* New York: ACM, 655. DOI: /10.1145/2207676.2207770. 124

Toyama, K. (2010) 'Human–Computer Interaction and Global Development'. *Foundations and Trends in Human-Computer Interaction* 4 (1), 1–79. DOI: 10.1561/1100000021. 124

Tractinsky, N. (2012) 'Visual Aesthetics in Human-Computer Interaction and Interaction Design'. *Encyclopedia of Human-Computer Interaction.* Aarhus.

Tractinsky, N., Katz, A.S., and Ikar, D. (2000) 'What Is Beautiful Is Usable'. *Interacting with Computers* 13 (2), 127–145. DOI: 10.1016/S0953-5438(00)00031-X. 5

Turkle, S. (1995) *Life on the Screen: Identity in the Age of the Internet.* New York: Simon and Schuster. 80

Turkle, S. (2004) 'Whither Psychoanalysis in Computer Culture?'. *Psychoanalytic Psychology* 21 (1), 16–30. DOI: 10.1037/0736-9735.21.1.16. 136

Turvey, M., Wartenberg, T.E., and Curren, A. (2005) 'Can Scientific Models of Theorizing Help Film Theory?'. In *The Philosophy of Film: Introductory Text and Readings.* ed. by Wartenberg, T.E. and Curran, A. Malden, MA: Blackwell. 36

Udsen, L.E. and Jørgensen, A.H. (2006) 'The Aesthetic Turn: Unravelling Recent Aesthetic Approaches to Human-Computer Interaction'. *Digital Creativity* 16 (4), 205–216. DOI: 10.1080/14626260500476564. 84, 89

Vertesi, J. (2014) 'My Experiment Opting Out of Big Data Made Me Look Like a Criminal'. *Time Magazine.* xv

Voida, A. (2014) 'A Case for Philanthropic Informatics'. In *User-Centric Technology Design for Nonprofit and Civic Engagements.* ed. by Saeed, S. Cham: Springer International Publishing, 3–13. DOI: 10.1007/978-3-319-05963-1_1. 124

Weiser, M. (1991) 'The Computer for the 21st Century'. *Scientific American* 265 (3), 94–104. DOI: 10.1038/scientificamerican0991-94. 20, 60, 80

Whittaker, S., Terveen, L., and Nardi, B.A. (2001) 'A Reference Task Agenda for HCI'. In *Human Computer Interaction in the New Millemnium.* Addison-Wesley. 80

Winograd, T. and Flores, F. (1986) *Understanding Computers and Cognition.* Ablex Publishing Corporation. DOI: 10.1002/bs.3830330107. 2, 3, 17, 23, 39

Wittgenstein, L. and Ogden, C. (1922) *Tractatus Logico-Philosophicus.* NY: Harcourt, Brace and Co. 22

Wittgenstein, L. and Ogden, C. (1999) *Tractatus Logico-Philosophicus.* Mineola, NY: Dover Publications. DOI: 10.1111/j.1747-9991.2010.00374.x. 22

Wittgenstein, L., Anscombe, G., Hacker, P., and Schulte, J. (2009) *Philosophical Investigations.* Malden, MA: Wiley-Blackwell. 62

Wittgenstein, L., Anscombe, G., Hacker, P., and Schulte, J. (1953) *Philosophical Investigations.* Oxford: Basil Blackwell 62

Wodak, R. and Meyer, M. (eds.) (2001) *Methods of Critical Discourse Analysis.* ed. by Wodak, R. and Meyer, M. London: SAGE. 51

Wright, E. (1984) *Psychoanalytic Criticism: Theory in Practice.* NY: Routledge. DOI: 10.2307/3729707. 117

Wright, P. and Finlay, J. (2002) Understanding User Experience: Literary Analysis Meets HCI. In *BCS HCI 2002.* 4

Zacharek, S. (2008) *Film Criticism in the Age of the Internet: A Critical Symposium Cineaste,* Vol. 33 No.4 (Fall 2008). 67

About the Authors

Jeffrey Bardzell is an Associate Professor of HCI/Design in the School of Informatics and Computing at Indiana University, Bloomington. His research examines design theory, with emphases on critical design, research through design, and design criticism. A common thread throughout this work is the use of aesthetics—including the history of criticism, critical theory, and analytic aesthetics—to explore art-based design methods. He is co-editor of *Critical Theory and Interaction Design* (MIT Press, in press) and is working on a book, tentatively titled, *Design as Inquiry*. Bardzell's work is funded by the National Science Foundation and the Intel Science and Technology Center for Social Computing.

Shaowen Bardzell is an Associate Professor of Informatics in the School of Informatics and Computing at Indiana University. Known for her work in feminist HCI, Bardzell's research focuses on emancipatory research and design methods, including critical design, participatory design, care ethics, and feminist utopianism. She has applied this work in several domains of inquiry, including creativity in IT innovation, maker cultures, human sexuality, and culture and creative industries in Asia. She is writing a book on utopian design and is co-editor of *Critical Theory and Interaction Design* (MIT Press). She co-directs the Cultural Research in Technology (CRIT) Lab. Her work is supported by the National Science Foundation and the Intel Science and Technology Center for Social Computing.